*Julie Helm...* (signature)

The twentieth century has seen biol... come of age as a concept... science. Biochemi... have been unified the molecular leve and development a...  play of molecules a molecules organized ...ys, subunits, and organelles. Emphasis on organization is, therefore, of increasing importance.

So it is too, at the other end of the scale. Organismic and population biology are developing new rigor in such established and emerging disciplines as ecology, evolution, and ethology, but again the accent is on interactions between individuals, populations, and societies. Advances in comparative biochemistry and physiology have given new impetus to studies of animal and plant diversity. Microbiology has matured, with the world of viruses and procaryotes assuming a major position. New connections are being forged with other disciplines outside biology—chemistry, physics, mathematics, geology, anthropology, and psychology provide us with new theories and experimental tools while at the same time are themselves being enriched by the biologists' new insights into the world of life. The need to preserve a habitable environment for future generations should encourage increasing collaboration between diverse disciplines.

The purpose of the Modern Biology Series is to introduce the college biology student—as well as the gifted secondary student and all interested readers—both to the concepts unifying the fields within biology and to the diversity that makes each field unique.

Since the series is open-ended, it will provide a greater number and variety of topics than can be accommodated in many introductory courses. It remains the responsibility of the instructor to make his selection, to arrange it in a logical order, and to develop a framework into which the individual units can best be fitted.

New titles will be added to the present list as new fields emerge, existing fields advance, and new authors of ability and talent appear. Only thus, we feel, can we keep pace with the explosion of knowledge in Modern Biology.

James D. Ebert
Ariel G. Loewy
Richard S. Miller
Howard A. Schneiderman

*Modern Biology Series*    **Consulting Editors**

James D. Ebert
*Carnegie Institution of Washington*

Ariel G. Loewy
*Haverford College*

Richard S. Miller
*Yale University*

Howard A. Schneiderman
*University of California, Irvine*

## Published Titles

## Forthcoming Titles

# Biological
# Conservation

## David W. Ehrenfeld
*Barnard College, Columbia University*

*Holt, Rinehart and Winston, Inc.*
*New York   Chicago   San Francisco*
*Atlanta   Dallas   Montreal*
*Toronto   London   Sydney*

Text and cover design by Margaret O. Tsao
Illustrations by Howard Stanley Friedman

*For the Carrs:  Archie, Margie, Mimi, Chuck,
Steve, Tom, Jasper, and David*

*In the discussions held by the General Assembly at its twenty-third session it was emphasized that for the first time in the history of mankind, there is arising a crisis of world-wide proportions involving developed and developing countries alike — the crisis of the human environment. Portents of this crisis have long been apparent — in the explosive growth of human populations, in the poor integration of a powerful and efficient technology with environmental requirements, in the deterioration of agricultural lands, in the unplanned extension of urban areas, in the decrease of available space and the growing danger of extinction of many forms of animal and plant life. It is becoming apparent that if current trends continue, the future of life on earth could be endangered. It is urgent, therefore, to focus world attention on those problems which threaten humanity in an environment that permits the realization of the highest human aspirations, and on the action necessary to deal with them.*

*Report of the Secretary-General
United Nations Economic and
    Social Council, 47th Session
May 26, 1969*

*But it seems that the wind is setting East, and the withering of all woods may be drawing near.*

The Two Towers
J. R. R. Tolkien

# *Preface*

No academic subject can be said to have
come of age until textbooks have been
written about it. If judged according to this
criterion, biological conservation, as it is
defined in this book, is only now in the
process of emerging from a prolonged in-
fancy. Except for a few of the more advanced texts of the "natural resource"
school, some edited compilations of papers,
and one or two semipopular short works,
there has been virtually nothing to indicate
to the college undergraduate that qualified
biologists are beginning to forge a discipline
in that turbulent and vital area where
biology meets the social sciences and the
humanities. The need is now very great for
a scientifically valid presentation of the
biological problems that are most relevant
to the life of modern man.

In discussing the fate of communities of animals and plants and of individual species, I have tried to portray the impact of the population and technology explosions on the natural world within the context of western, urban society. I have stressed environmental changes that are likely to be significant to man, and have placed special emphasis on the relationship between conservation and ecology.

Because of the nature of the subject matter, my sources have been varied. The reader should not be surprised to find excerpts from the research and writings of demographers, economists, novelists, and landscape architects blended with accounts of the findings of biologists and chemists. I believe that the greatest strength of conservation is its potential to serve as a rallying point for different kinds of intellect in an age when real human communication has been all but supplanted by a variety of unsatisfactory substitutes. I am personally not fond of the aura of magic and ritual that sets scientists apart from others and which often prevents us from relating our work to worldly needs. And I suspect that there are many persons in nonscientific fields who are equally dissatisfied with being held responsible for deciding what to do with a black box that they never open.

One problem, peculiar to this kind of biology book, is the increasing remoteness of fundamental biology—of animals and plants, of biological functions and biological events—from the lives of an urban populace. In order to want to conserve something, one has to appreciate it first, and the number of people who are intimately familiar with natural landscapes outside the city and with wild species other than rats and pigeons grows proportionally smaller every day. Few of us have followed a biological community through a full-year cycle of life and death; few of us know when the grunions are supposed to arrive or when the blackberries ripen; and few of us have had any contact with any of the environments in which the human species evolved and to which it remains obscurely committed by physiological cycles of daily, lunar, or seasonal periodicity, by metabolic adjustment, and by psychological associations of great complexity. Thus, teaching biological conservation in the early 1970s is a little like advertising color television on black-and-white screens: One can assert, persuasively, how beautiful and rich the colors are, but acceptance of the idea is still an act of faith on the part of the inexperienced audience. Here I can only hope that this book provokes some people into seeing for themselves what all the shouting is about.

In preparing the text I have had the help of many people, not all of whom can be acknowledged in this short space. Among my students at Barnard College, Miss Nancy Chu, Miss Diane Drigot, Miss Maria Hanushevsky, Mrs. Joan Gardner Rothman, Miss Rena Vassilopoulou, and Miss Marina Wong were of special assistance in all phases of the writing. Colleagues who provided valuable advice include Dr. Stanley A. Cain, Dr. Patricia Dudley, Dr. Robert Franke, Dr. Wayne King, Dr. A. L. Koch, Dr. Mike Levandowsky, Dr. Donald Ritchie, Dr. Paul B. Sears, Dr. George Small, Dr. T. J. Walker, and Dr. Frederick E. Warburton. My editors at Holt, Rinehart and Winston, Inc., Mr. Ian Baldwin, Mr. Donald Schumacher, Miss Yvonne Freund, Mrs. Pam Landau, and Mr. George Sullivan made production of the book pleasant for me, and have greatly contributed to the quality of the text. I could not have proceeded far without the assistance of my wife Ellie. Her scientific and stylistic critical ability is manifest in the best parts of each chapter. Above all, I am grateful to Dr. Archie Carr and Mrs. Marjorie Carr for having started and encouraged my interest in conservation and my delight in the things that conservationists enjoy.

*D. W. E.*
*New York City*
*January, 1970*

# Contents

*xi*

# chapter 1

# *Introduction*

The idea of conserving existing life forms meets little opposition when presented in abstract terms. But simple acceptance of a conservation ideal saves few species and fewer environments. Although the acts of conservationists are often motivated by strongly humanistic principles, the practice of conservation must also have a firm scientific basis or, plainly stated, it is not likely to work. Biological conservation is inseparable from the rest of modern biology: It borrows elements of its theoretical framework from such disciplines as ecology, physiology, biochemistry, and behavior, and in return contributes the preservation of many of the life phenomena that the rest of biology seeks eventually to understand. In this book, therefore, the biological aspects of conservation will be stressed, although not at the expense of the social and aesthetic content of the subject. Few of man's activities can claim so successful a fusion between science and humanism; the success, in turn, of any book on conservation will depend on the extent to which its author is willing to deal with the full scope of the problem.

Conservation is a broad topic, even when restricted to biological applications. There is no guarantee that people—including conservationists—are talking about the same thing when they refer to it. The discussion of conservation in this book presents the theme that a comprehensive sample of existing animal and plant species and natural communities should be preserved for the enjoyment and benefit of future populations of man. This is not just a noble gesture. Failure to conserve life forms is outright theft, irrevocable theft, since once species and communities have been obliterated, they cannot be reconstituted, regardless of whether future generations of man should want to have them again. Nor does the possibility of genetic manipulation offer much promise; one cannot reconstruct *de novo* something for which no models or descriptions exist. Indeed most of the species and all communities that have vanished to date have disappeared with their stories untold or badly told: We are informed that the thylacine or marsupial wolf, the only large marsupial carnivore to survive to modern times, hopped on its hind legs, kangaroolike, when frightened, but we are not likely to know

*Fig. 1-1    Garbage dump, McMurdo Sound, Antarctica. (The New York Times)*

much else about this bizarre and unique creature, since it has nearly vanished from its last retreats in western Tasmania.

Most persons are unaware of the magnitude of the threat to wildlife and of the urgency of the situation. It is tempting to cling to the childhood fantasy that there still exist vast areas where wilderness and wild creatures flourish unmenaced, faraway places with strange-sounding names: Sarawak, the Osa Peninsula, the Ross Shelf, the Dismal Swamp. But it is no coincidence that wherever one goes, such places are generally somewhere else. The largest, relatively blank area left on the land part of the map of the earth is the Amazon basin, containing extensive rain forests and a monumental river system that collects nearly 20 percent of the world's free-flowing, fresh water. Yet even here, where the best atlases show frequent gaps of more than a hundred miles without a named, human habitation, changes have occurred in recent years. Biologists traveling in the far interior reaches of the Amazon system, more than 1500 miles from the river mouth, report that extensive areas of rain forest, which present an unbroken, green canopy to the airborne observer, show marked depletion of wildlife when viewed from the ground. In such areas the forest sounds are now mostly insect noises, while once-common mammals, large birds, and large reptiles are scarce or absent.

It may be some time, however, before the fauna and flora of the Amazon basin are irretrievably lost; other regions present far more immediate problems. Lake Erie, with an area of 9940 square miles, has been biologically altered almost beyond recognition. Only time, in the absence of pollution, might bring back a vestige of its original plant, fish, and invertebrate populations. Experts estimate that Lake Michigan, twice as large as Erie, and much deeper, might be relatively clean in a thousand years if all pollution were stopped now. The Amazon basin and Lake Erie define the lower and upper limits of the disaster that now confronts all wild environments on earth. Between these limits, facing a multitude of both recognizable and obscure threats to their continued existence, are all other places that still have at least a part of their natural biota intact.

The extinction of individual species of plants and animals is only one aspect of the larger problem affecting communities, but it has garnered much of the attention devoted to conservation. The extinction of a particular species is comprehensible and dramatic; it is at least as irreversible and final as the destruction of a work of art. All species are potential Humpty Dumpties: The processes of evolution, as we know them, will not put them together again on this planet once they are destroyed. There are numerous, valid aesthetic and practical reasons for supporting the conservation of species (and of communities), but this specter of irreversibility is the most powerful reason of all. We are privileged to have witnessed some of the finest examples of the great adaptive radiations that took place during the Mesozoic and Cenozoic Eras. We have seen giant tortoises, giraffes, elephants, orchids, macaws, redwoods, orangutans, walruses, and whales—fabulous creatures that would enliven any mythology even if they were not real. Our immediate descendants will be unable to see living representatives of many of the species in these groups, and no one should blame future generations if they consider our personal accounts and recollections an inadequate substitute for living specimens, nor will their loss be less if they are unaware that such species once existed.

Although the word "conservation" implies a series of static holding maneuvers, this is scarcely the policy intended by conservationists, even if it were possible. Modern conservation, regardless of the scale of activities, must deal with a large number of variables that differ widely from situation to situation. A completely flexible position is necessary, as is the case whenever a considerable amount of advance planning and a delayed feedback are involved. Thus conservation policy ranges from a complete *laissez faire* style of protection for some wilderness areas and sanctuaries to nearly complete management and manipulation of others. Some of the factors that are taken into consideration in making these decisions are discussed in subsequent chapters.

Despite the fact that specific conservation strategy is too variable to present in outline form in an introduction, the broad aim of conservation (as the word is used in this book) can be stated. The aim is not to prevent changes from taking place—ecosystems and species will change even without the actions of man. It is, rather, to ensure that nothing in the existing natural order is permitted to become permanently lost as the result of man's activities unless all foreseeable consequences of the loss have been weighed in the balance. G. L. Kesteven (1) has stated it clearly: "There should be no further modification of, or interference with, water, air, soil, substrate, rock, [organism] or biotope unless the immediate and necessary benefits of that modification are accompanied by long-term benefits." One might add that the burden of proof should fall on those seeking to modify the environment.

Most humans find natural surroundings pleasant; this is hardly surprising, since this is the setting in which our species evolved and to which we are genetically attuned. It can be argued that even our most artificial environments, our cities, are most successful in satisfying their inhabitants when they begin to approach and mimic the complexity and variety of a natural ecosystem such as a mixed hardwood forest and its intricate organization of components in space and time. We are paying increasing though still inadequate attention to the planning of future cities; it will be equally important to give imaginative and careful consideration to the problem of finding a way to maintain some natural areas with indigenous species in a mechanized and densely populated world.

There is no way to predict whether such areas will serve as models, museums, or refuges, but one thing is quite certain: If our descendants tire of having wild places and wild creatures coexisting with them, they will have as little trouble getting rid of them as we do now.

The most urgent needs of conservation lie in the realm of education. The cause itself has been well publicized by energetic individuals, by private conservation organizations, and by some public agencies. Good intentions are legion, and new proposals backed by people willing to contribute time and money are appearing with increasing frequency and regularity. But many of these schemes are unrealistic; some are of marginal utility and may block more worthwhile programs, and a few would actually damage the things they seek to protect. Far too often conservationists find themselves on opposite sides of practical issues even though they agree on the long-range goal. The preservation of the redwood forests, which is discussed elsewhere in the book, is a case in point. Education will not solve all such difficulties, but it will help in at least two ways: (1) Specific training in the problems of conservation will augment the small nucleus of professional scientists who devote much of their time to biological conservation, by attracting new students at every educational level and by informing workers in related disciplines how their skills can be used to best advantage in conservation work. (2) Suitable books and well-informed teachers will be available so that amateur conservationists having some prior acquaintance with biology do not have to acquire their information haphazardly or by trial and error.

Unfortunately, improvement by education is a slow process, and the crises are already at hand. By every conceivable measure the rate of wildlife disappearance is increasing rapidly. One can plot the number of species that become extinct per year, the reduction in population size for given species, or the loss of wild and semiwild terrain — each tells the same story. Perhaps it is too late to do anything other than save a few odd bits and pieces of the landscape; nevertheless the possibility of achieving more than that makes the effort imperative.

## TRADITIONAL CONSERVATION IN THE UNITED STATES

One dictionary provides the following primary definition for the word "resource": "a source of supply, support, or aid, especially one held in reserve." If we expand this slightly to include the idea of a resource as unconverted or raw wealth, we arrive at the concept that forms the core of the philosophy of the more successful variety of conservation that has been practiced in the United States. A resource has value or utility, and there is enough of it to satisfy at least some of the anticipated future demand. Therefore, if one is concerned about taking action to conserve resources, there is no need to give high priority to things that have little tangible value or that appear to be present in inexhaustible supply. The majority of American conservation efforts have been resource-oriented; this has meant that, until recently, certain selected elements of our flora and fauna and certain selected parts of our unsettled territory have been the subjects of intensive, governmentally supported conservation efforts backed by scientific research, while the rest of our wildlife and natural communities have been left unattended or entrusted to private conservation organizations. This emphasis on resources has generated some paradoxical situations: For example, in 1963 the 154 national forests comprised 182 million acres of virgin and second-growth timber, and in 1964 Congress designated 9.1 million of these acres as wilderness areas; yet at the same time, only 7 percent of our 21,000 miles of ocean shore line (exclusive of Hawaii and Alaska) had been reserved for public recreation, and only a part of this was wild. The prairies have fared even worse; grasslands do not make popular national parks, nor are they appropriate to be considered as national forests. Unaltered plains communities are now virtually nonexistent, despite the romantic place they occupy in our history and popular fiction.

It is possible to trace the existence of conservationists and conservation ideas back to the early days of the colonial administration of North America. In 1681, William Penn decreed that for every 5 acres cleared of forest, 1 acre of timber should be set aside; even earlier conservation ordinances are on record. However, most seem to have received the same fate—they were largely ignored; not until the second half of the nineteenth century did any popular, conservationist sentiment arise. The intellectual base for this sentiment came in the form of a massive and surprisingly readable tome published during the closing years of the Civil War, and entitled *Man and Nature* (later known as *The Earth as Modified by Human Action*). Its author was George P. Marsh, whose previous works had dealt with the origins of the English language.

In *Man and Nature*, Marsh provided extensive documentation for his theme, the relatively unexplored idea that man was in the process of making global and often permanent changes in "the balance of nature." His examples included the digging of canals, the removal of seaside dunes, the draining of swamps, the introduction of exotic animals and plants, and the destruction of forests. He examined the consequences of these actions at length; some section headings in his chapter on "The Woods" are: "Electrical Influence of Trees," "Chemical Influence of the Forest," "Trees as Conductors of Heat," "Influence of Forests on the Humidity of the Air and the Earth," "Its Influence on the Flow of Springs," "Protection against the Fall of Rocks and Avalanches by Trees," and so forth. Marsh's insistence that man's activities were having a profound effect on nature was most timely because he had the full weight of nineteenth-century philosophy behind him, which preached that man had been endowed by God with dignity and power. It is appropriate that he chose a quotation from a sermon by Horace Bushnell for the inscription on the title page of *Man and Nature*: "Not all the winds, and storms, and earthquakes, and seas, and seasons of the world, have done so much to revolutionize the earth as Man, the power of an endless life, has done since the day he came forth upon it, and received dominion over it."

Having presented his argument that man was changing nature, Marsh went a step farther in a significant departure from the Judeo-Christian doctrine that God made man master of nature. Marsh wrote: "The equation of animal and vegetable life is too complicated a problem for human intelligence to solve, and we can never know how wide a circle of disturbance we produce in the harmonies of nature when we throw the smallest pebble into the ocean of organic life. This much we seem authorized to conclude . . . the law of self-preservation requires us to restore the equilibrium, by either directly returning the weight abstracted from one scale, or removing a corresponding quantity from the other. In other words, destruction must be either repaired by reproduction, or compensated by new destruction in an opposite quarter." The intellectual origins of the conservation movement are here, plainly stated. When man altered his natural surroundings, the results were frequently unforeseen and unpleasant. This was a situation that the disturbers were obliged to correct, either by protecting the disturbed environment and allowing ecological processes to effect restoration insofar as possible, or by following the more dangerous but sometimes necessary course of redressing the balance through additional alteration and management.

Marsh was responsible for establishing the broad features of the conservation idea, but he did not determine specific policies. This was done during the last decades of the nineteenth century and the first decade of the twentieth, and it was during this time that conservationists found themselves split into two groups, one of which was to dominate United States conservation efforts. Although many persons were associated with the conservation movement during this period, two men best represent the opposing points of view; they were Gifford Pinchot, America's first professional forester and later chief of what was to become the United States Forestry Service, and John Muir, naturalist, author, and founder of the Sierra Club.

In 1910, in a book entitled *The Fight for Conservation*, Pinchot defined what he meant by the word "conservation," which he had coined several years earlier. "The first principle of conservation is development, the use of the natural resources now existing on this continent for the benefit of the people who live here now. . . . In the second place conservation stands for the prevention of waste . . . there is a third principle. It is this: The natural resources must be developed and pre-

served for the benefit of the many, and not merely for the profit of a few."
Like Marsh before him, Pinchot was in accord with his times. His first
principle of conservation said nothing to damp the exuberance of a
country just beginning to become aware of its power, and the second
and third principles blended nicely with the muckraking, trust-busting,
outraged public spirit of the early 1900's.

Muir was a generation older than Pinchot, although their careers
overlapped at a critical time. In 1908 Secretary of the Interior James R.
Garfield granted a permit to the city of San Francisco to dam the Hetch-
Hetchy Valley in Yosemite National Park and turn it into a city reservoir. Muir (2), whose writing had prompted the creation of the Park in
the first place, had written earlier, "Any fool can destroy trees. They
cannot run away; and if they could, they would still be destroyed. . . . It
took more than three thousand years to make some of the trees in these
western woods—trees that are still standing in perfect strength and
beauty, waving and singing in the mighty forests of the Sierra. . . . God
has cared for these trees, saved them from drought, disease, avalanches,
and a thousand straining, leveling tempests and floods; but He cannot save them from fools—Only Uncle Sam can do that." Acting on this
belief, he appealed to his friend President Theodore Roosevelt, but
Roosevelt's term of office expired with the matter unresolved. In 1911
the Advisory Board of Army Engineers revealed the true issue in its report on the Hetch-Hetchy proposal: "The Board is of the opinion that
there are several sources of water supply that could be obtained and
used by the City of San Francisco. . . . From any one of these sources
the water is sufficient in quantity and is, or can be made suitable in quality, while the engineering difficulties are not insurmountable. The determining factor is principally one of cost." Pinchot supported this viewpoint, which was consistent with his resource-oriented philosophy of
conservation. He urged San Francisco to "make provision for a water
supply from the Yosemite National Park. . . . I will stand ready to render any assistance in my power." The kind of cost accounting that was
favored by Muir, an accounting based on present and future esthetic
intangibles as well as material considerations, was rejected not only by
Pinchot but also by Congress, which legislated the damming of Hetch-
Hetchy several months before Muir's death in 1914.

To Pinchot, conservation meant the development and wise use of
our material natural resources: forests, agricultural land, water, and
mineral reserves. To him belongs much of the credit for establishing
strong governmental agencies to promote conservation, and also the
credit for saving millions of acres of forest land in the system of National
Forests, which was largely of his design. During the first half of the
twentieth century the conservation of material resources was advanced
on a number of fronts. Sport fish and game management had widespread
public support and had many successes. Few of the threatened species

in the United States have ever been major game animals. The Bureau of Sport Fisheries and Wildlife's deer census showed an increase in the national deer population from 500,000 in 1890 to 14 million in 1963. The Migratory Treaty (1916) and subsequent Migratory Bird Treaty Act (1918) were aimed primarily at game birds that regularly crossed the United States-Canadian border, but offered protection to other species as well. Commercial and sport fishermen have been aided by extensive research on the physiology, behavior, population biology, and ecology of various species of salmon, trout, bass, and other edible fish. The Fur Seal Treaty of 1911, signed by Japan, Russia, Canada, and the United States, was the first international agreement to protect a marine resource. The Soil Erosion Service of the Department of the Interior (in 1935 it became the Soil Conservation Service of the Department of Agriculture) initiated thousands of projects to prevent the recurrence of the dust bowls that were common during the Great Depression; these projects included the establishment of soil conservation districts and the creation of the Shelterbelt program, in which thousands of miles of tree windbreaks were planted in the plains states. Finally, many areas were designated as national parks and monuments, most of them in wilderness regions of great beauty, and most of them highly suited for recreation such as camping, hiking, boating, and fishing.

At the height of the hard-fought campaign to save America's material natural resources, there was a technical advance in biological conservation practice that was of great significance. George Marsh had written about two ways of restoring natural "harmony": The first way was primarily protection; the second involved protection plus additional planned interference with biological and nonbiological parts of the ecosystem to achieve a desired result. The latter method was both hazardous and difficult to apply, and it was not until 1933, when Aldo Leopold of the University of Wisconsin published a book entitled *Game Management*, that the second of Marsh's two approaches to conservation became really practical. Leopold studied the interrelationships among wild animals and their habitats, and described the conditions that would produce a surplus of game animals which could be harvested by man without endangering the breeding stock. Leopold's conclusions were independently confirmed by a growing number of field ecologists and conservationists, including F. Fraser Darling (3), who spent two years in the Scottish Highlands observing the native red deer. In his classic account of his findings, entitled *A Herd of Red Deer*, Darling wrote, "A constant mistake in Scotland has been the equal toll [by hunting] of stags and hinds [females]. There should be a kill of twice as many hinds as stags, [as an effective population control measure] and the overall kill should be a fifth of the whole stock. The hind stock should be kept young, except for a few leaders, and, therefore, highly productive, and stocking should be below capacity, say 1 to 60 acres." Closely reasoned

*Fig. 1-2 (left)* John Muir in redwood forest. *Fig. 1-2 (below)* Ribbon Falls between oaks, Hetch-Hetchy Valley, 1894. (Both: The Sierra Club)

*Fig. 1-2 (above)  Gifford Pinchot during inaugural parade, March 1925. (U.S. Forest Service)*

*Fig. 1-2 (right)  Upper end of Hetch-Hetchy Reservoir at low water, 1955. (Philip Hyde)*

and well-documented game management plans such as this one were the response to Leopold's contention that simple protection for a community that was already unbalanced by loss of predator species could result in drastic overpopulation of deer and other game, with attendant weakening of individual animals.

During the time when Pinchot's style of conservation was making its greatest gains (roughly during the first half of the twentieth century), the preservation of communities and species that were not considered prime material resources in their original form was left, by default, to private organizations with limited resources, such as the Sierra Club and the Audubon Society. The natural communities that suffered most were swamps and wetlands, river estuaries, bays, offshore marine habitats, coastal beach and dune communities, inland waters, grasslands, deserts, and the island patches of semiwild land that once were a characteristic feature of American suburbs. Species that were especially affected included the fishes that spawn in estuaries and coastal waters, nonsport freshwater fishes (particularly those in the Southwest, in the Great Lakes, and in heavily polluted rivers), predatory birds and mammals, trees that grow slowly, species requiring solitude or unspoiled habitat during some phase of their life cycles, species like small song birds displaced by imported competitors or parasites, and many others.

By 1960 it had become apparent that the traditional policies of conservation in the United States were inadequate to meet the conservation needs of the country. Muir's conservation philosophy had been disregarded because the things he prized, unspoiled wilderness areas, had no cash value as natural resources. However, during the 1960s, under the twin pressures of a rapidly expanding population and heavy industrialization, the seemingly inexhaustible open space began to shrink at an alarming rate. This change in the status of natural communities and species encouraged a possible compromise between the Muir and the Pinchot schools of conservation. As wilderness areas dwindled in number and size, the once intangible value of the remaining areas and the creatures they contained became suddenly quite real. Government agencies, such as the conservation departments of a number of states, the National Park Service, and the Bureau of Sport Fisheries and Wildlife started to assume responsibility for some conservation efforts that had previously been left to private initiative. One began to hear expressions like "the quality of life," expressions which carried the implication that man had been unable to construct entirely artificial environments that were worth living in. Thus the total remaining biota of the nation could be considered a prime resource, security against the failures of technology; and the major differences that had divided conservationists no longer were insurmountable. Matters of policy and procedure still cause differences of opinion among conservationists, but there is now some hope that at least a small measure of unanimity may be attained before there is nothing left to preserve.

**COMMUNITIES AND**   Throughout most of this book the conserva-
**SPECIES—A NOTE**   tion of communities and of species are
**OF CAUTION**   treated separately. This facilitates the organization of a great deal of diverse material
in a relatively simple and rational way. It is, however, as artificial as any textbook categorization is bound to be. All natural communities are composed of species; all species are members of some community. Therefore, although it may be useful for the purpose of understanding to have the conservation puzzle separated into its component parts, it is essential that at some point the reader perform the necessary integration of these parts so that a coherent picture of the whole subject will emerge.

The scope of this book is limited to *biological* conservation, the conservation of flora and fauna. One could stretch a point to include soils; this has not been done, nor is the conservation of water (as distinct from aquatic habitats), minerals, or commercial lumber reserves discussed. Fortunately, these topics have been advertised for a half-century; there is a large and continuing flow of literature about them.

The United States is not alone in facing an acute conservation crisis. The problem is global, although its manifestations vary from place to place, depending on a multitude of local circumstances. For this reason, the examples used in subsequent chapters are not confined to this country or to the North American Continent.

## FURTHER READING

Clepper, Henry, ed., *Origins of American Conservation*. New York: Ronald Press, 1966.
Hays, Samuel P., *Conservation and the Gospel of Efficiency*. Cambridge, Mass.: Harvard University Press, 1959.
Leopold, Aldo, *A Sand County Almanac*. New York: Oxford, 1966.
Nash, Roderick, *The American Environment: Readings in the History of Conservation*. Reading, Mass.: Addison-Wesley, 1968.

## REFERENCES

1.   Kesteven, G. L., *Science 160*, 857 (1968).
2.   Badè, W. F., *The Life and Letters of John Muir, Vol. II* (Houghton Mifflin, Boston, Mass., 1924).
3.   Darling, F. Fraser, *A Herd of Red Deer* (Doubleday, Anchor Books, Garden City, N.Y., 1964).

# chapter 2

# *Factors that Threaten Natural Communities*

**COMMUNITIES** Plants and animals are not sprinkled haphazardly over the surface of the earth; each species has a geographical range and occupies restricted portions of the territory within that range. The primary environmental determinants of the distribution of species are geology and climate, accounting for variables such as soil type, topography, yearly temperature profile, and rainfall. To say that particular plants and animals will be found where conditions are right for them is a truism, but there is a less obvious corollary: Plants and animals are rarely found in all places where conditions are presumably right for them. The European starling, *Sturnus vulgaris*, was not found in the United States prior to 1890; yet after its introduction by man it adapted remarkably well, spreading from New York's Central Park to the West Coast, Mexico, and Alaska in 60 years. Evidently the starling was not a resident of a large part of the earth that constituted an ideal habitat for it. Charles S. Elton (*1*) has written: "When one was a child, this circumstance was very simply summed up in books about animals. The tiger lives in India. The wallaby lives in Australia. The hippopotamus lives in Africa." To the geologic and climatic determinants we must therefore add the biological determinant of dispersive power and the determinant of history. The area where a plant or animal naturally occurs is related to the place where it evolved and its movements since that time.

One major determinant of species distribution that remains to be mentioned is the distribution of other species. Biologists have long been aware that the distribution of animals is greatly dependent on that of plants; the dependence of plants on plants, of plants on animals, and of animals on animals is equally well documented. This dependence is not simply a matter of parasitism. Relationships between species may be subtly constructed in space and time. Tobacco grows well in fields that previously have been covered with wild ragweed. Amazon parrots nest in the hollows of diseased or dead trees; the 200 remaining Puerto Rican parrots (*Amazona vittata*) may not now find enough of these trees in their protected area in the Espiritu Santo Valley to maintain the species. Baby burrowing owls frighten away potential predators by imitating the warning buzz of a rattlesnake. Every type of animal and plant in a region is linked with all others in an evolved meshwork of immense complexity. Some are less dependent than others on the biological integrity of the region—there are always a few adaptable species that persist after most of their neighbors have gone—but all are involved with each other to some degree.

This kind of assemblage of plants and animals sharing a common environment and a degree of common history, and operating as a highly interrelated unit, is known as a *community*. Similar environments may generate similar-looking communities in different places (the rain forests of Panama resemble the rain forests of equatorial Africa), but the elements of these similar communities are rarely the same species. Although it is literally quite true that no square inch of the earth's surface is exactly like any other square inch in climate, topography, and soil type, nevertheless we find that the number of major kinds of communities is small. A particular community is most easily characterized by its most typical members, indicator species that are rarely found in other communities in the vicinity. The indicator species for the formerly predominant community of the north-central part of Indiana are sugar maple and beech trees and the small woodland salamander, *Plethodon cinereus*. Ecologists often group similar terrestrial communities together in broad categories, described for convenience by their vegetation type. In one widely accepted classification scheme these categories are known as *biomes* and include desert, grassland, savanna, and forest, in order of increasing rainfall.

From the standpoint of conservation the most important thing about communities is that their growth and maturation involve a series of metamorphoses. Each stage is a different community; only a few of the former species remain when a new community replaces the old. The metamorphic process, whose study was pioneered in the United States by H. C. Cowles and F. E. Clements, is referred to as *succession*. The total assemblage of communities that occupies a given region during succession is known as a *sere*. The final stage of a sere, which in theory will remain until some major geologic or climatic change takes place, is called the *climax community*. If the climax is representative of the virgin flora and fauna of its climatic region, it is a *climatic climax*; if it is different because of some local peculiarity in the physical environment, such as atypical soil or unusually frequent fires, it is an *edaphic climax*. The complexity of the sere varies from place to place; seral stages in tropical climates with high yearly rainfall contain the largest number of species interlinked in the most complex way. This "horizontal" increase in community complexity as the equator is approached is often paralleled by a similar increase along the time axis, with the climax community

*Fig. 2-1   Rain forest on French Guiana-Brazil border. The climax community contains hundreds of species of trees per square mile. (Jerry Frank)*

containing more elements more intricately related than in earlier seral stages.

It is probably climatic stability that accounts in part for the multitude of species in the tropical rain forest, where each square mile contains hundreds of different sorts of trees, and it is probably another and different kind of stability that accounts for the relative complexity of climax communities when compared to their predecessors. Here, the only thing that changes in time is the biological matrix. A climax beech and sugar maple community does not spring full-blown from the bare earth, but arises (in one sequence) in the shelter of a red oak and white oak forest, which may have arisen from a black oak grove derived in turn from a jack pine forest which was itself preceded by cottonwood. The maturation of each seral stage prior to the climax provides conditions unfavorable for growth of the young of its own species, but favorable for the young of the community to follow. Many species of southern pine sprout and grow readily in open fields, but pine seedlings cannot compete with oak and magnolia in a mature pine forest. Eugene Odum (see Further Reading at end of this chapter) has summarized these concepts in this way: " . . . the mature community with its greater diversity, larger organic structure, and balanced energy flows is often able to buffer the physical environment to a greater extent than the young (early) community, which, however, is often the more productive. Thus, the achievement of a measure of stability or homeostasis . . . in a fluctuating physical environment may well be the primary purpose (that is, the survival value) of ecological succession when viewed from the evolutionary standpoint."

From the point of view of the conservationist the significance of succession in terrestrial communities is plain. Most of the natural communities that are particularly threatened and in need of preservation, the original communities that first came with the land and identify it, are in or near a climax stage. The built-in stability of these communities is often sufficient to overcome small challenges to their integrity, but as Marsh long ago pointed out, man is not limited to small challenges. When enough damage is done to a climax community, it does not grow back. The climax community comes into being in the shadow and protection of the penultimate seral stage; its own structure and functions maintain it, and it is climax because no other assemblage of species can replace it. If its structure is lost to the bulldozer and chain saw, the only way to get it back is via the lengthy process of succession, if at all. Climax communities cannot be planted or stocked, and the number of variables to take into account are innumerable. Since the course of a sere is reckoned in hundreds or thousands of years, the loss of a mature _ecosystem_ (a community in its total physical environment) is as permanent, on the time scale of human civilizations, as the extinction of a species.

Additional ecological topics will be considered in their conservation context, but ecology is an extensive subject and cannot be covered completely in this text. In particular, the idea that one climatic zone ordinarily has only one climatic climax community is an oversimplification made only for the sake of brevity. The reader should consult the references at the end of the chapter for more information on community ecology.

### POPULATION AND TECHNOLOGY

#### Population

It is no longer necessary to provide a gentle and reticent exposition of the problems associated with a rapidly increasing population; students are frequently intimidated by professors brandishing exponential curves, and subway riders feel the pinch more directly. Already, fresh water, food, and space have been depleted in some places; unless present trends are altered, these prerequisites for life will soon be available in sufficient quantities only in a few fortunate enclaves in a sea of poverty. Agricultural researchers, urban planners, sociologists, and psychologists seem to agree on only one thing: Overcrowding is bad, and the human crowd is increasing so rapidly that new problems arise faster than old ones are being solved. Conservationists, as might be expected, are generally at the heart of the population control movement. All kinds of conservationists find themselves involved: Expanding human populations consume food, commodities, and space at a rate that frightens resource conservationists; expanding populations also destroy habitats and communities and overcrowd the fragile parks and wilderness areas at a rate that frightens wildlife conservationists.

The correlation between population expansion and loss of resources appears to be simple and direct, and it would seem that the resource conservationist should have no trouble in testing it. The extent of real and potential resources can be estimated, and this, if combined with the predicted rate of consumption, should in many cases give a good measure of the effect of increasing population. Such technical predictions, however, may fall short of usefulness. Thus, W. R. Schmitt(2), in a discussion of the planetary food potential in a world that may contain 30 billion people by the twenty-second century, claims that: "Technically, the long-range prospects for adequate nutrition are excellent — other factors than the food supply will likely control the size of the human population. . . ." But Schmitt also points out: "Socioeconomic restraints control food production before physical factors do, because the potential of each major mode — agriculture, silviculture, aquaculture, and microbial culture — in terms of the production of organic matter, is greater than the requirements of three billion people, or even of the 30 billion projected for the future. Yet, food shortages exist." Evidently, in this branch of conservation (resource conservation) the effects of population increase, although of major importance, are neither simple nor readily predictable. Many times in this century we have seen populations starve while mountains of food were available on the other side of a political boundary. Other supporting examples may be found in the areas of mineral, fuel, and water resources, where the aforementioned imponderables plus the prospects of improved technologies and development of the embryonic field of reclamation of raw materials from processed goods make it difficult to assess the impact of increased demand.

If the effects of population increase on resources are hard to predict, what about the effects on natural communities? It is possible to demonstrate that the growth of human societies has been accompanied by a parallel increase in the cultivation and settlement of land, with displacement of natural communities as the result. But the effects of the human population increase are not so simple or direct as the mere taking and modification of land in accordance with the number of people there are to support. For example, a glance at a world population map will reveal that Europe is one of the most uniformly densely populated areas, with 100–500 persons per square mile in most places. Central America, on the other hand, averages less than 100 persons per square mile, and for many regions the figure is near zero. Yet the European population lives in relative balance with the remnants of a Palearctic flora and fauna that was never very rich to begin with; a series of fairly stable compromise communities has been established, and in a number of national parks, primarily in Hungary, Czechoslovakia, Poland, and the Soviet Union, one can still see representative forests, marshlands, and alpine communities, some containing wild boar, wolves, and bears. In contrast, despite the lower population density, ecosystems are in turmoil throughout Central America, and as yet there are almost no national parks in the broad sense of the term as used in Africa, Europe, and North America. There are still many undamaged areas remaining in Central America, proportionally much more than in Europe, but they are disappearing rapidly and there is no indication that a European style of compromise conservation will be worked out. With one or two exceptions, Central American countries have demonstrated little effective concern for conservation practices.

Perhaps the density of population is no more important than other parameters, such as the rate of population increase (Central America has one of the highest rates in the world; Europe, the lowest), cultural history, and population movements. In Japan, with an average population density of 700 persons per square mile, alpine roses, sika deer, and the aggressive Asiatic black bear can be found in the timberline community of the Akan National Park in the eastern part of the large island of Hokkaido. It is true that most Japanese national parks incorporate manmade features like Shinto shrines, Buddhist temples, towns, and occasionally industrial areas; however, this should not be unexpected: Their cultural, religious, and social institutions and their low rate of population increase in recent years have enabled the Japanese to evolve a prosperous society that is somehow partly integrated into the natural landscape rather than at war with it. It may be worth mentioning that if the earth's population reaches 30 billion, the population density on all potentially inhabitable land will average a little more than 700 persons per square mile. Unfortunately, unless present indications prove false, there seems very little likelihood that much of this area will be as pleasant as Japan is now. Specific aspects of the population problem are described in subsequent sections.

***Technology***    Throughout the United States (and in other industrialized countries with a variety of political systems) there exists a curious assortment of monumental engineering projects whose function is obscure: Combined water conservation-hydroelectric dams which waste vast quantities of water through seepage into bed rock and through evaporation, which impair water quality through silting, and which produce relatively expensive electric power; flood-control dams on rivers that rarely flood; new, shallow-draft barge canals in the space age; and rural superhighways that carry barely enough traffic to crowd a bicycle path. In the case of most of these projects, there is no clear connection with the needs of an expanding population. Such connections are often suggested by proponents of the engineering schemes; nevertheless most of the projects are built in areas of extremely low population density, provide surprisingly few permanent jobs, and produce a service that is usually but one of several economically feasible alternatives. In a somewhat different but related category are what might be called the superfluous industries: industries that convert sweet, slightly yellowish sugar into sweet, white sugar at considerable cost to the consumer; industries that add unnecessary methyl groups to perfectly serviceable molecules (drugs are a prime example), thus creating a "new" product; and industries that produce marginally useful products and then create a market for them, as is the case with many varieties of cosmetics, household "aids," packaged goods, and even textbooks. Although in many cases these industries meet genuine consumer demand, they, also, cannot be considered a result of population increase.

These forms of modern technology appear to some extent to operate independently of the feedback controls that regulate industrial production in modern capitalist and communist economies. In short, they are hard to turn off—even part way. One reason, at least in the case of the heavy construction industry, must be the enormous inventory of expensive and specialized equipment like power shovels and bulldozers. In 1964, before the Vietnamese war began seriously to distort economic indicators, shipments of selected types of construction machinery monitored by the U.S. Department of Commerce were valued at $2,256,000,000. Another less tangible reason is the natural desire of people who possess highly developed skills to want to use them. Presumably, an undammed river gorge, an unpaved mountain ridge, or the chance to make a sudsier cleanser are professional opportunities to engineers, regardless of the actual merit of the plans. Yet despite these factors weighing against change, it is not clear, at least to this author, why alternatives to slowdown have been so little explored. Surely in urban reconstruction there exist challenges equal to the damming of the Grand Canyon. The repair and renovation of existing highways in congested zones is primitive, slow, and unimaginative; modern engineering has passed it by. But even the simple and cheap expedient of consultation with ecologists and other biologists during the initial project planning stage is unusual; more frequently they are summoned later to repair the damage. Few persons who have experienced the benefits of technology would wish to do without them, but it has become painfully obvious that technology is not an unmixed blessing.

The pressures generated by the growth of population and technology are not always easy to distinguish, but it is necessary, if practical solutions are to be found, to remember that population alone is not at the root of all conservation problems. Every conservation problem is unique, so the search for underlying causes of a disturbance is rarely routine. Certain classes of factors that threaten natural communities do recur, however, and they are discussed in the remainder of this chapter. Population and technology, the prime factors, are usually identifiable somewhere in the picture, and it will be left to the reader to make what will sometimes be an indirect connection.

## LANDSCAPE ALTERATION

### Agricultural Clearing

Many of the activities that affect ecosystems involve direct destruction of the physical and biotic substrate. In the past, the clearing of land for cultivation was responsible for most landscape alteration. This process has now largely ceased; in some places it has been actually reversed. Ireland, Japan, Sweden, and Switzerland now have a smaller land area under cultivation than in previous years. The Soviet Union, according to L. R. Brown (3), "is reportedly abandoning some of the land brought under cultivation during the expansion into the 'virgin-lands' area in the late 1950's." By 1966, one-seventh of all cropland in the United States was idle, primarily because of governmental restrictions. This unused acreage has subsequently been substantially reduced in response to world food shortages and declining grain reserves. The most populous countries, India and China, are cultivating nearly all of their suitable land: India planned to expand its farmland area less than 2 percent between 1966 and 1971. Of the major types of biotic community that are seriously threatened by agricultural expansion at this time, perhaps the most important are the low-lying, coastal deserts found on most continents, and the tropical rain forests of the Amazon basin, Africa south of the Sahara, and southeast Asia.

If fertilized and irrigated, deserts can prove very productive; the limiting factor is fresh water, and it will remain limiting until desalinization of sea water becomes economically practical—probably around 1980. Tropical rain forests present more of a problem, and there is no guarantee that they will ever be amenable to large-scale clearing for agricultural purposes. Despite the lush appearance of tropical rain forests, their soils are usually poor and thin, and are often undergoing a natural process known as "laterization." In this process, which occurs in the soil zone between high and low water table, silica and some of the organic materials are leached downward, and most of the remaining organic material is oxidized. If the thin topsoil is eroded away in an area of laterization, this exposes a layer of aluminum and iron oxides, which can form a hard, impermeable, red crust called *laterite*. Once formed, this crust appears to be relatively permanent, and will support only an edaphic climax vegetation of widely spaced, low, herbaceous shrubs. In addition to the danger of producing laterite soils, deforestation can modify climate: P. Dansereau (4) cites examples in which removal of native vegetation may have caused a warming trend in Brazil, in Africa, and in Ohio. In Central and South America, the traditional Indian agricultural methods still seem better suited to the local environment than many "modern" techniques. Small patches of rain forest are cleared, and several different types of crop are planted, as if in imitation of the original community (see Geertz, Further Reading, Chap. 7). Thus banana plants may be used to shade other vegetable crops. After several years, the clearing is abandoned and secondary succession begins. In contrast, the large banana plantations initially produce a more marketable fruit, but experience in Central America has shown that prolonged use of the land for growing bananas may favor the growth of banana parasites as well. Extensive plantation holdings and even cities have been deserted, and the biotic and economic future of these areas is uncertain.

**Defoliation**    Although unrelated to the increase of croplands, there is another landscape-altering process that could cause the deterioration of tropical rain-forest communities and soils. This is "defoliation," which has been practiced extensively in Vietnam. Approximately 13–14 million pounds of 2,4-D and 2,4,5-T (di- and trichlorophenoxyacetic acids), the entire production of these chemicals in the United States during 1967 and 1968, plus other

*Fig. 2-2   Multiple crop agriculture on the farm of Mr. Bertie Downs, Tortu-
guero, Costa Rica. Nearly every plant in this seeming jungle of vegetation is
used for food or medicine. Bananas, sugar cane, and young papayas are visible.
(David W. Ehrenfeld)*

compounds like the arsenic-containing cacodylic acid, have been
sprayed on the Vietnamese rain forests. According to T. O. Perry (5),
doses of 2,4-D and 2,4,5-T in excess of 3 pounds per acre are nonselective in their effects; if applied as oil basal sprays, the vegetation is killed
from the ground up. There are those who dispute Perry's figures as excessive, based on agricultural experience with herbicides, although it
does seem obvious that, to be effective, military spraying must destroy
all foliage above waist height. Even Perry's critics agree that this may
cause the loss of the climax community. Soil changes and the intrusion
of dense stands of bamboo are possible outcomes. Research in the
United States has largely been confined to studies of the effects of weed
control spraying along railroad tracks; it is unlikely that the conclusions
reached in these studies of disturbed, temperate climate ecosystems

*Fig. 2-3  Defoliated mangrove swamp in Vietnam. Mangroves are especially sensitive to defoliating chemicals. (Courtesy Society for Social Responsibility in Science)*

can be extended to predict long-range changes in Vietnam. Short-range changes, aside from the loss of nearly all flora and fauna in the repeatedly sprayed areas, have already occurred. A single forest fire destroyed nearly 100,000 acres of heavily treated woods near Saigon. Living rain forests do not ordinarily burn.

***Urban Expansion***  Far more important today than the expansion of conventional agriculture as a threat to communities is the world phenomenon of urbanization. During the first part of this century, this actually meant the recovery of rural land as the population migrated to the centers of widely spaced cities. This is no longer true. Two factors now affect the fate of land adjacent to urban areas: first, the steady increase in city population caused by continued migration and high birth rates; and second, the increase in per capita requirement of land. It is expected, for example, that between 1965 and 2000 the average town dweller in France will have doubled his space consumption. Because the population will also double, the total urban area of France will quadruple in one generation. Under this kind of pressure, neighboring cities coalesce. A single urban area will soon stretch from Amsterdam south to Paris and along the Rhine to Köln (Cologne) and the Ruhr. Similar regions are developing in the United States along the shore of Lake Erie and along the Atlantic Coast from Boston to Washington. Urban land area in the United States is expected to increase from 21 million acres in 1960 to 45 million acres by the end of the century.

Since 62 percent of the total land in the United States is privately owned, any comprehensive planning of urban spread must be accompanied by the advance purchase of property by the government or by strict regulation of land use. This has not generally been done, and these functions have been delegated to local governments (whose authority to plan derives from the police power of the states), with the Federal Government keeping only loose control over the financing of housing construction. Although there has been an increased tendency toward the formation of regional associations for metropolitan planning, it is not likely that the alteration of exurban communities in the United States will be an orderly or coordinated process in the foreseeable future. Nevertheless, there are several interdisciplinary groups that are planning for a more extensive reorganization of urban structure than has yet been attempted anywhere. Athelstan Spilhaus (6) has said: "The overgrown urban complex must be selectively dismantled and dispersed if we are to cure the ills of the megalopolis." He suggests that when the population of the earth reaches 15 billion, around A.D. 2068, it could be housed in 60,000 cities, each with a population of a quarter of a million, and each surrounded by 40,000 acres (64 square miles) of "open land." There are many other plans for model cities, including a few like Disneyworld's model city in central Florida, which have gone beyond the planning stage. Aside from pollution control, some of these model cities often seem to be no better designed to coexist with their regional ecosystems than do existing cities and are possibly much worse. Here, as in other land-using ventures, it is imperative that ecologists and residents of the region where the city is to be located be given a major role in formulating the initial plans. When this kind of cooperation occurs, the results can be spectacular, as in the case of Columbia, Maryland, where 15,000 acres of farmland were turned into an eminently livable model city without damaging the considerable natural and historical attributes of the region.

One effect of the rapid urbanization of the United States (and all other countries) will be to cause enormous harm to natural and seminatural communities, including those most accessible to the bulk of the population. The expansion of cities into land surrounding them does not necessarily mean the loss of natural communities; much of this land is

*Fig. 2-4   The Passaic River in New Jersey's Great Swamp. (Annan Photo Features)*

already semiurbanized, containing dilapidated buildings and weedy, treeless lots. There are, however, some surprisingly intact areas near even the largest cities. Regulations against hunting and overnight camping in densely populated suburban regions have had the effect of protecting bird and small mammal populations. For example, New Jersey's Great Swamp, an exceptionally rich biotic community, is less than 30 miles from the center of the world's largest metropolitan area. Central Park, in Manhattan, is not exactly a natural community, but 101 species of birds have been seen there on a single day. The Cornell Laboratory of Ornithology lists 200 places in Greater New York City where many varieties of birds may be found. At the Jamaica Bay Wildlife Refuge, within the New York City limits and accessible by subway, a number of large, showy birds have started to breed for the first time in this century, despite the noise of arriving and departing jets at Kennedy International Airport a few hundred yards away. These species include the glossy ibis, Louisiana heron and snowy egret, and an assortment of migratory ducks that ordinarily breed in the western prairie regions. Unfortunately, in most large cities the wildlife that remains is usually a testimonial not to far-sighted planning but to human oversight and to the stability of certain natural communities. Even in the New York area, which does not lack conservationists, the Hempstead Plains have been filled with grotesque and dismal suburban developments. The Great Swamp is coveted by airport builders, despite its status as a National Wildlife Refuge, and in Central Park air pollution is finally driving away species of song birds that were able to survive all other challenges presented by more than ten generations of New Yorkers.

In urban areas, public and private land acquisition patterns are based on property valuation and on neighborhood factors; long-range conservational projections to maintain city vitality are shunted aside by the pressure of these immediate economic demands. A prime example of profit making at the expense of both an important ecosystem and the city itself is the filling of the Tampa and San Francisco Bays. In addition to scenic beauty, which in each case is the major attribute of the surrounding city, the bays are strategic spawning areas for a host of marine animals, including game fish. San Francisco Bay is the most important stopping place for migratory birds on the Pacific Flyway. According to the U.S. Fish and Wildlife Service, approximately 1 million water fowl winter on the bay; there may be as many as 30,000 per mile along the tidal flats, and from 50–75 percent of all water birds migrating along the Pacific Coast depend on this habitat.

Surprisingly, much of the floor of both bays is privately owned: 20 percent of San Francisco Bay, including a large part of the biologically rich offshore region, is in the hands of developers and speculators; an-

*Fig. 2-5   Jamaica Bay Wildlife Refuge in New York City, looking toward Kennedy Airport. (Holt photo by John King)*

other 25 percent is owned by local governments whose major concern is
to increase their taxable lands by filling in the bay. Already 15–20 percent of Tampa Bay and one-third of San Francisco Bay have been filled
in. Since some of the fill comes from dredging in other parts of the bay,
the damage is even greater than the numbers indicate. The bottom of
Tampa Bay was referred to by one official of the Interior Department as
a "biological desert." Only part of the fill material is obtained by dredging, however; the remainder is garbage. There are now at least 32 garbage disposal sites jutting out into San Francisco Bay. If San Francisco
Bay becomes 70 percent filled (70 percent of the bay is less than 12 feet
deep and therefore fillable), some meteorologists predict a sharp rise in
summer temperatures and a drastic increase in smog. Geologists worry
about the effects of earthquakes on buildings constructed on the unstable land fill. The narrow, polluted tidal creek that will remain will still be
spanned by the Golden Gate and Bay bridges — a monumentally unfunny
joke on the future residents of the cities of San Francisco, Berkeley, and
Oakland, and on the rest of humanity.

The ecological and aesthetic damage done by the dredgers and
fillers has aroused enough opposition to generate some political action.
In California, the state legislature has finally taken up the problem. In
Florida, the city of Sarasota is holding its present bulkhead line at the
mean high-water mark. No commercial developing will be allowed beyond this line. Florida's Brevard, Martin, and Palm Beach counties,
which are urbanizing rapidly, have passed moratoriums on the sale and
dredging of submerged lands. Florida's Randell Act now requires "biological and ecological surveys" of submerged land before the state will
consider issuing permits for it to be dredged, filled, or sold. Important as
this pioneer law is, William Partington (7) has pointed out that it has a
number of biological defects:

1. The term *ecological surveys* is not well defined; consequently
these surveys are not performed.
2. The Florida Game and Fresh Water Fish Commission is not
asked to evaluate the effects of estuarine development on air-breathing
vertebrates that do not actually live in the water, although many such
mammals, birds, and reptiles depend on an undamaged marine habitat
for food and, indirectly, for shelter.
3. The biological value of land areas above the mean high-water
mark is not usually considered, but the mangrove swamps, button-
woods, or marsh grasses of this zone are an integral part of the coastal
ecosystem, regulating the flow of nutrients, the movement of soil, and
the growth of invertebrates and microorganisms important to the adjacent waters.

Points 2 and 3 underscore the importance of an ecological concept
that must be understood by the concerned public before conservation

**Fig. 2-6 (above)**  *Biscayne Bay, Miami, Florida, 1949.*
**Fig. 2-6 (below)**  *Biscayne Bay, Miami, Florida, 1969. (Both: Bob Graeber, Airflite)*

can become fully effective, namely: An essential structural unity among ecosystems gives them their distinctive character; disturb it and what remains is merely a loose assortment of those animals and plants that may manage to survive under less-than-optimum conditions. We would not think of preserving a historical mansion without its roof or colonnade or grounds. It is strange, then, that we can try to keep some south Florida coastal waters intact, but fail to preserve the intricate tangle of interlocking mangroves that hold the soil, catch organic debris, provide asylum for larvae and invertebrates, and harbor the nests of roseate spoonbills, herons, and ibises. The question of where one ecosystem stops and the next begins, therefore, becomes crucial. Obviously, any demarcation line will be somewhat artificial, yet such decisions can and must be made. For practical purposes, the littoral community of the south Florida Gulf Coast "stops" above the line of salt-tolerant plants that defines the farthest reach of storm tidewater and salt spray.

*Public Works*    Neither agricultural nor urban expansion
*Projects*    are altering the landscape of industrialized
countries as profoundly as an assortment of massive engineering ventures that usually fall under the heading of "public works," and which include dams, flood control projects, and highways. As discussed above, these enterprises are justified by their proponents in terms of urban and/or agricultural need, but in considerable measure serve the purposes of passing out Federal money to the various congressional districts, of utilizing an enormous inventory of heavy construction machinery, and of providing work for a large number of highly trained engineers and the extensive organizations that back them up in both government and private industry. In the United States, the principal governmental agencies that engage in this kind of activity are the Army Corps of Engineers, the Bureau of Reclamation, and the Bureau of Public Roads. The impact of these federal agencies (and many private corporations, especially power companies) on the land has been great, and the net result is difficult to assess. Certainly they are neither the monsters of the popular conservation literature nor the shining knights of the technology-oriented press. They perform a large number of essential services, but they also make mistakes, and these mistakes have caused unnecessary, widespread alteration of the landscape.

Over the years, the "earth movers" have advanced a philosophy that might be crudely summarized as "progress through technology and change." From an ecological point of view, the least appealing aspect of this philosophy is the tendency to minimize both the importance of existing ecosystems and the consequences of their destruction. From the very beginning of the twentieth-century technological upsurge in the

*Fig. 2-7    Mangrove root tangle in Everglades National Park. (National Park Service)*

United States, this idea has been incorporated in a quasi-scientific dialogue having social, economic, and political ramifications. Because the fundamental controversy has undergone little change during the past 75 years, it may be useful to reach back to the scientific literature of the first quarter of this century and uncover a debate that has long since been buried. Earlier, Marsh raised the specter of wholesale changes in climate and stream flow occurring as the result of removal of forest cover in watersheds. In 1909, Lt. Col. H. M. Chittenden (8), of the Army Corps of Engineers, denied Marsh's conclusions in a lengthy paper entitled, "Forests and Reservoirs in Their Relations to Stream Flow, with Particular Reference to Navigable Rivers"; in 1927, Chittenden was answered in turn by Raphael Zon, director of the Lakes States Forest Experiment Station of the U.S. Forest Service, in a monograph titled *Forests and Water in the Light of Scientific Investigation.*

Chittenden based his argument concerning forests and stream flow on two claims: first, that snow accumulates to a lesser degree in forests than in open spaces and melts more quickly in the former (see Fig. 2-8); second, that it is not the cutting of forests but the subsequent

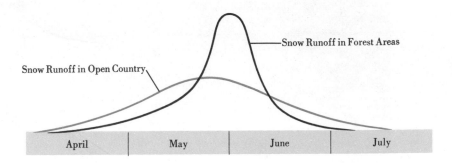

*Fig. 2-8    Graphic illustration of snow melting in forests and open country, Rocky Mountain region. (From "Forests and Reservoirs in Their Relation to Stream Flow, with Particular Reference to Navigable Rivers" by H. M. Chittenden; Trans. Am. Soc. Civ. Eng., 62. 245-546 (1909).)*

cultivation of the cleared land that permits erosion by altering its water-holding and run-off properties. Even this supposed loss of topsoil through cultivation he regarded as beneficial because it "builds up deltas and surely, though slowly, extends the habitable area of the globe." Zon's conclusions were in direct opposition. He claimed that: "Among the factors, such as climate and the regularity of stream flow, the forest plays an important part, especially on impermeable soils. The mean low stages as well as the moderately high stages in the rivers depend upon the extent of forest cover on the watersheds. The forest tends to equalize the flow throughout the year by making the low stages higher and the high stages lower."

The bulk of the Chittenden paper is taken up by a "Discussion" section; a number of the 23 discussants were highly critical of Chittenden's conclusions. The remarks of one participant, Gifford Pinchot, reveal the intensity of the debate: " . . . Colonel Chittenden's fundamental conception as to the forest floor and its influence is mistaken. His idea that records in the United States do not show an increase in the frequency of floods and low waters is mistaken. His idea that the critical point to be considered is flood heights, and not flood frequencies is mistaken. And his conception of forestry . . . is so fundamentally mistaken that the speaker might discuss it at far greater length without exhausting the mistakes." Taken as a whole, the Chittenden paper suffers from the lack of a list of verifiable references and from an approach that makes little use of the fundamental scientific concept of the "control," specifically from a paucity of data comparing stream flow in forested and deforested watersheds in the same climatic region and at the same time. Because of drastic yearly fluctuations in rainfall and temperature, analysis of the same river system for a few years before and after deforestation is not meaningful for the small number of documented examples that Chittenden considers.

In addition to employing the necessary controls (see Table 2-1), Zon uses an analytic approach that is far more amenable to scientific test; he records separately "the influence of the forest upon each of the different factors affecting stream flow, and the final effect of the forest upon stream flow is deduced from the combined effect on all the factors. While less direct, this method lends itself more readily to experimentation. . . ." (See Table 2-1.) Zon's bibliography, in which he cites more than a thousand scientific papers, is a virtually complete review of the literature up to that time. Since 1927 there has been little serious disagreement with Zon's major conclusions, whereas the fate of Chittenden's paper illustrates the danger of advancing unsupported scientific arguments as an ex post facto justification of nonscientific policy.

Space does not permit an exhaustive discussion of all large-scale engineering projects that are now altering or threatening to alter the American landscape, but a few will suffice to illustrate the general lack of concern for biological principles that characterize them.

One of the best examples of a "make-work" scheme that will have disastrous effects on an ecosystem of great international value is the proposed Rampart Canyon Dam construction on the Yukon River. (At the time of this writing, the Corps of Engineers had not received authorization or funds for this controversial project.) If built, the dam will flood 10,500 square miles, obliterating 400 miles of the Yukon River and more than 12,000 miles of its tributaries as well as the 36,000 lakes and ponds of the Yukon Flats. The Yukon Flats ecosystem has been described by A. Starker Leopold and Justin W. Leonard (9): "The Yukon Flats are a complex admixture of lakes, ponds and sloughs, coniferous and hardwood timber, willow brush and muskeg, with tundra on some elevated ridges. Viewed from a low-flying airplane, the intermixing of types on the Flats, it becomes quite clear, is maintained in considerable part by action of the meandering and braided channels of the Yukon River and some of its principal tributaries.

"The Yukon is a restless river, constantly undercutting banks on the outsweep of meanders and depositing new bars on the inner curves. Oxbow sloughs are left in the wake of the migrating channels, and in time these develop marshy borders favorable for waterfowl, muskrats and beavers.

"Newly deposited sandbars soon develop fresh young stands of

Table 2-1    **Effects of Forests on Climate and Local Environmental Conditions**

A. PRECIPITATION IN INCHES WITHIN AND OUTSIDE THE FOREST AT DIFFERENT ALTITUDES

| | Altitude (ft) | | | | | |
|---|---|---|---|---|---|---|
| Location | 3-300 | 330-650 | 980-1300 | 1970-2300 | 2300-2600 | 3000-3250 |
| Stations in the forest (R. Weber) | 25.9 | 26.2 | 29.4 | 42.9 | 55.5 | 69.9 |
| Ordinary stations (Dr. van Bebber) | 25.5 | 22.9 | 27.4 | 36.0 | 38.6 | 37.9 |
| Difference | 0.4 | 3.3 | 2.0 | 6.9 | 16.9 | 32.0 |
| Percent | 1.25 | 14.2 | 7.3 | 19.0 | 43.7 | 84.2 |

B. FREEZING OF SOIL INSIDE AND OUTSIDE THE FOREST

| Stations | Altitude, Nature of Soil, and Composition of Forest | Depth to which Soil Freezes (in.) Outside forest | With-in forest | Differ-ence (in.) | Depth of Frost in Forest Soil in Percent of Depth in Open |
|---|---|---|---|---|---|
| Haguenau (Alsace) | Rhine Valley, 492 ft; gravelly sand mixed with humus; Scotch pine | 19.7 | 8.3 | 11.4 | 42 |
| Eberswalde (near Berlin) | 160 ft; sandy soil mixed with humus; Scotch pine | 27.6 | 18.5 | 9.1 | 67 |
| Neunath (Lorraine) | Plateau, 164 ft; lime rock; beech | 8.7 | 5.9 | 2.8 | 68 |
| Melkerei (Alsace) | Moderate southeast slope, 3114 ft (167 ft below summit of slope); decomposed granite; beech and fir | 17.7 | 13.0 | 4.7 | 73 |

C. COMPUTED RUN-OFF (GAL.) DAILY PER SQUARE MILE FROM FORESTED, CULTIVATED, AND BARREN WATERSHEDS DURING THE LAST EIGHT MONTHS OF 1881

| Month | Passaic, Forested | Raritan, Cultivated | Barren Watershed |
|---|---|---|---|
| April | 597,000 | 754,000 | 631,000 |
| May | 297,000 | 325,000 | 145,000 |
| June | 272,000 | 272,000 | 139,000 |
| July | 207,000 | 134,000 | 22,000 |
| August | 140,000 | 89,000 | 22,000 |
| September | 139,000 | 87,000 | 23,000 |
| October | 129,000 | 84,000 | 22,000 |
| November | 127,000 | 93,000 | 23,000 |

SOURCE: *Forests and Water in the Light of Scientific Investigation*, by Raphael Zon, U.S. Govt. Printing Office (1927).

*Fig. 2-9   The Yukon Flats, August, 1962. (Fish and Wildlife Service)*

willow that constitute excellent winter forage for moose. The willow stands advance slowly through successional stages of aspen or cotton-wood to spruce forest, and the sloughs fill gradually with organic matter and the silt of spring floods. But sooner or later transient channels of the river migrate back through the forest, again initiating the processes of succession. It is this dynamic process of self-renewal that maintains such varied and productive wildlife habitat on the Yukon floodplain."

The dam would substitute for this natural community a large and relatively sterile lake, useless as a breeding site for ducks and geese, and unsuitable as a habitat for the mammals of the region, including more than 10,000 moose, two caribou herds, minks, beavers, otters, martens, wolverines, weasels, lynx, and red foxes. A salmon run that provides 800,000 fish per year for the local inhabitants would be lost. The total waterfowl breeding land that would be inundated amounts to 6.9 million acres, accounting for 1.5 million ducks and 12,500 geese annually. Boating and fishing in the new lake, which will have little sce-nic value, is likely to be impaired by countless snags — remnants of the old forests — that will remain on the bottom for many decades.

The economic arguments against the dam are also strong:

1.  It would create few jobs, and any industry it might attract would be highly automated.

2.  It would produce far more electricity than the projected needs of the population and industry of Alaska during the next half-century,

and its surplus power would probably be too expensive to compete with locally produced nuclear power on the U.S. Pacific Coast, 2000 miles away.

3. There are a number of excellent, untapped sources of power near the population centers of Alaska.

4. The construction cost estimate of $1.3 billion, if previous Corps of Engineers estimates are any indication, is very conservative.

In short, the best that can be said about the Rampart project is that Rampart Canyon is an unoccupied dam site that presents some interesting engineering challenges.

Besides electric power, another common justification for rural engineering projects is the appealing phrase, "water conservation and flood control." Perhaps the most grisly example of compounded errors and ecological mismanagement in the United States is the vast series of canals, levees, dikes, and spillways that comprise the domain of the Central and Southern Florida Flood Control District. That part of Florida south of Lake Okeechobee is the only part of the continental United States that has a nearly subtropical climate, and its dominant biological community, the Everglades, is so complex that its most important biotic relationships are only beginning to be understood. The Everglades were formed and molded by the moderate climate and, equally important, by the high summer rainfall and run-off from Lake Okeechobee. When Lake Okeechobee overflowed, the waters crept south in a broad, shallow sheet, supporting what has aptly been called a "river" of tall sawgrass, and forming teardrop-shaped islands that became covered with a variety of trees, including mahogany and a number of other tropical species. Southwest of the lake there was an extensive region of cypress swamp whose quiet waters were dyed black by organic acids leached from the trees. In the south, sawgrass gradually gave way to mangrove, and fresh water to brackish, in an area that was a remarkably rich spawning ground for fish and invertebrates. The list of animal species was long (and still is), befitting such a highly developed ecosystem. The most representative member of the local fauna was the alligator, whose role is discussed later, but a host of other animals—ranging from the panther to the snail-eating Everglades kite to the loggerhead sea turtles nesting at Cape Sable—were integrated into the Everglades community. As the noted Spanish ecologist Ramon Margalef (10) has pointed out, in a mature (complex) ecosystem the number of species is high, many species are physically and behaviorally specialized, food chains are long, population sizes are relatively stable, and there is a more efficient utilization of solar energy input by the whole community (the ratio of photosynthetic production to community biomass is low). A mature ecosystem confers environmental stability on its member species; indeed the stability and efficiency of these communities go a long way toward explaining why they have evolved (see Chapter 6). But even though mature eco-systems can locally damp the effects of normal environmental fluctuations, the specialization of their individual species makes the community particularly susceptible to extreme environmental changes. In the words of Margalef, "Succession can build history only when the environment is stable. In the case of a changing environment, the se-lected ecosystem will be composed of species with a high reproductive rate and lower special requirements. Such an ecosystem is less diverse and less complex. . . ."

Eighty years of ill-conceived tampering with the water system of south Florida has resulted in such violent environmental fluctuations that the predicted disintegration of the mature Everglades ecosystem has begun to occur. An early attempt to drain the glades for agricultural development culminated in the Tamiami Canal, opened in 1928, and running from the Gulf of Mexico to the Atlantic Ocean. It intercepts much of the southward flow of water from Lake Okeechobee. In 1949, one year after the Everglades National Park was dedicated, the Central and Southern Florida Flood Control District replaced the old Everglades Drainage District as the state authority that was to manage the increas-ingly intricate water diversion system built by the Corps of Engineers.

*Fig. 2-10  The Everglades on the Shark River Tower Loop road. (National Park Service)*

Three "conservation areas" were created between Lake Okeechobee and the Park; these further ensured that the Park could receive no water unless authorized by the Corps or the Flood Control District (Fig. 2-11). Moreover, the water is now delivered by canals, not by slow, steady seepage through the river of grass. The complexity of the artificial system now in operation (many of the canals were built in response to agricultural, real estate, and industrial pressures and do not even meet sound water management criteria) makes it difficult to control; consequently the conditions in the conservation areas, especially Area 3, fluctuate wildly between flood and drought, while the Park rarely has enough water. Floridians have been treated to the spectacle of millions of fish stranded in parched mud holes, and thousands of dead herons and egrets, while a few miles north the Corps of Engineers released "surplus" fresh water into the Atlantic Ocean. Between 1961 and 1967, the wood ibis, North America's only stork, had one successful nesting season.

Although the Flood Control District and Corps of Engineers have become somewhat more sensitive to the needs of the Park, it remains to be seen whether their unwieldy system can ever be tuned finely enough to restore the delicate balance of Everglades ecology. Meanwhile, other factors threaten the ecosystem. On August 11, 1969, the *New York Times* reported that construction had begun on a 39 sq mile jetport in Big Cypress Swamp (see Fig. 2-10), which provides 38 percent of the water flowing into Everglades Park. Initial construction grants by the U.S. Department of Transportation were made without prior consultation with the Department of the Interior. At the time of this writing, further construction on the jetport has been prohibited, but the existing training runway is still in use. In other areas, unregulated suburban residential and industrial expansion have caused intrusion of salt water via canals and via seepage into the depleted underground reservoir or aquifer. Ironically, the Flamingo Canal, built by the Corps under Park authorization to increase visitor access to the Park, was not provided with protective locks, and the saline waters of Florida Bay have flowed into and wrecked Coot Bay and the surrounding area, killing the water plants *Chara* and *Naiad*, which once fed a nesting waterfowl population of several hundred thousand birds. Caught as they are between the twin pressures of a million visitors a year and alteration of the surrounding landscape, there is serious doubt whether the Everglades will survive in the original, unique form that made them worthy of perpetual preservation.

**The Land Ethic** There are other factors that alter landscapes and thus threaten ecosystems and natural communities. "Modern" lumbering operations that substitute monoto-

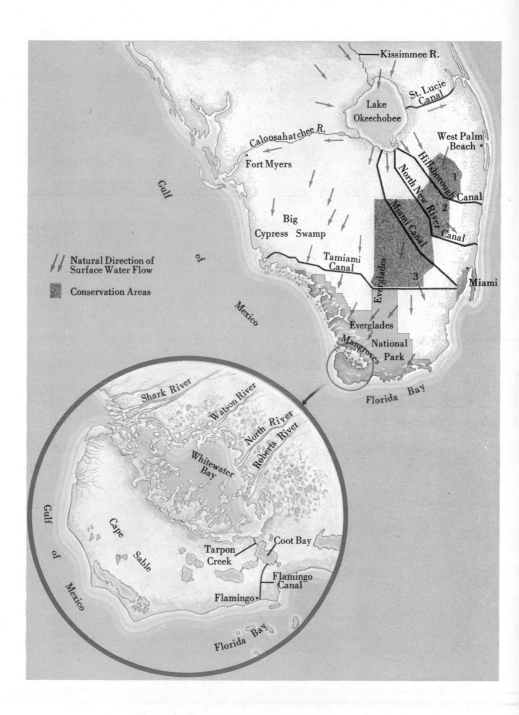

*Fig. 2-11   The Florida Everglades.*

*Fig. 2-12 (above)   Deer in the Everglades during a high water period in 1966. Fig. 2-12 (left)   Dried-up creek in the Everglades during a drought, 1967. (Both: Charles Trainor)*

nous and potentially highly vulnerable stands of a single species of fast-growing tree for the forest ecosystem, inappropriately placed highways, certain strip-mining operations, the building of unneeded gas stations for real estate speculation and tax relief, and many other questionable procedures deserve examination in a longer work. Aldo Leopold, in his essay on "The Land Ethic" in *A Sand County Almanac* (see Further Reading, Chapter 1), has summed up the problem that currently confronts nearly all countries and societies in the world: "There is as yet no ethic dealing with man's relation to land and to the animals and plants which grow upon it. . . . The land relation is still strictly economic, entailing privileges but not obligations. . . . All ethics so far evolved rest upon a single premise: that the individual is a member of a community of interdependent parts. His instincts prompt him to compete for his place in that community, but his ethics prompt him also to co-operate (perhaps in order that there may be a place to compete for)." In the years since Leopold's death there has been scant progress toward his goal of a meaningful and binding land ethic.

*POLLUTION*    Pollution is perhaps the best-publicized of the various threats to ecosystems and natural communities, but the subject is so broad and objectives so diverse that there has been little common ground for discussion, even among conservationists. In this book the two points of view adopted should help clarify the biological aspects of the problem.

First, uncritical appeals for "an end to pollution" are of limited value. Granted, all pollution is bad—but some kinds of pollution are worse, and therefore a list of priorities must be established. This list can be made according to the following set of criteria:

1. The extent, degree, and type of damage caused by the particular pollution.

2. An estimate of the relative effectiveness of methods of stopping the pollution versus methods of treating it after the fact.

3. The existence of reasonable alternatives to pollution and/or economically feasible control methods (this implies that some sources of pollution will have to be allowed to continue operating, at least for the present, and some commercial and noncommercial enterprises must cease operations).

Second, pollution must be judged according to its ecological effects; chemical and other nonbiological quality standards and monitoring systems should be used to supplement rather than to supersede biological evidence of damage. When chemical tests show permissible concentrations of pollutants, but biological indicators show signs of pollution damage, then there is indisputable pollution. Not only are biological indicators often more sensitive to pollution than are other assay methods, but it is the ecosystem with which we are ultimately concerned, not chemical tables of maximum permissible concentrations listed in parts per million.

Pollution may affect water, air, and soil, and insofar as they are separable, our understanding of each category decreases in the order listed. The effects of pollution on natural, aquatic communities will therefore receive the most attention in the following pages. The category of water pollution may be further subdivided: natural pollutants; oxygen-consuming wastes; suspended solids; poisons, including cumulative food chain toxins (pesticides, for example); agents of eutrophication (agents that cause acceleration of the ecological aging process); radioactive wastes; thermal pollutants; salt; oil; detergents; and chemicals whose exact composition and source are unknown. There is, naturally, some overlap among these topics; however, it will simplify matters to discuss them in turn.

***Natural Pollution*** People who think of ecosystems as being maintained by static balance rather than by a dynamic interplay of active processes may have trouble imagining that there can be pollution in the absence of man—yet it occurs often. H. B. N. Hynes describes a number of examples in his excellent book, *The Biology of Polluted Waters* (see Further Reading at end of this chapter). In one case, where fish and invertebrate populations were adversely affected by a toxic substance diffusing out of spruce and red cedar needles that had fallen in the water, Hynes remarks, "Had any mine or factory existed in the area it is probable that its effluent would have been the first suspect, and the investigation might not have been pursued further." The leaves of deciduous hardwoods can also cause pollution, especially at times of low stream flow. It has been shown that leaves falling in ponds and streams during autumn can exert effects by blocking light transmission, interfering with oxygen exchange at the air-water interface and, most important, causing a depletion of dissolved oxygen as they decay. At the time of peak contamination with leaves, fish kills were observed in an otherwise unpolluted stream; in addition to a very low oxygen concentration, levels of iron, manganese, bicarbonate, and pH were significantly altered. One significant difference, however, between natural and man-made pollutants is that the former are all biodegradable, usually in a short period of time, and they are among the normal components of ecosystems. In this respect, "pollutant" may be an inappropriate word for these substances.

***Deoxygenation*** Despite its common occurrence, natural pollution is of minor importance when compared with the pollution caused by man. Of the many forms that this can take, one of the most destructive and most prevalent is pollution by wastes whose consumption by chemical or bacterial oxidation lowers the oxygen concentration of the water. Most of these wastes are organic and consist of raw sewage and industrial effluents such as those from many food-processing plants; but some, like sulfites from pulp and paper mills and ferrous salts from acid mine drainage, are inorganic. In rivers, deoxygenation reaches a peak a short distance downstream from the pollutant outfall, and this coincides with the disappearance of the normal flora and fauna and the appearance of large populations of a few species of organisms that are successful under largely anaerobic conditions. These include the familiar white "sewage fungus" (actually a bacterium, *Sphaerotilus natans*), gas-producing bacteria that reduce sulfate, and invertebrates like the bacteria-eating protozoan, *Paramecium putrinum* and the small, red sludge worms, *Tubifex tubifex* (Fig. 2-13). As expected in communities subjected to extreme fluctuations of environmental conditions, the number of member species is low, but populations of the few adaptable species are likely to be enormous. Fishes, of course, can be killed by low oxygen concentrations, but if the area of deoxygenation is not extensive, they are more likely to migrate. Toxins and low oxygen concentrations often act synergistically on fish. It is unusual for deoxygenation to occur in the absence of other manifestations of pollution.

Because lakes and rivers may be deoxygenated in a variety of ways, it is sometimes important to be able to measure the actual amount of reducing wastes in the water. The BOD (Biochemical Oxygen Demand) test was devised for this purpose; BOD, which is expressed in milligrams per liter (parts per million, ppm) of dissolved oxygen consumed per unit time (for example, a 5-day period is widely used), is supposed to measure deoxygenating pollutants indirectly. In theory and practice it is a simple test: The oxygen saturation of a sample of water is measured (a known quantity of oxygen may be added) and the water is then sealed in a light- and airtight container kept at 20°C. After a given period of time the oxygen saturation of the sample is measured again and the difference between the two readings is taken as a measure of the oxidizable material originally present in the water. Unfortunately, the results of this test, which are the summation of hundreds of different chemical events, are easy to misinterpret; for example, the presence of a poison that lowers the rate of bacterial decomposition of organic matter will give a misleadingly low BOD. Even if the results are accurate, some persons still make the mistake of considering a very low BOD as a sign of clean water, although the test does not measure concentrations of phosphates, nitrates, and other substances that may cause serious

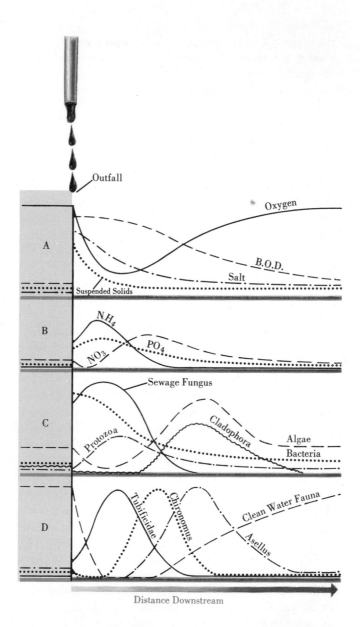

**Fig. 2-13** *Diagrammatic presentation of the effects of an organic effluent on a river and the changes as one passes downstream from the pollution outfall. (A & B) physical and chemical changes, (C) Changes in micro-organisms, (D) Changes in larger animals. (Modified from* The Biology of Polluted Waters, *H. B. N. Hynes, Liverpool U. Press (1963, page 94).)*

pollution (see below). The BOD test is not a comprehensive test for pollutants, but is adequate for monitoring certain controlled waters like the effluents of sewage plants. Analyses of the flora and fauna are the most sensitive tests for pollution in complex natural communities. In the United States, Dr. Ruth Patrick (28) has developed a pollution monitoring system based in part on the population sizes of a variety of indicator species of diatoms, single-celled organisms commonly found in both fresh and salt water. Such observations must be made over a long period of time to discern local trends, since individual bodies of water (particularly estuaries and marine littoral zones) are likely to exhibit unique biotic responses to all but the most extreme pollution. To confuse matters further, the community of a polluted lake in Michigan may resemble the community of an unspoiled lake in Georgia. Thus the word "pollution" must be used with reference to a regional norm. Throughout the temperate latitudes it is especially important to look for the effects of deoxygenation in the summertime because the solubility of oxygen in water is inversely related to temperature and because chemical deoxygenation will proceed at a higher rate.

***Suspended Solids***    Suspended solids in lakes and streams are produced by soil erosion in watersheds, by mine slurries, china-clay quarries, factories where root crops are washed, and other contributors. If chemically inert, these solid wastes may damage ecosystems by clouding water so that game fish and other animals that depend on vision while hunting are unable to find prey, by settling on and killing rooted bottom plants and bottom animals (including salmon and trout eggs), by reducing light transmission needed for photosynthesis, and by drastically altering depth and flow rate because of silting. Suspended solids are becoming an increasingly severe problem in suburban streams that drain areas where construction has exposed the soil. M. F. Katzer and J. W. Pollack (11), who studied Mill Creek (near Washington, D.C.) during a storm, report that at the beginning of the storm the concentration of suspended solids was approximately 11.5 milligrams per liter; 1 hour later the concentration of solids at the same point was 13,000 milligrams per liter. When suspended solids are of industrial origin they are generally easy to trace because of the contrast between the turbidity of the effluent and the relative clarity of the waters that are being polluted.

***Poisons***    Poisons are usually considered to be substances that interfere directly with the essential metabolic chemistry of organisms and which are effective in small doses. These doses may be subdivided and their administration spread over a long period of time in the case of "cumulative" poisons like arsenicals and many pesticides. Poisons vary in their selectivity, but the responses of animals and plants are rarely "all or none" — rather they are related to a difference in toxicity thresholds. The *Handbook of Poisoning* (R. H. Dreisbach, Lange Publications) lists hundreds of the more common poisons, and new industrial processes are adding so many obscure ones to the list that all the challenge has gone out of murder mystery writing. Any of these could find its way into an aquatic ecosystem, and most of them have done so at one time or another; so, any remarks about the effects of poisons on biotic communities are bound to be generalizations riddled with exceptions.

Nevertheless, some generalizations about poisons are important. To paraphrase Hynes (see Further Reading at end of this chapter):

1. Toxicity is dependent upon many environmental factors, particularly temperature, oxygen content, pH, and calcium concentration in the water. Therefore, toxicity experiments performed in the laboratory may have little predictive value when applied to real pollution situations.

2. Although fish are repelled by some poisons, others, such as dilute solutions of ammonia or phenol, can attract them.

3. All but the most extreme cases of poisoning usually leave a few resistant members of susceptible species, and if the resistance is genetically transmissible and the poisoning is continued at the same level, resistant populations may develop. (This phenomenon has played havoc with the users and abusers of antibiotics and pesticides. No hospital is now without its own special strains of penicillin-resistant *Staphylococcus*; and insecticide-resistance has appeared in every major group of insect pests. In Central America, malaria is common wherever continual agricultural spraying has caused the selection of DDT-resistant *Anopheles* mosquitoes.)

4. Poisons rarely affect all species in a habitat; the few species that remain, now free from the danger of predation by those affected, may reach enormous population sizes (see Fig. 2-14), and may otherwise behave like members of an "immature" community.

5. All members of an aquatic community — not just fishes — must be examined for the effects of poisons. In one example cited by Hynes, populations of the stonefly *Leuctra* and the alga *Lemanea* clearly demonstrated the effects of ammonia and cyanide poisoning from a mildly polluted effluent, whereas neither the local fish populations nor the chemical tests gave indication of the presence of these toxic compounds. Just as there are fresh-water pollution faunas containing organisms like *Tubifex*, so there are a variety of clean-water faunas with stonefly nymphs, caddis worms, and other forms intolerant of pollution.

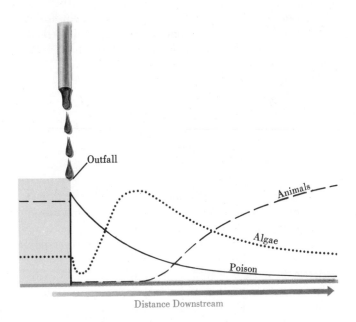

*Fig. 2-14   Diagrammatic presentation of the decrease in concentration of a poison in a river and the corresponding changes in numbers of algae and numbers of species of animals. (Modified from* The Biology of Polluted Waters, *H. B. N. Hynes, Liverpool U. Press (1963).)*

The effects of some cumulative poisons are subject to biological amplification. A nonlethal dose of DDT insecticide ingested by a filter-feeding plankter (member of the plankton) will be deposited in its fatty tissues. When the plankter is eaten by a predatory fish, the DDT will be incorporated in the tissues of the fish. During its lifetime the fish is likely to consume much plankton; part of this plankton mass will be converted into energy, part into fish protoplasm, and part will be excreted, but nearly all the fat-soluble DDT from the plankton will remain in the fatty tissues of the fish. The fish thus becomes a kind of insecticide trap, accumulating concentrations of DDT that are much higher than those found in its prey. The story repeats itself when the fish in turn is eaten by an osprey, pelican, eagle, or other bird of prey. Although DDT accumulates in the same way in the fatty tissues of man, its biological effects are less well understood than in the case of predatory birds. (A similar but little studied kind of biological amplification of poison concentration may occur with mercury (*12*). In the case of one food chain, methylmercury fungicides used on seed grain can accumulate in the grain grown from these seeds. If this grain is subsequently eaten by chickens, the organic mercury will collect in the whites of their eggs, and if the eggs are eaten in turn by man, the mercury will accumulate in the brain, kidney, and other tissues, or may be transferred across the placenta to the fetus in the case of pregnant women. In another food chain involving man, mercury-containing industrial wastes can be concentrated in the muscle of fish and in shellfish. Since 1953, more than 100 people in two small villages in Japan have been killed or severely disabled by this kind of mercury poisoning.)

Levels of insecticides in fresh and salt waters are now so high that predatory water bird populations are beginning to decline sharply. Dr. H. Nicholson (*13*) has pointed out that: "Even animals far removed from areas where pesticides are known to have been used may have chlorinated hydrocarbon insecticide residues in their tissues." He cites the cases of two Antarctic species, the Adelie penguin and crab-eating seal, both of which feed on small crustaceans, and both of which now contain measurable amounts of DDT residues. The story is similar everywhere. C. F. Wurster and D. B. Wingate (*14*) state: "Residues of DDT . . . averaging 6.44 parts per million in eggs and chicks of the carnivorous Bermuda petrel indicate widespread contamination of an oceanic food chain that is remote from applications of DDT. Reproduction by the petrel has declined during the last ten years at the annual rate of 3.25 per-

Fig. 2-15   *Ospreys with young. (Allan D. Cruickshank, National Audubon Society)*

cent; if the decline continues, reproduction will fail completely by 1978." Although associations between insecticide residues and declining reproduction rates do not prove a causal relationship, there is now considerable laboratory evidence that DDT interferes with gonadal development and calcium metabolism in birds. This evidence, in the absence of other recognizable threats to a well-protected species like the Bermuda petrel, appears conclusive.

Food-chain amplification of insecticide concentrations is also believed to affect carnivorous land birds. According to Roger Tory Peterson (29), "The Peregrine Falcon, finest of all birds, is gone from nearly every eyrie in the Hudson Valley and its environs, where as late as 1950 a dozen or more pairs existed." Reproductive rates in populations of bald eagles, the national symbol of the United States, have declined to the point where the species is threatened. Even the robin is showing signs of DDT toxicity, although this species is not yet in serious difficulty. Poisons of this kind, which affect an entire category of ecosystem members (namely, the carnivorous element) are especially but subtly disruptive in their effects on natural communities. Since DDT and related chlorinated hydrocarbons are highly resistant to bacterial degradation, and since the major sources of these compounds in the environment are traceable to run-off from agricultural land and aerial fallout, both of which are hard to control, the only practical alternative to this destructive use of certain pesticides would seem to be large-scale conversion to other methods of chemical and biological pest control.

In 1968 Wurster (15) reported another potentially catastrophic effect of DDT on living organisms. In controlled experiments, concentrations of DDT as low as a few parts per billion reduced the rate of photosynthesis in four major classes of coastal and oceanic algae (see Fig. 2-17). If this phenomenon also occurs under natural conditions, it would be the principal, direct toxic effect of DDT and similar halogenated hydrocarbon insecticides because photosynthesis in marine phytoplankton accounts for a substantial part of the total reconversion of carbon dioxide to oxygen that occurs on earth. (See below for the effects of increasing $CO_2$ concentration.)

**Eutrophication** It is as easy to disrupt communities by promoting growth as it is by retarding it. The addition of free nutrients to an ecosystem may have a number of different kinds of unbalancing effects. If the nutrients (that is, fertilizer or organic wastes) are added rapidly and achieve high concentrations, the integrity of the community will be destroyed and a few opportunistic species, evolutionarily geared to take advantage of the bonanza, will predominate. If the addition of nutrients is relatively slow, the community may gradually become more complex, and its species composition

Fig. 2-16   *Peregrine falcon. (Jeanne White, National Audubon Society)*

will change. This latter process mimics the phenomenon of eutrophication (see below), a naturally occurring feature of succession in aquatic communities. For theoretical reasons it is important to distinguish between these two types of pollution with nutrients, but in practical situations it is common to find examples that do not fit clearly into either category.

Oligotrophy and eutrophy are at the opposite ends of an ecological scale. An oligotrophic body of water is clear, often with a stone or gravel bottom; there is little nutrient turnover, and the biotic community is simple, with short food chains. A eutrophic body of water is turbid, with a muddy bottom; both the water and the bottom are rich in nutrients and organic debris, and the biotic community is complex, with many elements and with involved food chains and webs. The manifestations of these conditions are different, however, in rivers and in lakes. In rivers, the transition from oligotrophy to eutrophy is spatial and occurs as clear, cold mountain streams, flowing rapidly over boulders, merge and gradually give way to the slow-moving, silt-depositing rivers that are characteristic of delta regions. Nutrient pollution can seriously affect rivers, but the damage usually proves transitory if the source of pollution is eliminated.

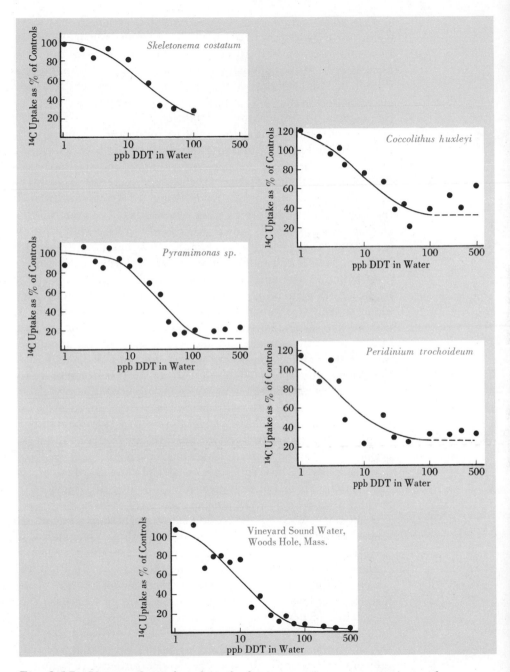

**Fig. 2-17** *Photosynthesis by phytoplankton at various concentrations of DDT, measured by uptake of* $^{14}CO_2$ *relative to uptake by controls. (From Charles F. Wurster, Jr.,* Science, 159 *(1968). Copyright American Association for the Advancement of Science, 1968.)*

In lakes and ponds a slow succession from oligotrophy to eutrophy occurs in time under natural conditions and is usually irreversible. Lakes trap nutrients: Evaporation and overflow prevent the water level from increasing continuously, but dissolved nutrients are left behind by evaporation and are fixed in the bodies of plants and animals, and particulate matter settles and is retained even in the case of overflow. The rich community of plankton, crustaceans, fish, and other creatures that results, and which is the hallmark of eutrophication, is merely a prelude to the eventual filling in and disappearance of the lake. This happens in the case of all lakes, and depending on depth and size, normally takes thousands or millions of years. The Great African Rift, a gigantic gash in the earth's crust, which runs from equatorial Africa northward beyond the Dead Sea, contains a number of deep lakes of great antiquity, including Nyasa, which is so old that an extraordinary adaptive radiation (evolutionary species diversification) of fish has taken place within it, producing nearly 200 endemic species. Few lakes are so durable.

Pollution with nutrients can accelerate eutrophication and aging of lakes, and this has a number of unpleasant consequences. First, only biologists and small children enjoy wading in the organic ooze of a eutrophic lake. The majority of the public prefers to swim in the crystal-clear, sand-bottomed, oligotrophic waters of a young, unpolluted lake. Second, the fish of oligotrophic waters, the trout of Lake Superior and the "omble chevalier" of Lake Lucerne, taste better than the species found in eutrophic lakes, such edible but unpretentious types as perch, roach, and bream. Third, eutrophication, when caused by pollution, is rarely as uncomplicated as a straightforward increase in number of species; there are periodic sudden increases in the populations of some organisms, followed in some cases by massive die-offs. When this occurs, beaches are littered with tons of foul-smelling algae or, as in the case of Lake Michigan, with great piles of a little, herringlike fish called the alewife.

In addition to organic carbon sources, polluted effluents may contain other growth-promoting substances such as phosphates, nitrates, trace minerals, and even vitamins. As we have seen earlier, a waste treatment plant may produce an effluent with a very low BOD which still contains large amounts of inorganic phosphate and nitrate. Detergents, fertilizers, and many industrial products are prime sources of these ions. As much as 80 percent of the nitrogen and 75 percent of the phosphorus added to surface waters in the United States now comes from man-generated sources. F. A. Ferguson (16) has reported that excessive algal growth may occur if "the average concentration of inorganic nitrogen exceeds 0.3 p.p.m. and the inorganic (soluble) phosphorus content exceeds 0.01 p.p.m. . . . However, some waters containing as much as 0.05

Fig. 2-18   Dead alewives on a Chicago lakefront beach. (Chicago Sun-Times Photo; © Chicago Sun-Times)

p.p.m. soluble phosphorus do not support excess algal growths." This last figure confirms, at least in broad detail, a principle first given by Liebig in 1840, and since known as "Liebig's Law of the Minimum." This states, roughly, that growth will be limited by the concentration of any factor(s) present in minimum amount, regardless of the concentration of other necessary factors. In other words, excessive phosphate will not produce an algal bloom if something else is present only in growth-limiting concentration. This accounts, in part, for the complexity of the whole problem of eutrophication.

Most of the Great Lakes, with the partial exception of Lake Huron and Lake Superior, which are bordered by relatively small populations, have been subjected to both rapid and gradual pollution. Lake Erie is in the worst condition, with much of its water completely deoxygenated; but even here, where the catch of blue pike dropped from 18,857,000 pounds in 1956 to less than 500 pounds in 1965, the numbers of sheepshead, carp, yellow perch, and smelt are increasing—at least temporarily. In Lake Michigan it is estimated that 85-95 percent of the total weight of fish is composed of alewives. J. Chiappetta (17) writes that a small fishing boat can net 5-6 tons of these little fish in two 6-minute runs. Surprisingly, most of the pollution of southern Lake Michigan is caused by industry, not by the city of Chicago, which discharges its treated waste into the Mississippi River system via the Chicago River Canal and the Illinois River. According to Chiappetta, the Inland Steel Company alone dumps 480 million gallons of heavily contaminated waste water into Lake Michigan each day, and this company accounts for only a fraction of the waste produced by industry in the city of East Chicago, Indiana. If any serious waste control is ever put into effect in this region, we can expect a sharp reduction in the concentrations of poisons like cyanide and phenol that are released into the lake, but other nutrients may be more difficult to control. Thus eutrophication will probably continue at an accelerated rate for a long time. In the case of Lake Erie there is at least the small satisfaction of knowing that not only does the lake flush quickly, but also that it will disappear after another 25,000 years anyway; but not even these small consolations apply to the much deeper Lake Michigan.

**Radioactive Wastes**  Contamination with radioactive fallout and waste, especially the latter, is becoming increasingly important, but it is still rather difficult to evaluate the dangers in a comprehensive way. Although radiation can undoubtedly cause damage to ecosystems, there are so many ways to administer radiation and radioactive materials, and so many different communities to study, that it is hard to see how conclusions of any generality could be obtained experimentally, except in the case of massive doses of radiation. Indeed, most studies of radiation damage concern particular species, usually man, whose slow rate of maturation and long lifespan render him susceptible to the genetic and somatic changes that accompany prolonged, low-level radiation. Ecological methods may be used, as is the case with investigations of food-chain amplification of radioactive waste concentrations, but here it is not the fate of the community but the fate of the radioactive material that is of prime concern. We tend to be interested in $^{90}$Sr and $^{131}$I because man is at the end of the short food chains that concentrate them. On the other hand, it is probably safe to say that nobody has ever given a thought to the potential consequences of contamination with $^{49}$V, since most of it that might enter biological systems would end up in the green, blue, and orange blood corpuscles of certain sedate and unobtrusive marine animals called *tunicates*.

The major sources of radioactive waste pollution are nuclear explosions that produce fallout, accidents at atomic power and other nuclear installations, and a variety of research laboratories, including medical and biochemical facilities, which release radioactive wastes into the air and sewage. The first two sources are erratic and difficult or impossible to control to everyone's satisfaction. Accidents, fortunately, are rare; and it is to be hoped that the great increase in the number of nuclear power stations that will occur in the next decades will stimulate the development of new safety procedures and remote handling techniques. F. L. Parker and D. J. Rose (*18*) discuss this problem with reference to fusion power systems: "For each 1000 Mw$_e$ of power produced daily by a deuterium-tritium nuclear-fusion reactor, some $3 \times 10^6$ curies of tritium will be produced in a surrounding moderator, and a larger quantity will be continually circulated through various parts of the system. . . . The amounts of tritium in use will be vastly larger than those to which we are now accustomed, and present methods of controlling tritium . . . will certainly not suffice for handling of fusion-system components. Suitable schemes must be (and certainly will be) developed to match the peculiar problems posed by fusion-power systems."

The use of radioisotopes by research laboratories in the United States is controlled by the Atomic Energy Commission. This is a formidable job for a number of reasons. Most important of these is that it is not feasible to measure any parameter besides the least common denominator of radioactive waste, namely, the type and quantity of the radiation itself. Yet of the radioactive wastes that are discarded down drains every day by laboratory workers, some molecules (for example, those that can easily be incorporated in DNA, the stable, genetic material of genes and chromosomes) are far more likely to inflict biological damage than others of equal radioactivity, provided they find their way into food chains, including those that culminate in man. Nor is it feasible to collect and bury the large quantities of isotope-containing liquids, solids, and gases that are produced in laboratories—only the most highly radioactive wastes can be handled in this way. Finally, it is impossible to check each laboratory more often than weekly or monthly, and in the interim it is easy for technicians and scientists to be careless with a menace that cannot ordinarily be perceived by any human senses. But in spite of these potential hazards, there is no evidence that laboratory-produced radioactive waste is currently a threat to natural communities or to man directly; and at the time of this writing, radioactive waste from all sources appears to the conservationist to pose less of a problem than most other forms of pollution.

**Thermal Pollution**    More significant than pollution with radioactive wastes is the problem of disposal of excess heat produced by nuclear power stations. *Environmental Science and Technology* (2, 399, 1968) reports that, according to power industry estimates, by 1980 "approximately 20% of all the fresh water runoff in the United States will be used for cooling purposes." Conventional power plants, gas works, and other industrial facilities also produce thermal pollution. The direct effects of heat on aquatic ecosystems are variable, but can be readily imagined by the reader. Most aquatic creatures exist at or near water temperature; changes in water temperature affect both their activity and their energy requirements. Oxygen requirements also change. If the temperature rises, oxygen consumption increases, but oxygen solubility in water declines. Many organisms have a narrow range of temperature tolerance. At some point a lethal temperature is reached; this varies according to rate of change of temperature, species of animal or plant, and physiological condition of the individual. Since a rise in temperature of 10°C is sufficient to double the rate of many chemical reactions, it can readily be understood why even a small amount of thermal pollution is sufficient to disrupt the organization of aquatic communities.

Thermal pollution also damages ecosystems indirectly. Most important, it aggravates the effects of poisons and accelerates deoxygenating processes, thus converting what might have been mild pollution into a more serious situation. Also, many companies chlorinate water before it enters their cooling systems, in order to prevent the growth of bacteria that could clog pipes. If this is done incorrectly, free chlorine, a highly toxic substance, may be released in the effluent. Even if this does not occur, chlorine will react with certain sulfur-containing compounds (thiocyanates) in the water (especially common in gas-works effluents) to produce a deadly poison, cyanogen chloride, plus acid, according to the following reaction:

$$KCNS + 4Cl_2 + 4H_2O \rightarrow CNCl + KCl + H_2SO4 + HCl$$

The bacteria, small plants, and animals killed by thermal pollution form dead organic matter, which further increases the BOD. Some of the effects of thermal pollution can be summarized in a diagram (see Fig. 2-19).

**Salts**   Inorganic salts of many kinds are among the major constituents of industrial pollution. They arise primarily from acid-base neutralization processes, which are among the most common types of reactions used by industry. Enormous quantities of waste salts are produced. Apart from the separate chemical effects of the different salts, they all alter the osmotic balance of fresh-water organisms. Tolerances to salt vary widely within the animal and plant kingdoms; fresh-water fish are often more resistant than the

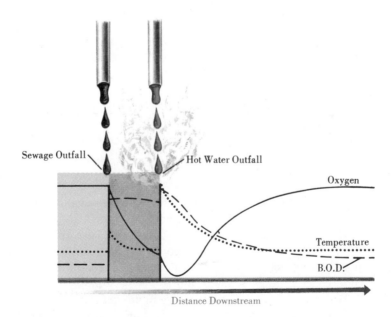

Fig. 2-19   *Diagrammatic presentation of the effect of a heated effluent on an organically polluted river. (Modified from* The Biology of Polluted Waters, *H. B. N. Hynes, Liverpool U. Press (1963).)*

invertebrates or plants that may constitute their food. If salt-polluted water is used for irrigation, the productivity of the land will decline: This has happened in parts of the Rhine Valley. Another cause of salt pollution is salt-water intrusion, which occurs when coastal, fresh-water aquifers are overdrawn, as described in the discussion of the Everglades. Finally, an increasingly important source of sodium chloride is desalinization installations. When this form of fresh-water production becomes more widespread, the supply of sodium chloride will exceed commercial demand and disposal of the surplus may be a problem. The ocean seems to be the most logical place to put it, but if this is done haphazardly, zones of hypersaline water may disrupt marine communities.

*Oil*    Oil, even in thin films, retards the rate of oxygen uptake of the water beneath it; in thick films it will kill some aquatic organisms that spend part of their lives at the surface or in the marine intertidal region. Oil-soaked, dying water birds are becoming a commonplace feature of most beaches, even in areas remote from population centers. In the case of oil, a little pollution goes a long way; 1 gallon is sufficient to cover approximately 4 acres of water. Industry contributes a substantial share of oil pollution, but the private citizen in highly developed countries is equally responsible. Each year Americans leave 350 million gallons of used motor oil in service stations; those few persons who think about it probably assume that "something is done about it," and they are right. Unfortunately, the re-refining of used motor oil is no longer a very profitable business, so when enough oil accumulates it is usually poured into the municipal sewer system, and hence finds its way into the nearest lake or stream. The problem of oil spills is considered further in the section entitled "Industrial Accidents."

*Detergents*    Detergents are among the few pollutants that advertise their presence from a distance: Mountains of white foam floating down a river can mean little else. The actual impact of detergents on ecosystems is far harder to pinpoint. Hynes claims that when the rate of oxygen uptake by rivers is low, detergents will lower it still more, but he admits that the relationship between oxygen uptake and detergent concentration is not a simple one. Biochemists and microbiologists are well aware that fairly high concentrations of detergent will kill cells by dissolving away part of their lipid cell membranes. But what about low concentrations of detergents (see "Industrial Accidents")? There is some evidence that detergents act like heat and some poisons and reduce the capability of certain fish to cope with low-oxygen tensions. Hynes also suggests that the eggs of parasitic worms may be dispersed from sewage works in detergent foam blown off the tops of activated sludge tanks. Any detergent threat to man, however, is very likely to be indirect, via his natural communities, and not through toxic effects. R. D. Swisher (*19*) has reviewed the literature on the effects of detergents on humans and other mammals, and concludes that "the margin of safety is very great, and there is no indication that hazard exists." The figures given appear to bear out this conclusion.

Two principal chemical classes of detergents have been widely used since World War II. The first, known as alkyl benzene sulfonate (ABS), resists breakdown during sewage treatment and persists for long periods of time afterward. The second group is linear alkylsulfonate (LAS), called *biodegradable* detergents, although the term is a misnomer because the difference between the two classes is not absolute but merely one of rate of decomposition. Largely because of mounting public reaction to detergent foam in drinking water, lakes, and streams, the detergent industries in a number of countries have converted from ABS to LAS production. The conversion went into effect in England in 1962, in West Germany and Hungary in 1964, and in the United States in 1965. W. T. Sullivan and R. L. Evans (*20*) report that surfactant concentration in the Illinois River fell 61 percent during the year following the introduction of LAS detergents, despite an increase in detergent use. But this encouraging news does not end the detergent story. The rapid biodegradation of LAS detergents can have two deleterious effects. It can increase the short-term BOD (Sullivan and Evans state, however, that the use of LAS has not lowered dissolved oxygen in the Illinois River); and, more important, the biological breakdown of the detergent molecules releases large quantities of eutrophication-promoting phosphates (280 million pounds per year in the United States). Since it is conceivable to synthesize detergents without high phosphate concentrations, there may be increasing pressure on the detergent industry to effect yet another conversion.

*Unknown* *Compounds*    The proliferation of new and sometimes secret chemical processes and new products has caused a host of new pollutants to enter our waters. Some are difficult to identify and trace. Obviously, no detailed statement can be made about them except to say that they are indeed there and may be dangerous. Research on them is understandably rare. In one paper, S. S. Epstein and F. B. Taylor (*21*) reported that polycyclic hydrocarbons of unknown origin were detected in drinking water by means of a bioassay involving phototoxicity in *Paramecium*.

They stated that: "These findings are of interest in view of a demon-strated association between photodynamic toxicity and carcinogenicity."

***Air Pollution***    The fact that this book devotes so few words to soil and air pollution does not mean that these subjects are of lesser importance, but rather that less is known of the responses of natural communities or species to these kinds of pollution. Most of the air-pollution literature deals with man, with species whose physiology is similar to that of man, or with agricultural crops. For example, D. C. MacLean and his co-workers (22) studied the effects of acute exposures of gaseous hydrogen fluoride and nitrogen dioxide on 6 species of citrus and 14 species of ornamental plants common to central Florida. They found a wide spectrum of sensitivity to the two atmospheric poisons, both of which are common industrial air pollutants in that area. Several gladiolus varieties have been reported to be sensitive to as little as 1 part per billion of HF after six to seven days of exposure, while MacLean and associates found that Carissa plants could survive 8 parts per million of HF for 4 hours with only moderate damage. They also found that leaf abscission in young citrus plants was largely independent of HF concentration over the range tested (0.5–10 parts per million). The pattern of damage was quite different for chronic low-level exposures, with chlorosis and subsequent necrosis occurring in immature tissues. Considering these findings, the reader can appreciate the difficulty of evaluating the effects of complex and fluctuating mixtures of air pollutants on an entire community of plants and animals, even though it is obvious that there is bound to be damage.

One general effect of air pollution on ecosystems is sufficiently well known to cause anxiety among ecologists and other environmental scientists. This is called the "greenhouse effect." Nearly all of the earth's total energy input comes from the sun. It is supplied largely in the form of visible light (4000–7000 angstroms); the ozone in our atmosphere prevents the transmission of most ultraviolet solar radiation below 3000 angstroms, and the atmospheric water vapor absorbs much of the incoming infrared radiation above 8500 angstroms. Approximately one-third of the incoming energy is reflected back, so the total energy falling on the surface of the earth is the total incoming energy minus the absorptive and reflective losses. Most of this net energy is absorbed by inanimate matter and is re-radiated as energy of long wavelength and low energy (heat). A small amount of the light energy falling on the surface of the earth is absorbed by plants and is eventually also re-radiated as heat generated by metabolic processes and decay.

During the past century the extensive use of fossil fuels has caused an increase in the atmospheric carbon dioxide concentration from 5 to 10 percent. This carbon dioxide acts in turn as a one-way filter, preventing the re-radiated heat energy from leaving the earth's atmosphere, but continuing to transmit the incoming higher energy radiation from the sun. Theoretically, this ought to produce the same kind of warming trend on earth that is experienced in a glass-covered greenhouse.

The actual results of the increase in atmospheric carbon dioxide are very difficult to interpret because of other variables (such as atmospheric humidity) that are involved, and it is harder yet to make sound predictions. During the past 50 years the average temperature of the earth has warmed about 1°C, and some glaciers are melting. There may, however, be indications of a more recent cooling trend; and considering the Pleistocene history of glacial fluctuations, it would be foolish to insist on a causal relationship between glacial movements and the activities of industrial man. Moreover, the greenhouse effect of $CO_2$ may be in part counteracted by the great increase in the atmospheric concentration of another by-product of industrialization, particulate matter.

In the future, the atmospheric $CO_2$ balance will depend on the extent of our conversion to the use of nuclear fuels and the amount of vegetation remaining on earth. Whether there will be further warming, with associated changes in climate, melting of polar ice, and submergence of low-lying coastal areas, remains to be seen, but in the interim it should not be forgotten that pollution, including air pollution, can have global effects of most serious and unpredictable nature (30).

INDUSTRIAL ACCIDENTS   Not all industrial accidents affect factory employees only; some cause serious damage to ecosystems. Although accidents constitute just another source of pollution, they are considered separately because they are an increasing threat to the environment and because different kinds of laws and regulations are needed to deal with them.

Nearly all the accidents that concern us here involve some phase of the transport and storage of bulk chemicals. Stories of chlorine gas escaping from tank cars, pipeline explosions, and storage tank fires are disturbingly common; as industry expands to keep pace with population, the industrial traffic grows and accidents increase. Nor are the accidents confined to industry. The United States has confirmed that debris from shattered but unexploded hydrogen bombs has been scattered around the landscape in two separate accidents. It is beyond the scope of this book to catalog all types of accidents, both military and industrial, that can contribute to pollution; two examples will suffice.

*Oil Spills*    On March 18, 1967, the giant tanker *Torrey Canyon*, carrying a cargo of 117,000 tons of crude oil, went aground on Seven Stones Reef off the Cornish Coast and began to break apart. During the weeks that followed, most of the oil floated out of the tanks and great masses of tarry sludge began to drift in to the beaches of Cornwall and Brittany. Efforts to burn the oil were unsuccessful, so 12,500 tons of detergent were used by the British in an ill-considered attempt to emulsify and disperse it. According to scientists of the Plymouth Laboratory (see Further Reading at end of this chapter), the immediate harmful biological effect of the oil alone was on marine birds primarily, but the detergents proved extremely toxic to intertidal forms (see Table 2-2) such as limpets and barnacles and to plankton in the open seas (Fig. 2-21). The disaster is estimated to have killed at least 20,000 penguinlike murres and 5000 razorbills. Eight thousand birds were "rescued" by the people of the British coastal areas; however, oil-soaked birds have a high mortality, and the 450 of the 8000 that were cleaned and that recovered lacked the natural oils that keep their feathers from becoming water-logged in the sea. Less than 1 percent survived to return to their natural habitat. The French, battling the same oil, but profiting from the British mistakes, avoided using detergents and instead dropped powdered chalk on the oil. (The chalk-oil

*Fig. 2-20   Trevone, North Cornwall, England, April 15, 1967. Spraying detergent mixed with fresh water onto rocks and sandy patches to remove oil spread by the* Torrey Canyon. *(Douglas P. Wilson)*

*Table 2-2*    **Toxicity of BP 1002 (Detergent) to Some**
**Sublittoral Species at 12° C**

| Species | Common Name | Concn. (ppm) Needed to Kill Majority in 24 hr | Notes |
|---|---|---|---|
| Coelenterata | | | |
| *Calliactis parasitica* | Sea anemone | 25 | Stayed closed at 5 ppm |
| Crustacea | | | |
| *Corystes cassivelaunus* | Masked crab | 10 | |
| *Portunus holsatus* | Swimming crab | 5 | |
| *Diogenes pugilator* | Hermit crab | 25 | |
| Mollusca | | | |
| *Nassarius reticulatus* | Netted whelk | 2.5 | Some survived 2.5 ppm |
| *Chlamys opercularis* | Queen scallop | 1 | Affected at 0.5 ppm (tended to gape) |
| *Laevicardium crassum* | Smooth cockle | 1 | Affected at 0.5 ppm (tended to gape) |
| *Spisula subtruncata* | Smooth cockle | 2 | Affected at 1 ppm (tended to gape) |
| *Ensis siliqua* | Razor-shell | 0.5 | |
| Echinodermata | | | |
| *Asterias rubens* | Common starfish | 25 | Climbing stopped at 10 ppm |
| *Ophiocomina nigra* | Brittle-star | 5 | Affected at 2 ppm |
| Algae | | | |
| *Delesseria sanguinea* | Red seaweed | 10 | Took several days to change color |

SOURCE: *'Torrey Canyon' Pollution and Marine Life*, J. E. Smith, ed., Cambridge U. Press, 1968.

complex sinks to the bottom.) Fortunately, an unusual northerly wind kept most of the oil out at sea; otherwise the damage to beaches and shallow-water communities might have been much worse.

Indirect effects of the oil and detergents may continue for many years. The murre population had been declining before the accident, presumably because of many other oil spills during the past half-century (an accident off the Scandinavian coast in the 1950s killed 30,000 birds). Sea gulls, which have evidently learned to avoid oil, were not killed, but the gull populations in the disaster area did not nest in 1967, for unknown reasons. Since oil is degraded very slowly in sea water, tarry "souvenirs" of the *Torrey Canyon* may continue to disrupt the biology and scenery of the British and French coasts for decades.

Fig. 2-21a   *Godrevy Point, England, May 10, 1967. Barnacles at high water mark almost completely covered by oil but untouched by cleansing operations, still alive after six weeks' exposure to pollution from the Torrey Canyon. (A. J. Southward)*

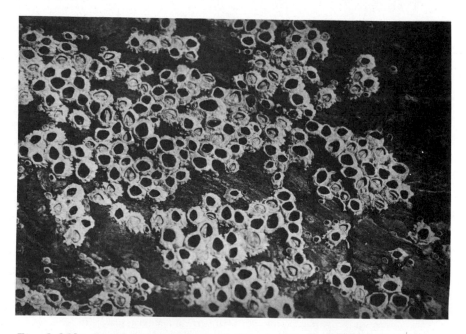

Fig. 2-21b   *Porthleven Reef, England, May 8, 1967. Barnacles at high water mark almost all killed by detergent cleansing operations. (A. J. Southward)*

The wreck of the *Torrey Canyon* was an accident, but it was a pre-ventable one. A Liberian board of inquiry reported that the tanker ran aground solely because of human error, and recommended, perhaps somewhat belatedly, that the license of its master be revoked. One of the major difficulties in formulating policy to deal with accidents of this sort is the high incidence of deliberate fouling that simulates the accidental release of oil. In 1966, in one of the rare cases in which such an offense was proved, a Japanese tanker was identified as the source of an 8-mile oil slick that appeared off Land's End, the outermost part of the Cornish coast. After the *Torrey Canyon* shipwreck, there were reli-able reports of ships sluicing out their tanks in the English Channel, secure in the knowledge that the pollution would be attributed to the accident. Even if this kind of deliberate pollution is not considered, the frequency and magnitude of accidents involving hazardous cargoes is increasing as the number of ships increases and as larger ships are built (see Fig. 2-22). The *Torrey Canyon*'s cargo weighed a little more than 100,000 tons. The *Idemitsu Maru*, a Japanese tanker, carries 210,000 tons, and 500,000-ton cargo vessels are being planned (see Chapter 6). The thought of a ship of this size loaded with insecticides or herbicides is an ecologist's nightmare.

***Reactor Accidents***   Other kinds of industrial accidents may have devastating effects on the environ-ment. To date, nuclear reactor accidents have been providentially few; although lack of publicity prevents a critical review of damage done to surrounding areas, presumably it has not been great. But the number and variety of reactors is increasing rapidly. P. H. Abelson (23) writes: "As of 1 April 1968, about 35 per cent of scheduled additions to electri-cal capacity were nuclear. Recent events, however, have caused some observers to fear that optimism was overdone. The utilities have gam-bled heavily on unproven equipment, some of which will be brought on line far behind schedule. . . . A conspicuous example is the installation at Oyster Creek, New Jersey. . . . During field hydrostatic testing of the water reactor pressure vessel on 29 September 1967, a leak was de-tected. . . . Detailed examination revealed localized intergranular crack-ing in 123 of 137 field welds joining the stub tubes and the control rod housings. . . . Even had . . . failure occurred, there would not have been a violent nuclear accident. However, if a leak or a weld failure had oc-curred after the reactor had operated for some time, the difficulty of repairing the defect would have been great, owing to intense radioactiv-ity."

In the years to come we may find that we have controlled routine industrial pollution only to replace it with episodic and unexpected pol-

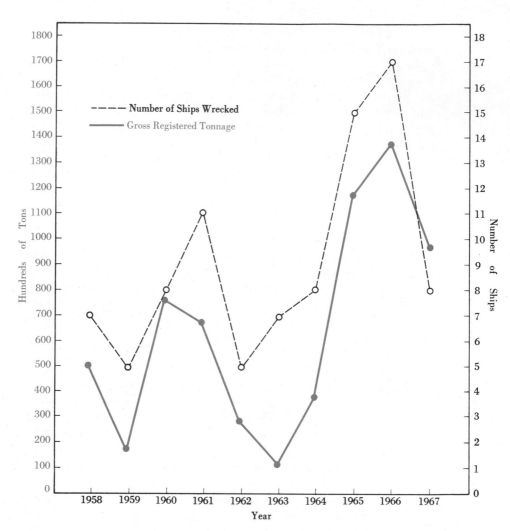

**Fig. 2-22**  *Shipwrecks of vessels transporting oil and related products. (Data from* Lloyd's Register of Shipping.)

lution caused by massive accidents. We can accept Abelson's statement that the defects found in the Oyster Creek reactor would not have caused a nuclear explosion. But we must not overlook the warning implicit in the data he supplies on welding defects: Not only does human error cause defects, but it also causes defects to be overlooked. Accidents are usually unpredictable, and the discovery of a multitude of errors that might have caused them, rather than being a reason for rejoicing, is a sign to the dispassionate statistician that other mistakes may yet lie hidden.

## INTRODUCTION OF EXOTIC SPECIES

### The Water Hyacinth

In 1884 a visitor returning to Florida from the Cotton States Exposition in New Orleans brought back a live water plant that had been on display. It was a floating plant with large, curled, green leaves and a handsome lavender flower—a native of Central America—and it looked fine against the black waters of a Florida cypress swamp (see Fig. 3-1). Its descendants still look fine, and they please the tourists who drive south to Miami. There is no need to go out of the way to find them now; the water hyacinth, at last count, covered 90,000 acres of Florida's fresh-water lakes and streams with an impenetrable mat of curly leaves and purple blossoms. The plants all look healthy, and with good reason; they have no natural enemies in Florida.

Despite their attractiveness, water hyacinths now represent one of the major obstacles to the passage of boats on the inland waterways of the southeastern United States. They have spread as far as the Potomac River, limited in their advance only by the northern winter. Millions of dollars have been spent to control them and millions more will be needed; they are sprayed with herbicides and devoured by obliging manatees (sea cows) which are even transported to inland waters for that purpose, but still the hyacinths are everywhere. Not only do they interrupt navigation, but they shade the naturally occurring water flora from the sun, and without this normally abundant and varied source of food, the animal community of herbivores and carnivores breaks down. In most hyacinth-covered ponds, the number of minnows, turtles, waterfowl, predatory fish, and alligators is greatly reduced. There are, of course, a few adaptable animals that take shelter among the hyacinths, including certain insects, fish, and small water snakes. However, these are the exceptions, and there is little else that a biologist can say in favor of the water hyacinth in the United States.

Hyacinths are widespread and common throughout Central America. They often block streams or rivers, but only temporarily, and in most waterways the hyacinths are found in sheltered coves and along the banks, alternating with other water plants. After a little observation, some but not all of the reasons for this natural control become clear. Where the hyacinths touch the banks one can sometimes see undulating trails of parasol ants coming out of the underbrush to meet them, and on the hyacinths themselves teams of ants snip out and carry away sections of leaves to nourish their underground fungus gardens. The whole scene looks like a hyacinth assembly line run backward; the plants are chewed up at a great rate. On the other side, where the plants jut out into deep water, the manatees eat them by the bushel (in the larger, coastal rivers). In the upland streams, the frequent torrential rains cause floods

*Fig. 2-23  Walking catfish. This destructive and aggressive Asiatic species
was introduced into Florida in the 1960's. It facilitates its own spread by
traveling overland for considerable distances. (Fortunately, in the winter of
1969-1970 most of these catfish were killed by cold weather.) (Charles Trainor)*

which wash the hyacinths downstream, where great islands of them,
dozens of feet in diameter, drift past in the muddy water on the way to
the sea. And during times of drought, when the blue wedge of ocean
water infiltrates the lagoons and scours the intracoastal waterways, the
salt-sensitive hyacinths die by the millions. The water hyacinth is not
new to Central America, and there it is under control by virtue of its integration in the natural community, where checks and balances exist to
prevent one species from aggrandizing itself at the expense of the rest.

**Species**    Ever since man first began to travel long dis-
**Introductions**  tances he has wittingly and unwittingly
brought other creatures along with him. The
dingo, Australia's only placental carnivore, evidently came to the island
continent as the companion of prehistoric man during the late Pleistocene, so transplantation is not new. As the human population increases
and as rapid travel becomes commonplace, nonhuman hitchhikers
abound: Insects and spiders accompany bananas; rats, mice, and even
cats sneak off ships that are loading cargo at remote, oceanic islands;
and the American traveler returning from Europe brings back European
cold viruses along with new watches, scarves, and ash trays (the European traveler in America does the same). Foreign organisms are spread
in other ways. Agricultural animals (like pigs) and plants (like coconuts)
escape readily from domestication. People also transport and release
animals and plants because they like them or because they like to hunt
them or fish for them. Flocks of hundreds of Australian budgerigars
(parakeets) wheel over St. Petersburg, Florida, and schools of Coho (Pa-

cific) salmon thrive in Lakes Michigan and Superior, where they give joy to fishermen and feed on another recent arrival, the alewife.

Generalizations in ecology are always somewhat risky, but one must be offered at this point. The introduction of exotic (foreign) plants and animals is usually a bad thing if the exotic survives; the damage ranges from the loss of a few native competing species to the total collapse of entire communities (see Table 2-3). The stock explanation for the explosive success of introduced species is that freedom from predators and parasites gives them an unfair advantage in competition with native species. Although the truth probably exists somewhere in the vicinity of this vague notion, it is far from satisfying. There are times when introduced species do well in the face of many, direct challenges. For example, the muskrat was introduced into Bohemia (Czechoslovakia) in 1905 and spread exceptionally rapidly, despite heavy predation by foxes, polecats, domestic cats, owls, hunters and trappers, and the deliberate use of the virulent bacterium *Salmonella typhimurium* (see Fig. 2-24). Europe now has millions of muskrats. There are also the invariable counterexamples; not all species do well where they might be expected to thrive. The Burmese mongoose, which wreaked havoc among the small mammals and birds of Cuba and Haiti, has fortunately been unable to penetrate the dense jungles of Central America.

When the phenomenon of the rapid spread of exotics is better understood, it seems very likely that the role of the introduced species itself will not be pictured as passively as it is now. A successful exotic is not simply the lucky recipient of a ticket to a foreign Shangri-La where food is abundant and danger nonexistent. The introduced species often changes, too—changes its behavior if it is an animal and adapts its growth patterns if a plant. For example, the North American moth *Hyphantria cunea* (fall webworm) was introduced in Hungary in 1940. In Europe, its caterpillars show marked preference for leaves of the mulberry tree, even though in America they specifically avoid them. Many other examples could be cited.

### Table 2-3  Some Injurious Animals and Plants Imported into the United States

| Name | Origin | Mode of Transport | Type of Damage |
|---|---|---|---|
| **Mammals** | | | |
| European wild boar (*Sus scrofa*) | Russia | Intentionally imported (1912); escaped captivity | Destruction of habitat by rooting; crop damage |
| Nutria (coypu) (*Myocaster copyus*) (a giant rodent) | Argentina | Intentionally imported; escaped captivity (1940) | Alteration of marsh ecology; damage to levees and earth dams; crop destruction |
| **Birds** | | | |
| European starling (*Sturnus vulgaris*) | Europe | Released intentionally (1890) | Noise; competition with native songbirds; crop damage; transmission of swine diseases; airport interference |
| House sparrow (*Passer domesticus*) | England | Released intentionally by Brooklyn Institute (1853) | Crop damage; displacement of native songbirds |
| **Reptiles** | | | |
| Cuban ground anole (*Anolis sagrei sagrei*) (a small lizard) | Cuba | Three separate, accidental introductions via ports (1931, 1960, 1964) | Replacing native anole; ecological effects unknown |
| **Amphibians** | | | |
| Giant toad (*Bufo marinus*) | Surinam, Colombia | Imported by animal dealers; accidental and intentional releases (1955, 1963, 1964) | Displacement of native toad species; poisoning of dogs(?); ecological effects unknown |
| **Fish** | | | |
| Carp (*Cyprinus carpio*) | Germany | Intentionally released (1877) | Displacement of native fish; uprooting of water plants with loss of waterfowl populations |
| Sea lamprey (*Petromyzon marinus*) | North Atlantic Ocean | Via Welland Canal (1829...) | Destruction of lake trout, lake whitefish, burbot, and suckers in Great Lakes |
| **Insects** | | | |
| Argentine fire ant (*Iridomyrmex humilis*) | Argentina | Via coffee shipments from Brazil? (1891) | Crop damage: destruction of native ant faunas |
| Camphor scale insect (*Pseudaonidia duplex*) | Japan | Accidentally imported on nursery stock (192?) | Damages nearly 200 species of plants in Louisiana, Texas, and Alabama |

Table 2-3    (Continued)

| Name | Origin | Mode of Transport | Type of Damage |
|---|---|---|---|
| **Insects** | | | |
| Japanese beetle (*Popillia japonica*) | Japan | Accidentally imported on irises or azaleas (1911) | Defoliation of more than 250 species of trees and other plants, including many of commercial importance |
| **Plants** | | | |
| Alligator weed (*Alternanthera philoxeroides*) | South America | Dumping of ship ballast? (1897) | Clogs waterways |
| Chestnut blight (*Endothia parasitica*), a fungus | Asia | Accidentally imported on nursery plants (*ca.* 1900) | Destruction of nearly all eastern American chestnuts; disturbance of forest ecology |
| Dutch elm disease 1. *Cerastomella ulmi* (a fungus; the disease agent) | Europe | Accidentally imported in infected elm timber used for veneers (1930) | Destruction of millions of elms; disturbance of forest ecology |
| 2. Bark-beetle (*Scolytus multistriatus* the disease vector) | Europe | Accidentally imported in unbarked elm timber (1909) | |

There is no need to rely on the classic example of rabbits in Australia in an account of the damage done by imported species; few parts of the world have escaped harm. One cannot help but recognize the unpredictability of the consequences of introductions; not until we understand and computerize all the interactions of an ecosystem (a remote possibility) will we be able to make introductions of new species with safety. In the marshy areas of the Canea Valley, Colombia, eucalyptus trees were planted to dry the land enough for sugar-cane planting. Now the water table is so low that irrigation wells have become useless. Similar phenomena are occurring in the beleaguered Everglades, where an introduced ornamental tree, the meleleuca, is infiltrating and drying cypress swamps and other areas, and in the Rio Grande Valley, where the introduced *Tamarix* is having the same effect.

**Oceanic Islands**   The heaviest damage has been done to oceanic islands, whose limited and often unique floras and faunas form communities that are particularly susceptible to attack by competition-hardened invaders from the mainland. The most extreme example is that of Hawaii. Dr. Wayne King (24) has described the situation there: "Approximately 60% of the 68 endemic land birds of Hawaii are extinct following the intrusion of rats, mon-

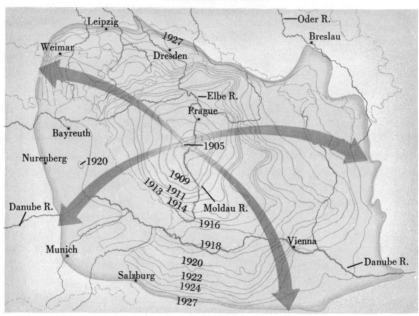

Muskrat
*(Ondatra zibethica)*
16-24 Inches with Slightly
Flattened Tail 10 Inches

**Fig. 2-24**  *Spread of the muskrat,* Ondatra zibethica, *up to 1927, from five individuals introduced into Bohemia in 1905. (From Charles S. Elton,* The Ecology of Invasions by Animals and Plants, *Methuen, London, 1958. After a colored map in J. Ulbrich,* Die Bisamratte: Lebensweise, Gang ihrer Ausbreitung in Europa, wirschaftliche Bedeutung und Bekämpfung, *Dresden, 1930.)*

goose, European rabbits, cats, goats, sheep, horses, cattle, and pigs. The list of exotic animals in Hawaii goes further, however. It also includes over 500 species of insects, more than 50 species of birds, and numerous reptiles, amphibians, and mollusks.''

Although biological control is occasionally the best way of curbing the effects of exotic intruders, this can be dangerous and tricky. King describes the outcome of one such attempt in Hawaii: "The giant African snail (*Achatina fulica*) was introduced into Hawaii in 1936, where it rapidly became established. . . . Not only does it damage crops, but the large calciferous shells of dead snails can change the pH of the soil in areas where they are plentiful, making it difficult to grow crops that require acid soil. When bounties, chemical and mechanical methods failed to control the snails, biological control was attempted by introducing predators from other parts of the world. . . . sixteen more animals were introduced [including beetles, flies, and other snails from Africa, India, Japan, Cuba, California, Florida, and New York]. The original pest is still present, and several of the predaceous species are attacking not only the African giant but also the endemic Hawaiian snails. . . . These colorful endemic snails are rapidly diminishing in numbers. . . ." What other effects the 16 "control" species are having is not known.

**Fish**    One of the few kinds of species introduction
**Transplantations**    that is not always an unmitigated disaster is
that involving sport and food fish. Many varieties of trout and salmon have been carried around the world: Brown trout have been taken from England to Tasmania to New Zealand and from Germany and Scotland to the United States. Although the trout introductions have not been a complete success everywhere (brown trout destroy rainbow and brook trout in the United States), most fishermen have welcomed the addition of this wily and handsome fish to their native waters. Commercial food fish have also been widely and successfully transplanted. H. Blegvad (25) has described the massive transplantation of plaice (the European flounder, *Pleuronectus*) from the North Sea to the Belt Sea (the waters around the Danish Islands of Fünen and Sealand). The North Sea subspecies grows much more rapidly than its local Belt Sea relative, and spawns in its new home. The Danish fishing industry has gained 200,000–400,000 Kr. ($40,000–$80,000) annually, while the transplantations cost the Danish government only 70,000–80,000 Kr. ($14,000–$16,000). On the other hand, trout introduced in Lake Tota and other Andean lakes have destroyed a number of endemic species of fish and have upset aquatic communities. And G. Laycock (26) reports that largemouth bass introduced in Guatemala's Lake Atitlan have nearly led to the extinction of the lake's unique flightless bird, the giant pied-billed grebe. The bass eat the young of the grebes as soon as they leave their floating nests. These two examples of misfortunes that happened to relatively simple lake communities should warn us that the success of many sport and food fish introductions performed in marine waters may be an illusion fostered by our ignorance of the complex ecology of the communities that lie hidden beneath the surface of the sea.

*REMOVAL OF*     Some animals and plants hold central posi-
*"KEY SPECIES"*     tions in the meshwork of interrelationships
that forms a community; if these species are
selectively removed, the community structure begins to collapse. These
kinds of organisms are referred to here, for convenience, as "key species." It is easy to appreciate the significance of key species in very
simple ecosystems like the Antarctic Ocean, where the handful of short
food chains converge in a very few kinds of organisms. However, complex communities also have their key species; it just may take a little
longer to figure out which ones they are.

*The Role of*     One of the best examples of a key species in
*the Alligator*     a complex community is the alligator in the
Everglades. This remarkable animal, whose
only close relative is nearing extinction in China, is one of the few large
and dangerous predators that never attacks man in the wild unless badly
imposed upon. Despite its agreeable disposition and its willingness to
live in a variety of habitats (wild alligators inhabit a pond on the campus
of the University of Florida), the alligator is being exterminated over
most of its former range, primarily by poachers who send the illegally
taken hides to the New York and other markets. No population of alligators is now safe from these poachers, who even raid zoos, private game
farms, and the Everglades National Park. Ironically, it is only as the
once abundant alligator disappears that its ecological importance is
being appreciated.

The alligator's vital role in its community has been described by
Archie Carr, F. C. Craighead, Sr., and others. Carr (27) writes: "All
animals to some degree affect the landscape they live in. The alligator
does so to a greater extent than most. Its habit of controlling its environment is part of the special resilience which has allowed the species to
live through the ages. To an alligator, home is a nest, a "gator hole" or
pool, a cavelike den, and a system of trails. All affect the look of the
landscape." This rearrangement of the landscape is one of the alligator's major contributions to its environment.

The holes excavated by the giant reptiles form the deepest pools in
the Everglades and are the last places to become dry during a drought.
In all but the worst dry spells, these gator holes serve as collecting
points and biological reservoirs for the dwindling life of the glades.
Nourished by the droppings of the alligator and by the remains of its
meals, the water of the gator holes supports a rich growth of algae, ferns,
and higher plants, and these in turn maintain a variety of animal life.
Fishes, amphibians, reptiles, and aquatic invertebrates all find shelter
here, ready to begin an explosive breeding cycle that will repopulate the

Fig. 2-25  Florida wildlife officers catch and tag alligator at its "gator hole" in the Everglades. The alligator's den can be seen at the left of the pond in the photo above. (Both: Charles Trainor)

glades when the drought ends. Birds and mammals also rely on the gator holes for food and water.

In addition to enlarging their home ponds, female alligators make large nest mounds out of sticks and mud, and hollow them out to receive their 30–70 eggs. When built in the same place for long periods, these mounds, together with the mud dredged from the den and pool, often form islands which are high enough to support trees in the midst of the glades. The trees that grow on alligator islands are popular sites for the nests of herons, egrets, and other birds; there is some indication that the presence of the alligator guarding her nest is sufficient to frighten away raccoons and wildcats that could climb the trees to destroy the bird rookery. In return for this favor, the alligator will eat baby birds that fall from the nest and fish dropped by the adult birds. The alligator's nest mound is itself frequently used by other animals, such as turtles and snakes, as a shelter for their own eggs, which receive the benefit of the alligator's maternal care — exceptional for a reptile. Also, in moving to and from its nest to the pond, and in moving along its trails through the aquatic vegetation, the alligator helps keep the pond area open and clear, and delays the inevitable succession to a marsh community.

The alligator's feeding habits exert another powerful influence on the community. There is no doubt that his fondness for crunching turtles and his ability to eat and be bitten by poisonous snakes with impunity are important in Everglades ecology. But far more significant is the large number of gar that are consumed by alligators. The spotted gar, which grows to a length of $2\frac{1}{2}$ feet, is the principal predatory fish of the Everglades, feeding on bass, bream, and other game fish. Where there are many alligators, the gar population is low, and smaller fish can thrive. In areas where the alligators have been exterminated, gar are numerous, the composition of the aquatic community changes, and the quality of fishing declines.

Hopefully, future research will uncover more of the ecological ties of the alligator with its community, and hopefully something will be done in time to prevent the extinction of both the species and the community that depends on it, for this loss of a beneficial species can never be compensated by the market value of the hides it supplies. Such a loss would be a grim indictment of the health and spirit of the kind of society that values alligator shoes and handbags more than living alligators.

*EPILOGUE*   Prior to the twentieth century there were few who noticed or were concerned with man's impact on the natural environment. Yet during the eighteenth and

nineteenth centuries we were even more heedless of the fate of our surroundings than we are now. What saved our ancestors from experienc-
ing the consequences of their folly was the vast expanse of the natural
world, the comparatively small human population, and the undeveloped
state of technology. Now the picture has changed. Human population
strains the habitable confines of a limited earth, and the side effects of
technology threaten the remaining biotic communities.

All life on earth is linked together by an infinity of connections,
and this vast structure is influenced by and influences inanimate properties of the planet, such as climate, atmosphere, and land form. Small
alterations in the environment, like the loss of a bolt from a machine or
the addition of some grains of sand to a gear box, may have effects far
out of proportion to their own physical significance. Biologists fear that
the simple act of dredging shallow portions of the Suez Canal will cause
catastrophic changes in the fauna of the Mediterranean Sea by allowing
foreign predators from the Red Sea to enter. Similarly, no one knows
what will happen if a new sea-level canal across Central America permits large volumes of Pacific Ocean water to flow into the Caribbean
Sea. We have not yet learned to live with the idea that the results of our
actions may be amplified many times and that the unforeseen consequences can come full circle to haunt us. Never has the question of the
dredger, "Which is more important, fish or people?" sounded so foolish;
we are all involved together in the same system.

## FURTHER READING

Allee, W. C., Emerson, A. E., Park, O., Park, T., and Schmidt, K. P.,
*Principles of Animal Ecology*. Philadelphia: Saunders, 1949.

Dasmann, R. F., *Environmental Conservation*. New York: Wiley, 1968.

Ehrlich, Paul R., and Ehrlich, Anne H., *Population, Resources, Environment*.
San Francisco: Freeman, In Press.

Elton, Charles S., *The Ecology of Invasions by Animals and Plants*. London: Methuen, 1958.

Hynes, H. B. N., *The Biology of Polluted Waters*. Liverpool: Liverpool
University Press, 1960.

Kormondy, Edward J., *Concepts of Ecology*. Englewood Cliffs, N.J.: Pren-
tice-Hall, 1969.

Marine, Gene, *America the Raped—The Engineering Mentality and the
Devastation of a Continent*. New York: Simon and Schuster, 1969.

Odum, Eugene P., *Ecology*. New York: Holt, Rinehart and Winston, 1963.

Rose, Steven, *CBW, Chemical and Biological Warfare*. Boston: Beacon
Press, 1969.

Smith, J. E., ed., *'Torrey Canyon' Pollution and Marine Life*. Cambridge:
Cambridge University Press, 1968.

# REFERENCES

1. Elton, Charles S., *The Ecology of Invasions by Animals and Plants* (Methuen, London, 1958).
2. Schmitt, W. R., *Ann. N.Y. Acad. Sci. 118*, 645 (1965).
3. Brown, L. R., *Science 158*, 604 (1967).
4. Dansereau, P., *Biogeography* (Ronald Press, New York, 1957), 272.
5. Perry, T. O., *Science 160*, 601 (1968).
6. Spilhaus, Athelstan, *Science 159*, 710 (1968).
7. Partington, William, *Florida Naturalist 41*, No. 2B (1968).
8. Chittenden, H. M., *Trans. Am. Soc. Civil Engineers 62*, 245 (1909).
9. Leopold, A. Starker, and Leonard, Justin W., *Audubon 68*, 176 (1966).
10. Margalef, Ramon, *Am. Naturalist 97*, 357 (1963).
11. Katzer, Melvin F., and Pollack, James W., *Environmental Science and Technology 2*, 341 (1968).
12. Environment *11*(4), 2-44 (1969).
13. Nicholson, H. Page, *Science 158*, 871 (1967).
14. Wurster, C. F., Jr., and Wingate, D. B., *Science 159*, 979 (1968).
15. Wurster, C. F., Jr., *Science 159*, 1474 (1968).
16. Ferguson, F. A., *Environmental Science and Technology 2*, 188 (1968).
17. Chiappetta, J., *Audubon 70*, 30 (1968).
18. Parker, F. L., and Rose, D. J., *Science 159*, 1376 (1968).
19. Swisher, R. D., *Surfactant Effects on Humans and Other Mammals* (Soap and Detergent Association Scientific and Technical Report No. 4, 1966).
20. Sullivan, W. T., and Evans, R. L., *Environmental Science and Technology 2*, 194 (1968).
21. Epstein, S. S., and Taylor, F. B., *Science 154*, 261 (1966).
22. MacClean, D. C., *et al.*, *Environmental Science and Technology 2*, 444 (1968).
23. Abelson, P. H., *Science 161*, 113 (1968).
24. King, Wayne, *Florida Naturalist 41*, 99 (1968).
25. Blegvad, H., *Proc. U. N. Conf. on the Conservation and Utilization of Resources VII*, 51 (1951).
26. Laycock, George, *The Alien Animals* (Natural History Press, Garden City, N.Y., 1966), 205.
27. Carr, Archie, *National Geographic 131*, 133 (1967).
28. Patrick, R., Proc. 9th Industrial Waste Conf. *Purdue Univ. Eng. Extn. Ser. 87*, 325 (1954).
29. Peterson, R. T., in Bull, J., *Birds of the New York Area* (Harper and Row, New York, 1964), xiii.
30. Peterson, E. K., *Environmental Science and Technology 3*, 1162 (1969).

chapter *3*

# Endangered Natural Communities: Case Histories

## THE OKLAWAHA RIVER AND THE CROSS-FLORIDA BARGE CANAL

### *The Oklawaha River*

The predominant impression that can be gleaned from the writings of the early travelers in Florida is one of great natural abundance, the kind of primeval lushness and bounty that was occasionally portrayed in the works of Coleridge and Wordsworth, and which in distorted detail forms part of everyone's image of America. The following passage, published in 1791 by the great naturalist William Bartram (*1*), is a case in point: "We had a large and fat one [soft-shelled turtle] served up for our supper, which I at first apprehended we had made a very extravagant waste of, not being able to consume one half of its flesh, though excellently well cooked. My companions, however, seemed regardless, being in the midst of plenty and variety, at any time within our

79

reach, and to be obtained with little or no trouble or fatigue on our part; when herds of deer were feeding in the green meadows before us: flocks of turkeys walking in the groves around us, and myriads of fish, of the greatest variety and delicacy, sporting in the crystalline floods before our eyes." When Bartram observed this scene he was passing through northeast Florida, not far from a stream the Indians called the Ockli-Waha, or Great River.

Today the landmarks described by Bartram are mostly gone, replaced by shoddy development communities, by endless miles of monotonous, slash pine tree farms, and by the sprawling Duval County urban complex, whose fetid paper mill fumes penetrate the cabins of arriving jet liners even before they touch the runway at Jacksonville's International Airport. Yet, surprisingly, in the midst of this disorderly change, one extensive and self-contained wilderness area, the Oklawaha Valley, was preserved in northeast Florida, through accident or oversight, until the latter part of the 1960s.

The Oklawaha River could hardly have been considered "Great" by the Indians, who had the mighty St. Johns for comparison; perhaps "magnificent" is a better translation. The Oklawaha arose in several large lakes of central Florida and flowed northward for 60 miles, joining the St. Johns River 8 miles north of Lake George. Along its course it received additional waters from Silver Springs and from Orange Lake. It was a sand-bottomed river with transparent, tea-colored waters stained by the humic acids leached from the surrounding hardwood forest. The river's course was tortuous, with many turns and oxbows, and it flowed through a mile-wide valley that it had cut during its long geological history. The valley itself was often flooded by the river during wet years; and the edaphic climax vegetation included water-resistant trees like the tupelo, swamp red bay, sweet gum, red maple, loblolly bay, water hickory, water oak, cabbage palm, and the spectacular bald cypress (see Fig. 3-1). At the sides of the valley, where the land sloped upward and was free of flooding, and on the islands of higher ground scattered through the valley, one could find the typical trees of the Florida climatic climax: laurel oak, blue beech, hop hornbeam, and magnolia.

As could be predicted from the plant community, the fauna of the Oklawaha River and its valley was exceptionally diverse. Several species that require extensive wilderness habitat did well there: The wild turkey, largest of North American birds, is a good example; the Oklawaha valley was one of the last strongholds of this traditional game bird in Florida. Other birds included limpkins, bitterns, rails, herons, snake birds (*Anhinga*), and until recent years, roseate spoonbills, and ivory billed woodpeckers. There was a variety of reptiles: snakes, turtles, and alligators, which could be seen sunning themselves at the water's edge. Among the more notable mammals were black bears, wildcats, otters,

*Fig. 3-1   The River Styx, a cypress swamp near the Oklawaha River. Dense mats of water hyacinths can be seen in the center. (David W. Ehrenfeld)*

and raccoons. The occasional panther still found refuge in the forest, enticed by the same deer herds that attracted hunters from all over the state to the surrounding scrub land. In the river itself and in its feeder springs there was a luxurious growth of multicolored aquatic plants and an abundance of fish, including chain pickerel, redbreast sunfish, shellcracker, speckled perch, largemouth bass of enormous size, and perhaps the tastiest of all fresh-water fish in the southeast United States, the channel catfish.

Within or adjacent to the Oklawaha region were five major Florida springs of considerable recreational value and of great interest to ecologists, geologists, paleontologists, and other scientists. Fifteen miles to the west of the Oklawaha River, two large and relatively unspoiled lakes, Lochloosa and Orange, added to the wildlife carrying capacity of the region. To complete the picture, it should be mentioned that the Oklawaha region was sparsely populated, containing no large towns or major highways. Viewing the region from an airplane, Dr. David Anthony described it as follows: "Flying north from the Silver Springs area the Oklawaha Valley appears as a broad, densely-forested belt that curves for more than forty miles around the northern third of the Ocala National Forest. To the west lie open pine lands, and the dry low forest of the Big Scrub spreads out to the east. Clearly, the valley forest serves as a safe highway and sanctuary for wildlife over an enormous area."

*The Cross-Florida* In 1942, Congress approved the plans of the
*Barge Canal* Army Corps of Engineers for the proposed route of a cross-Florida barge canal, to be constructed in part by means of damming and flooding the Oklawaha valley. Financial support was not forthcoming, however, and interest in the project waned during the next two decades as it became clear that the canal would be of questionable economic and aesthetic value. During these post-World War II years, the Corps was busy in southern Florida, rearranging (and, as we have seen, damaging) the landscape to suit the immediate needs of a mismatched assortment of special interests: real estate, industry, and occasionally agriculture. Meanwhile, a few hundred miles to the north, analogous interests—in particular, the powerful phosphate and pulpwood producers and the heavy construction industry—had not lost sight of the barge canal plans, which had the conspicuous advantage of prior congressional sanction. The presidential campaign of 1964 afforded these interests the opportunity to make public their demands for Federal support for the canal, and they were promptly joined by individuals whose land holdings on or near the canal right-of-way were likely to increase in value, as well as by several communities (for example, Palatka) that expected to benefit economically from the anticipated barge traffic. By 1966 the Corps of Engineers had awarded contracts for construction of the Rodman and Eureka dams in the Oklawaha valley.

As might have been expected, virtually all private conservation organizations in the state, with a combined membership exceeding 100,000 Floridians, opposed the destruction of the river valley; but the private citizens who actively led them constituted a much smaller group, largely inexperienced in lobbying, and able to muster only limited funds. Rather than register total opposition to the canal project, they proposed an alternate route (see Fig. 3-2) which would have preserved the lower 45 miles of the Oklawaha valley.

On the basis of topographic and economic data, which the Corps first referred to as part of a "careful study" but which later was described as rough estimates, the alternate route was rejected by the Corps at the annual Water Resources Meeting in Tallahassee on January 25, 1966. They concluded that the effect of relocation would be to dry up the Oklawaha River and to increase construction and mainte-

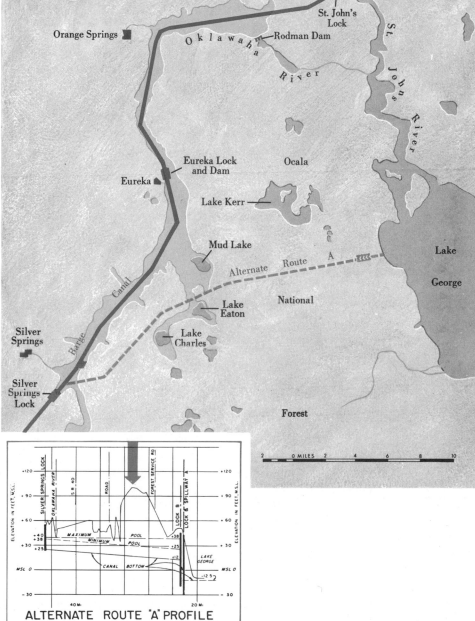

**Fig. 3-2** *Oklawaha River and Cross-Florida Barge Canal, with proposed alternate route. Inset shows Corps of Engineers' land profile for area of alternate canal route; arrow indicates questionably high figure for land elevation.*

nance costs of the canal. "Recreational" and "flood control" benefits were also deemed to be jeopardized by the conservationists' alternate route. Unprepared for this objection to their compromise solution, the conservationists could not reply at the meeting. Several weeks later, their careful evaluation of the district engineer's grossly misleading report was too late. Among the many points that they raised were the following:

1. The water level in the Oklawaha, downstream from the alternate route cut-off, could be maintained by a single pumping station.

2. The Corps' map of the land profile over the alternate route showed several miles of ground with an elevation greater than 90 ft above sea level (see Fig. 3-2), where the canal excavation costs would supposedly be high. However, the U.S. Geological Survey map of the same area (1964) shows an elevation of less than 75 ft.

3. The uniform, dwarfed, scrub pine forest along the alternate route would be much easier to clear for excavation than the mixed hardwood forest of the Oklawaha valley.

4. The Corps failed to explain how the two locks, built side-by-side, and the 23 miles of canal that comprised the alternate route would cost more to maintain than would their original route of 39 miles of canal, a 27,000-acre reservoir, and two locks and two dams located in three different places.

5. Calculations by the Corps of direct and collateral benefits that would result from construction of the original canal route were based on invalid and discredited methods of benefit analysis. (This latter statement will be examined in greater detail.)

At this point a brief explanation is indicated for those readers who are wondering what place should be given to considerations of economic matters in a text on biological conservation: We live in a capitalist economy and therefore are accustomed to valuing material things according to the price that has been determined by a semi-free market rather than through the deliberations and decisions of state planners. Traditionally, natural or "undeveloped" land has commanded a low market value, which was perhaps permissible and was certainly understandable when such land was in abundant supply. Unfortunately, now that natural communities of self-perpetuating size are scarce, we find ourselves still tied to the traditional monetary valuations.* Since natural communities

*It is curious to note that in communist countries, where most land is public domain and not subject to sale, centralized state planning can lead to a distressingly similar scale of priorities and values with respect to land use. The Soviet government's belated and perhaps inadequate response to the impending destruction of the magnificent Lake Baikal by effluvia from pulp mills is one example.

are evaluated only in terms of their fancied or real potential for development, conservation battles are frequently fought entirely on conventional economic grounds, and conservationists no longer can consider
themselves above the mundane considerations of budgets and accounting.

In 1963 the departments of Agriculture and Interior issued a joint
"River Area Inventory" statement about the Oklawaha, which they
concluded as follows: "This river is of sufficient size and unique character and should be included in any system of wild rivers. It is felt that this
use outweighs any other possible functions that have been proposed for
the general area." Obviously these findings were subsequently ignored
by the Federal Government when it decided to build the canal. Ordinarily, one would suspect that the Government's decision was based on the
usual failure of the conservationists to translate aesthetic and long-term
speculative considerations into dollars and cents. But for once this was
not the case. The conservationists had provided a sound and detailed
economic argument to support the value judgment contained in the area
inventory. After a summary of this argument, we can consider briefly
what nevertheless went wrong.

In 1946, in a project study and report on the proposed canal, the
Army Corps of Engineers found a benefit/cost ratio of 1.05:1.00, which
was considered economically unsound. A 1958 review reconfirmed the
Corps decision not to recommend construction. In 1962, however, in a
second review, the Corps suddenly announced that the benefit/cost ratio
was approximately 1.20:1.00, and that the project could proceed. This
sudden change in the estimated economic worth of the canal surprised a
great many people, including Raymond W. Stuck, who was chief of the
Civil Works Division of the Corps prior to the final project study. In a
letter reprinted in the U.S. Senate Congressional Record, August 23,
1965, Stuck wrote: "In the 1962 Addendum Report the same quantities
were used as in the 1946 Report but *five* additional highway bridges were
found to be necessary. Yet, surprisingly, the estimated cost was $13\frac{1}{2}\%$
less than the 1946 estimate and the benefit-cost ratio was now 1.20 to
1.00.

"Conservative evaluations show that all construction costs have
increased since the war years at about 2% per year but we have the very
unusual situation on this project where construction costs [were] pres-
umed to decrease even for an expanded project."

Moreover, as was pointed out by the conservationist and econo-
mist Col. F. W. Hodge (U.S. Army, Ret.) (2), the Corps neglected in 1962
to include interest charges in its cost figures, which would have added
an extra $13,000,000 to the construction figure of $157,900,000. Furthermore, in computing the discount rate (a way of accounting for loss of
income due to postponement of the return on an investment), the Corps

unaccountably used the value of 2.875 percent, little more than half the commonly accepted figure of 4.2 percent. Finally, federal construction estimates, even if computed in a realistic way, have generally tended to be grossly undervalued. It is clear, therefore, that if the Corps had performed a valid appraisal of the costs alone, the cross-Florida barge canal would have been found to be even more unsound a venture in 1962 than in previous years.

Between 1958 and 1962 there was also a curious manipulation of the benefit side of the ratio. In addition to direct benefits such as transportation savings, a new category of yearly benefits amounting to $907,000 was listed for the first time. These "collateral benefits" included "land enhancement" and "flood control." In the past, "land enhancement" claims have been rejected as vague during congressional hearings and have been described by the noted economist Otto Eckstein as an unfair way of counting again an item that has already been included as a direct benefit. Also, in the case of the barge canal, the "enhanced" land would largely border on a 1½-2 feet deep flooded area filled with standing dead trees. Even if these considerations did not apply, it is doubtful whether the private profits of a few real estate speculators are a public "benefit," since no price reduction in goods or services will ever be passed on to the consumer. The "flood control" benefit is, if anything, more dubious than the claimed land enhancement value. As Colonel Hodge has pointed out: (1) The flood control is "effected by the permanent flooding of the Oklawaha River valley," and (2) the agricultural development of other areas that will be protected from flooding will depend on the extra investment of private capital and will not automatically result from the canal project.

Of the several direct benefits, "transportation savings" was by far the largest item, amounting to $7,016,000 per year. This is probably the most heavily exaggerated figure of the entire Corps of Engineers report. According to U.S. Senator William Proxmire (Wis.) (3), who challenged the report in Congress, "The savings claimed are almost four times greater than those claimed for any other inland waterway." Among the various ingenious methods used by the Corps to inflate the figure was the assumption that as much pulp wood would pass through the canal as is carried by the entire Mississippi-Ohio traffic system. Using standard accounting practices of the Corps of Engineers, Colonel Hodge calculated the transportation savings to be $2,776,008; and Dr. Charles A. Welsh, director of the Graduate Program of Business Administration at Rollins College, computed a figure of $3,163,031, both less than half of the 1962 estimate made by the Corps.

Besides underestimating construction costs and exaggerating benefits, the Corps of Engineers neglected to account for indirect costs such as damage to many kinds of fish and game habitats in the vicinity of the canal. One example, according to the U.S. Fish and Wildlife Service, is the destruction of "a sizeable amount of littoral zone" in the Gulf of Mexico, caused by dredging and spoil disposal activities extending to a point 6 miles offshore. Another indirect (and incalculable) cost of the canal would be the attraction to Florida of the kind of heavy industry that is least desirable in an area whose healthy economy is based on the tourist trade, citrus industry, cattle ranches, and stock farms. Already there have been widespread complaints in the southern part of the state that fumes from phosphate and other factories are harmful to citrus and cattle (see "Air Pollution," Chapter 2).

In summary, the Corps of Engineers' precariously favorable benefit/cost ratio of approximately 1.20 seems little more than an economic subterfuge. Senator Proxmire has stated, "The actual benefit-cost ratio should be, at the very most, 0.79." If correct, this would hardly provide economic justification for the construction of a bicycle path, let alone a $157,900,000 barge canal.

Evidently the economic pressures to "develop" the remaining natural landscapes—if the cross-Florida barge canal is a representative example—can be generated by the economic demands of particular individuals and corporations rather than by the needs of the public. The cross-Florida barge canal is likely to be in both the short and long run an economic disaster for the U.S. taxpayers; however, in spite of ample evidence to prove this, construction plans were neither cancelled nor substantially modified, nor have they been postponed. One reason for this insensitivity of governmental agencies like the Army Corps of Engineers to the very realistic requests of large numbers of citizens is the lack of any firmly institutionalized mechanism whereby the public can delay the federal (or state) land condemnation process. Public hearings involving the Corps and related agencies are too often a sham, used only to invest prearranged policies with a semblance of procedural regularity.

*Land development is irreversible—waiting is not.* Any battle in which the setbacks on one side are always temporary and the losses on the other are always permanent can have only one outcome. The fate of the Oklawaha valley serves as a warning that conservationists in all countries must find a way to help the concerned public even the odds against a bureaucracy unresponsive to their needs. Until this happens there is no tactic and no variety of economic, scientific, or aesthetic argument that will protect the remaining natural communities.*

---

*Even at the time of this writing, as the water backed up behind the new Rodman Dam for the first time, there was evidence of severe and unforeseen difficulties resulting from the canal construction. In the Rodman water-storage area, the trees of the original Oklawaha forest, which had been felled and pressed into the earth by a giant forest-crushing machine developed for the Corps, began to pop up to the surface of the water at irregular inter-

**THE PACIFIC COAST REDWOOD COMMUNITIES**

*A Different Kind of Problem*

In the preceding example of an endangered community, the Oklawaha River valley, we have seen how complex economic issues can lie at the core of a conservation problem. Prior to its damming, the Oklawaha, which was a large and self-contained wilderness unit, needed little more than minimal management by state conservation and game officers. Had it not been "developed," its preservation would probably have been a relatively simple matter. The Pacific Coast redwood communities of California and southwestern Oregon present a very different kind of challenge to the conservationist.

Although many of the oldest and most magnificent of the redwood groves are under heavy pressure from lumber companies, this aspect of the redwood controversy will not be discussed here. Most of the readers are familiar with the lumber companies' exploitation of what should have been a public trust and with their attempts to quiet public reaction by promoting tree farms filled with redwood saplings as an adequate substitute for the 1000–2000-year-old giants that were cut down. There is, however, more to the story. During the 1960s, foresters and other kinds of ecologists began to realize that the redwoods are but a part of a complex ecosystem, an ecosystem that might still be in trouble even if the lumber companies were to vanish overnight.

*The Redwood Ecosystems*

One of the few studies in depth of the redwood ecosystems was made by an Australian forester, Dr. R. G. Florence (4), who did post-doctoral research at the School of Forestry of the University of California. Dr. Florence saw no reason to assume that redwood forests were a classical climax community, and set out to study the growth rate of redwood seedlings in a variety of soils, including soil from established

---

vals — hardly an auspicious beginning for the boating paradise that had been promised. Embarrassed, the Corps retired its Rube Goldberg monster from the canal project, and in a heavy-handed attempt to cover its tracks, bestowed a beautification award on the hideous, log-choked mudhole now known as Lake Rodman. Elsewhere along the canal construction route, the pH of the Oklawaha water, deprived of the natural organic acids once supplied by the surrounding forest, began to rise; this alkaline water, in turn, favored the growth of water weeds, including dense mats of enormous water hyacinths, capable of stopping any barge. In its original canal construction and maintenance budget, the Corps had not provided any funds for weed control, but even if money were available there would still be no acceptable hyacinth-removal method on which to spend it. In the face of these initial but serious problems, and with the canal's impact on the water system of central Florida yet to come, several citizens' groups began, in the summer of 1969, a last-minute effort to prevent completion of the canal project and to save the remaining portions of the Oklawaha valley. In March 1970, President Nixon ordered a re-study of the project.

redwood forests. He examined in the laboratory various parameters (soil respiration, nitrogen mineralization, microbiological flora) of soils from upland, old-growth, redwood-Douglas fir forests, from flood-plain redwood forests, and from earlier seral stages consisting largely of tan oak brush or madrone. These soils were also tested for their ability to support growth of redwood seedlings under several conditions. His results clearly showed a "development in the redwood forest soil of a condition in which microbiological populations are depleted, respiratory activity low, mineralization of nitrogen adversely affected, and in which root rot fungi can attack the redwood seedlings."

As Florence points out, these results are not entirely surprising — many species of trees in old-growth forests seem to create soil conditions unfavorable for the growth of their own seedlings. A subtle and rhythmic alternation of species may therefore occur, even in a "climax" forest. In the case of the upland redwood-Douglas fir forests, there is some evidence that this alternation does happen under undisturbed conditions, with various hardwood species like tan oak emerging and becoming dominant in the older redwood stands, only to give way to new redwood and Douglas fir growth when the soil has been rejuvenated after 50 years or more. This postulated alternation is probably not total, for all species coexist during all phases; only the relative proportions change. Obviously, management of such upland redwood groves in park land is not simply a matter of preserving the redwoods. Similarly, lumber companies have found that after logging in old redwood stands, regrowth of redwoods is slow until a hardwood phase has been completed.

Although soil depletion is almost certainly a feature of alluvial flat (flood plain) redwood groves, the upland type of species alternation does not seem to occur here, and nearly pure stands of redwood maintain and replenish themselves for immense periods of time in regions that have been periodically flooded in the past. Arguments over the causes of the success and vigor of these alluvial flat redwoods have produced sharp differences between foresters and professional conservationists as to how the old-growth alluvial forests should be managed in order to keep them in good condition.

In an article published in *Science*, Dr. Edward C. Stone and Richard B. Vasey (5) of the School of Forestry, University of California, Berkeley, claimed that the reason why the redwood is predominant on the alluvial flats is because it has a number of special features that render it resistant to both fire and flood. In the case of the former, it is protected by its thick, fire-resistant bark, and by the fact that its crown can regenerate from adventitious buds along the branches and stems. In the case of the latter, it can compensate for the tendency to lean in the unstable alluvial soil by adding enormous supporting buttresses to the trunk in the direction of tilt and by strengthening those roots under most

**Fig. 3-3** *Coastal redwood grove southeast of Camp Klamath, in proposed Redwoods National Park, California. (National Park Service)*

tension. Also, after heavy silt deposition during floods, redwoods can rapidly readjust their root systems to take advantage of the newly deposited soil layer (see Fig. 3-4). This is not only beneficial but necessary: During the past 1000 years — well within the life span of many large redwoods — 15 major floods have raised the level of the alluvial flats in the region under study by more than 9 m. According to Stone and Vasey, none of the major competitors of alluvial redwoods (tan oak, Douglas fir, bay, and grand fir) can withstand *both* fire and flood.

In addition to reducing competition, many foresters claim that periodic flooding in the past has, by virtue of new soil deposition, circumvented the problem of soil exhaustion in old stands of redwood. It is one thing, however, to allow fire and flood to maintain redwood forests over a

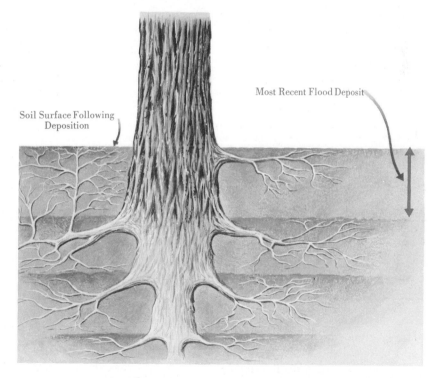

Soil Surface Following
Deposition

Most Recent Flood Deposit

*Fig. 3-4   Root system of a redwood tree that has survived three major root burials. After each burial, there is first a vertical invasion of new soil by roots from below, then, several years later, the development of a horizontal root system from the buried trunk. Once established, the horizontal root system replaces the vertically oriented one, which dies. (Modified after Edward C. Stone and Richard B. Vasey,* Preservation of Coast Redwood on Alluvial Flats, *from* Science, 159, *p. 157 (1968).© American Association for the Advancement of Science 1968.)*

broad undisturbed area prior to the twentieth century—it is another to rely on these same natural agents to preserve the few old groves of alluvial flat redwoods that remain in parks (see, however, the discussion of controlled burning in Chapter 6). Severe fires and floods can be locally destructive even to redwoods; besides, fire and flood control are now an accepted fact of life. What, then, should be done with flood-plain redwoods in the absence of fires and floods?

Up to now the professional conservationists' viewpoint has not been represented. Bestor Robinson (6), a director of the Sierra Club, has challenged the conclusions reached by Stone and Vasey. In a letter also published in *Science*, he claims that "although fire and siltation may help, neither of these agents is necessary. The redwood, given proper growing conditions . . . has weapons and competitive advantages (including long lifespan, rapid growth rate, vigorous root competition, disease resistance, and great height) that enable it to become a climax species as against its competitors in this region. . . ." Furthermore, flooding has the major disadvantages, according to Robinson, of (1) providing new soil free, for several years, of redwood roots and therefore accessible to invasion by competing seedlings; (2) undermining and toppling thousands of large redwoods; and (3) raising the water table, which kills redwoods through a disease known as "sour root."

Responding to Robinson's criticism, Stone and Vasey wrote: " . . . they [the conservationists] have failed to appreciate the dynamic character of the ecosystem involved. They have focused their attention on preserving the trees now standing, ignoring the rest of the ecosystem which was responsible for these redwoods being present and upon which their replacements depend."

### Management of Alluvial Flat Redwoods

Clearly, there is an honest and fundamental difference in viewpoint concerning the nature of the alluvial-flat redwood ecosystem (this difference is perhaps less pronounced in the case of the uplands redwoods). Believing in the importance of fire and flood, Stone and Vasey have written: " . . . time is running out for the alluvial-flat redwoods and . . . flood control could be the final blow unless man actively intervenes with herbicides, the ax, or the chainsaw [in order to control redwood competitors]." Many conservationists feel, to the contrary, that the ecological effects of flood and fire control alone do not justify additional and potentially dangerous interference with a delicate ecosystem.

In the background of this controversy looms the larger conservation problem of whether succession (or other kinds of ecological change) can or should be arrested in an area that was originally set aside and protected because of the special qualities of the present seral stage. It would take a clairvoyant to ascertain where the truth lies, but one thing is certain: If the various interests that are trying to save the redwoods cannot find a practical forest management compromise, they will never be able to work together to resist the kind of politico-economic pressures that destroyed the Oklawaha valley.

## FURTHER READING

Maass, Arthur, *Muddy Waters—The Army Engineers and the Nation's Rivers.* Cambridge, Mass.: Harvard University Press, 1951.

## REFERENCES

1. Van Doren, Mark, ed., *Travels of William Bartram* (Dover, New York, 1955), 159.
2. Hodge, F. W., *Business and Economic Dimensions 1* (4), 1 (1965).
3. Proxmire, Hon. William, *Congressional Record* (Senate), Aug. 23, 1965.
4. Florence, R. G., *Ecology 46*, 52 (1965).
5. Stone, Edward C., and Vasey, Richard B., *Science 159*, 157 (1968).
6. Robinson, Bestor, *Science 160*, 833 (1968).

# *Factors that Threaten Species*

**SPECIES**   A biological species can be defined as a group of sexually reproducing organisms, all of whose members share in a common gene pool; however, most of the several million types of organisms in the world that have been called "species" by biologists have never been put to the official test of the definition. Although we assume that members of the same species can interbreed and produce fertile offspring and that they cannot do this under natural conditions with members of closely related but different species, it has not been possible to check many species in this regard. This problem—that the functional definition is usually nontestable—is one that we would gladly leave to the systematists and evolutionists; but occasionally the meaning of species worries the conservationist as well. For example, the coyote, *Canis latrans*, and the red wolf, *Canis niger*, are named and treated as separate species by mammalogists, who thereby commit themselves to the idea that there is no gene exchange between the two populations. Yet it is now claimed that the coyote, which has increased its range by tens of thousands of square miles during the twentieth century, is threatening to wipe out the last remnants of the Texas red wolf population through hybridization.

If, indeed, it turns out to be true that the constellation of genes that we now know as *Canis niger* is being swallowed up and lost in the constellation of genes that we know as *Canis latrans*, should we be concerned? If, when the 150 extant red wolves die, they have left behind offspring that are part coyote, will there be any difference in the zoological status of the world? The answer is clearly "yes": Uniqueness, for the conservationist, is usually a function of populations, not necessarily of species. This does not mean that species are unreal or uninteresting to conservationists. The species is the fundamental unit of any natural system of classification of diploid, sexual organisms; without it, neither higher nor lower levels of classification could be fully defined or understood. Not only is it important to know the species identity of animals and plants in order to make conservation policy decisions (as in the example just described), but in the majority of cases, the valid identification of a creature rests on its species designation and not on any other taxonomic or popular nomenclature. Thus, throughout this chapter, as the chapter title implies, the concept of "species" is used, although it is sometimes used rather loosely.

## ECOSYSTEM ALTERATION

The principal cause of the loss of species is the alteration of the ecosystems in which they live (see Chapter 2). So many examples of this could be provided that it is difficult to choose only a few. But it is not possible to be inclusive in an introductory survey work; the Red Data Books of the International Union for the Conservation of Nature list hundreds of cases where man's alteration of the environment is causing the extinction of particular species — two examples must suffice here. Both have been chosen because they have had little attention, to date, and deserve more.

Game and sport fish are among the most carefully tended and conserved of all natural resources, but the rest of our native fishes receive virtually no attention, and a number have become extinct in recent years or are in danger of extinction. This is especially true of the fresh-water fishes of the southwestern United States, where there is hardly a river or stream that has not been affected by the activities of man. Because aquatic habitats in the desert are isolated for long periods of time, punctuated infrequently by floods, the distribution pattern of the fishes of the Southwest once provided an exceptional opportunity for the study of speciation and zoogeography. Now the pattern has been thoroughly disrupted, often unnecessarily, and if anything like it still exists in the world, it is not in North America.

W. L. Minckley and James E. Deacon (*1*), who have made one of the most comprehensive studies of the current status of southwestern fishes, divide organisms into four general categories with respect to habitat needs:

1. Species having habitats produced by or changed by man, which have responded to man's influence by extending their range and abundance
2. Organisms that have not responded to man's influence and which inhabit large geographic areas and are at present common
3. Animals that require large special habitats
4. Species living in small, unique habitats as relics or isolated endemics.

The first two categories of organisms are discussed elsewhere. Category 3 and category 4 approximate most closely the situation in the rivers, streams, and springs of the Southwest.

The alteration of natural aquatic communities in the Southwest has been so extensive that the widespread distribution of many of the fishes in category 3 offers them no protection. Were it not for historical records, a number of species that 40 years ago occupied entire river systems would now be classified as peculiar local forms. For example, the Gila topminnow, *Poeciliopsis occidentalis*, formerly was found throughout the Gila River basin, and as late as 1941 was described as one of the most common fishes in the southern part of the Colorado River drainage. According to Minckley and Deacon (*1*), the Gila topminnow now "persists only in one spring area in Santa Cruz County, Arizona." Under the kinds of conditions that today prevail, categories 3 and 4 tend to merge, and it is no longer possible without prior information to distinguish between species whose range has been restricted naturally by geographic and ecologic barriers, and species whose range has been restricted recently by man. Because of the spotty distribution of many of the remaining species, the pattern of extinction is now as haphazard and unpredictable as man's activities in the region. Here and there in a comparatively undisturbed creek or spring, a unique species or subspecies survives for the present, while others less fortunately situated disappear without fanfare.

The causes of the extinction of the southwestern desert fishes are as varied as the causes of the alteration of their habitat. Human population growth and agricultural and industrial development are rapidly outpacing the development of water resources, which is limited in the long run by the arid climate. After a certain point, which probably already has been reached in the Colorado River system, the construction of more dams in a river basin does nothing but juggle the existing supply of water about, giving it to some regions at the expense of others. Dams do not create water, and reservoirs waste it through evaporation and seepage. Because of the overconstruction of dams, many streams and rivers have become dry or have been reduced to a small trickle. Nearly all the surface run-off waters in the Southwest are now being used by man; this leaves long stretches of river bed below the dams where the remaining thin streams of water, often saline and polluted, must be supplied entirely by seepage of waste and irrigation discharge. The lakes above dams are similarly unsuitable for a number of local species that are adapted for life in turbulent, clean-bottomed streams. In addition to surface waters, underground water supplies have been tapped extensively, resulting in a lowering of the water table. When the water table drops far enough, springs in the vicinity dry up: This has happened in many places (Table 4-1). In some watersheds, twice as much water is being used each year as is being returned (through rainfall and waste outflow) to the underground reservoirs.

Clearly, this means that unless water is brought in from elsewhere, or unless population increase, industrial expansion, and agricultural growth are curtailed, the price of the current exploitation of southwestern water reserves will be paid in full by the next generation. Unfortunately, the native fauna has paid in advance, as so often happens in exploited environments. Table 4-2 lists some of the faunal changes that have occurred in one stream, the Salt River, Arizona, which has been extensively altered by damming during the past century.

Environmental alteration by man can be less obvious than the construction of dams. The Moapa dace, *Moapa coriacea*, was common in the Moapa River, Nevada, when Hubbs and Miller collected it in 1933, but it declined abruptly in the early 1950s. In this case, stream flow was unchanged and the physical environment had not visibly altered. Minckley and Deacon correlate the decline of the Moapa dace with the introduction of another fish, the shortfin molly, *Poecilia mexicana*: "The introduction of *P. mexicana* resulted in a decrease in the population density of *Moapa*, apparently through an increase in parasitism . . . and possibly through direct competitive interaction. A primary danger to *Moapa* is the possibility that additional introductions will cause another population decline from which it might not recover; such circumstances are not predictable." Figure 4-1 illustrates another example of a native fish that is being displaced by an exotic species; in this case, the invader

*Table 4-1*  **Water Discharge and Utilization in Pahrump Valley, Nye and Clark Counties, Nevada, in the Period 1875-1967**

| Year of Period | Manse Spring (ft³/sec, av) | Pahrump Spring (ft³/sec, av) | Raycraft Spring (ft³/sec, av) | Thousands of Acres Irrigated | Pumpage (in thousands of acre-feet) | Number of Wells Operating | Depth of Water Table (ft) |
|---|---|---|---|---|---|---|---|
| 1875 | 6.0 | 7.9 | | | | | |
| 1916 | 3.2 | 4.7 | 0.002 | 0.5 | 4.3 | 15 | |
| 1917-1937 | – | – | – | – | 3.3-4.6 | | |
| 1937-1940 | 3.1 | – | – | – | 2.2-3.5 | | |
| 1940-1946 | 3.1 | 5.5 | – | – | 2.2-16.3 | | |
| 1951 | 2.6 | – | – | – | 16.1 | 39 | 37 |
| 1952 | – | – | – | – | – | 39 | 30-60 |
| 1959 | 2.5 | 0.0 | 0.0 | 5.8 | 25.6 | 45 | |
| 1960 | 2.4 | – | – | 6.2 | 27.4 | 39 | |
| 1961 | 2.0 | – | – | 6.5 | 30.1 | 55 | |
| 1962 | 1.9 | – | – | 6.5 | 29.2 | 54 | |
| 1963 | 1.8 | – | – | 7.8 | 31.9 | 59 | |
| 1964 | 1.9 | – | – | 7.7 | 37.5 | 62 | |
| 1965 | 1.2 | – | – | 8.2 | 36.5 | 64 | |
| 1966 | 1.5 | – | – | 7.6 | 37.9 | 71 | 70-85 |
| 1967 | | | | | | | 75-84 |

SOURCE: W. L. Minckley and J. E. Deacon, *Science 159*, 1424 (1968).
Copyright: American Association for the Advancement of Science, 1968.

(the red shiner, *Notropis lutrensis*) is an aggressive fish that escapes from fishermen's bait buckets and subsequently spreads rapidly. Although the present manner of surface and subsurface water use is a debatable subject, the introduction of non-native species is not. It is a biologically hazardous undertaking whose effects—often deleterious—can be only partially known after extensive ecological study; pending such studies, introductions should be curtailed through public education and, if necessary, by law.

The plight of the indigenous fishes of the southwest is especially serious because in many cases the affected populations represent the entire gene pool of a species, not just a fragment thereof. If these curious little desert fishes had been salmon or bass, there would undoubtedly be large organized groups of sportsmen clamoring for their protection. But they are not salmon or bass, and their loss impoverishes the environment only in subtle ways: by obscuring relationships of scientific significance, by further unbalancing delicate ecosystems, and by promoting the kind of biological uniformity that has its architectural counterpart in the deadly housing developments of the 1950s and 1960s.

**Table 4-2**  **Fishes Recorded from the Salt River, Maricopa County, Arizona, in the City of Tempe, in the Period 1890-1967**

| Species | Year of Collection or Probable Occurrence[a] | | | |
|---|---|---|---|---|
| | 1900 | 1920 | 1940 | 1960 |
| NATIVE SPECIES | | | | |
| Gila elegans | O---- | | | |
| Meda fulgida | O---- | | | |
| Plagopterus argentissimus | O---- | | | |
| Ptychocheilus lucius | X---- | | | |
| Rhinichthys osculus | O---- | | | |
| Catostomus latipinnis | O---- | | | |
| Xyrauchen texanus | O---- | | | |
| Agosia chrysogaster | X-------- | ----O-- | | |
| Gila intermedia | X-------- | ----O-- | | |
| Gila robusta | X-------- | ----O-- | | |
| Poeciliopsis occidentalis | O-------- | ----O-- | | |
| Cyprinodon macularius | O-------- | ----O---- | ---X---- | ---O-- |
| Catostomus insignis | O-------- | ----X---- | ---X---- | ---O----O-- |
| Pantosteus clarki | O-------- | ----X---- | ---X---- | ---O----O-- |
| INTRODUCED SPECIES | | | | |
| Gambusia affinis | | ---O---- | ---O---- | ---O----O-- |
| Lepomis cyanellus | | ---O---- | ---X---- | ---O----O-- |
| Cyprinus carpio | | | --O---- | ---X----O-- |
| Ictalurus melas | | | --O---- | ---O----O-- |
| Lepomis macrochirus | | | --O---- | ---X----O-- |
| Pomoxis nigromaculatus | | | --O---- | ---X----X-- |
| Poecilia latipinna | | | | ----O----O-- |
| Micropterus salmoides | | | | ----O----O-- |
| Dorosoma petenensis | | | | ----O-- |
| Carassius auratus | | | | ----O-- |
| Notemigonus crysoleucus[b] | | | | ----O-- |
| Notropis lutrensis | | | | ----O-- |
| Pimephales promelas[b] | | | | ----O-- |
| Ictalurus natalis | | | | ----O-- |
| Ictalurus punctatus | | | | ----O-- |
| Lebistes reticulatus[b] | | | | ----O-- |
| Poecilia mexicana[b] | | | | ----O-- |
| Xiphophorus variatus[b] | | | | ----O-- |
| Lepomis microlophus | | | | ----O-- |
| Tilapia mossambica[b] | | | | ----O-- |

SOURCE: W. L. Minckley and J. E. Deacon, *Science 159*, 1424 (1968).

[a]Dashed lines span the period during which a species probably inhabited this segment of the stream; (O), occurrences documented by specimens in museums or recorded in the literature; (X), probable occurrence of a species at a given time, on the basis of collections made before that time or in other parts of the drainage, both upstream and downstream from Tempe.

[b]These species were taken prior to severe flooding in the Salt River Channel at Tempe in the winter of 1965-1966, but not subsequently.

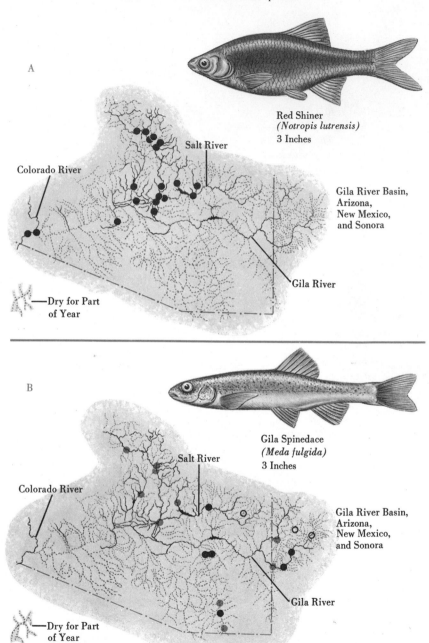

*Fig. 4-1   (A) Present distribution of the introduced red shiner in the Gila River basin. (B) Present and past distribution of the native Gila spinedace in the Gila River basin. Blue circles are localities of former occurrence where the present absence of the fish has been confirmed; open circles are localities that have not been reexamined; black circles are localities where the spinedace persists. (Modified after W. L. Minckley and J. Deacon, Science 159 (1968). Copyright American Association for the Advancement of Science, 1968.)*

Unfortunately, the majority of the public has not been made aware of these considerations; if any of the threatened species are preserved in their natural environments, it will probably not be through direct action, but will be an indirect consequence of action taken to correct the 75-year-old pattern of abuse of water resources.

Among the measures that might be taken are a limitation of the rights of property owners as they pertain to water resources and water use, regional coordination and regulation of irrigation throughout entire watersheds so as not to deplete the surface reserves or lower the water table, strict "zoning" of the other kinds of water use (also on a regional watershed basis), and the rapid implementation of a high priority program to bring additional water from the north. Above all, the inhabitants of the Southwest will have to recognize that the population size and industrialization of their communities will soon be limited by the supply of water and that they will be more comfortable if they deal realistically with the situation in advance.

As in the case of the fishes of the southwestern United States, the wild animals of India have suffered primarily from the destruction of their native ecosystems. Here a significant part of the fauna of an entire subcontinent has disappeared almost unnoticed. The decline has been particularly striking because India, like Africa, used to have extensive forests and savannas containing some of the most spectacular species in the world. Unlike Africa, however, India has done little to preserve its native fauna; were it not for the American field biologist, and ethologist George B. Schaller (2), few would even be aware of the problem. Schaller, who first attracted wide attention with his book on the mountain gorilla, one of the earliest studies of the habits of a great ape in its natural environment, went to India to study the behavior and ecology of the native deer and the tiger, but found himself increasingly involved in the gigantic problem of Indian wildlife and wildlife habitats.

Although poaching and unrestricted hunting are now the immediate threat to many of the mammals and birds of India, these creatures would not be in such a precarious position were it not for the devastation of the Indian landscape. As an example, we can consider the present status of the Gir forest, a "wildlife sanctuary" on the Kathiawar peninsula in western India near the Gulf of Cambay. The area of the Gir Forest is 483 square miles, but it is utilized by more than 7000 people and at least 57,000 domestic cattle, many of which are diseased and transmit their parasites to the wild ungulates, in addition to competing with them for food in the overgrazed forest. Tragically, the cattle of the Gir Forest and throughout India are of little use to the majority of the inhabitants, who cannot kill them because of Hindu religious beliefs. As far as India is concerned, domestic cattle are the economic equivalent of giant rats, multiplying uncontrollably (like the human population) and devouring every blade of grass in their paths.

The Indian lion, a distinct subspecies different from the more common African lion, once ranged widely from Asia Minor, Palestine, and Arabia to Persia and India; it is now largely confined to the Gir Forest. In 1960 it was estimated that there were 350 lions in the forest; in 1968, 162 were counted. The decline is occurring in spite of the lion's high reproductive potential (its gestation period is only 100 days), which might even be able to overcome the loss of 100 animals per year by poisoning were it not for the destruction of the forest itself. Because of the proliferation of cattle, both the vegetative cover and the deer that constitute the natural food of the lion are fast disappearing. Lee M. Talbot (*14*) estimated in 1960 that "at the present rate of attrition the Gir should only last another 20 years. . . ." When the forest is gone, the world population of Indian lions will consist of approximately 50 animals distributed among a little more than a dozen zoos.

Sound wildlife management and habitat conservation are virtually unknown in India. According to Schaller *(2)*: "The rare Indian wild dog is persecuted wherever it is found. In one park all these dogs were shot on sight because they destroyed deer. At the same time the deer were shot because they destroyed tree seedlings!" The most vivid example of wanton and unnecessary habitat destruction cited by Schaller is

Fig. 4-2   *Indian lion in Gir Forest, India. (E. Hanumantha Rao, Photo Researchers)*

that of the Keoladeo Othana Sanctuary, which like the great Nairobi National Park 6 miles from the capital of Kenya, is close enough to a large city, Agra, to be a potential major tourist attraction. Yet, this tiny, 11 square mile patch of woods now contains more than 5600 head of cattle and buffalo and is rapidly becoming a wasteland. Ironically, India was probably the first nation on earth to practice land conservation and wildlife management: The late E. P. Gee, one of India's few noted conservationists, found that in the year 300 B.C. government decrees set aside certain areas where "the extraction of timber, burning of charcoal, collection of grass, fuel and leaves, the cutting of cane and bamboo, trapping for fur skins and tooth and bone were all totally prohibited." Since that time, the sense of these regulations has been forgotten, and large parts of India have been lost to both man and nature through indiscriminate lumbering and overgrazing, leading in turn to desiccation of the remaining vegetation, fire, and massive soil erosion. Crowded into patchy and ever-contracting fragments of the original landscape, the last representatives of India's fauna fall easy prey to poachers, from all social classes, whose activities are totally unregulated (see Table 4-3). This, then, is perhaps the bleakest chapter of the whole conservation story. Remedies could be suggested, but to suggest them would be to introduce what seems to be a fatuous note of optimism. India's problems are too immense and intertwined to be attacked piecemeal, and even if a concerted effort were possible, it is hard to see how it could accrue enough force in time to oppose the gathering momentum of the landslide.

The examples of the fate of the fishes of the southwestern United States and of the wildlife of India provide one lesson in common: The widespread and often preventable destruction of natural communities and the subsequent general loss of species foreshadows and often is accompanied by severe environmental problems for the human inhabitants of the region, regardless of their technology. If the other motives and objectives for maintaining the diversity of the environment fall on deaf ears, this ominous correlation should at least provoke concern.

*THE PET TRADE, ZOOS, AND MEDICAL INSTITUTIONS* The destruction of habitat usually effects an over-all reduction in the number of species present; but there are a variety of means by which particular species can be endangered, even within relatively intact communities. The remainder of this chapter is largely devoted to a consideration of the ways in which this can happen.

One of the most unrelenting and insidious drains on remaining

Table 4-3 **Status of Some Characteristic Indian Species**

| Species | Description | Status | Cause of Decline |
|---|---|---|---|
| Tiger (*Panthera tigris*) | The Indian tiger is the most numerous sub-species of a group that is nearing extinction everywhere else (Siberia, China, Java, etc.); the largest and handsomest of the big cats; habits poorly understood. | Population in 1920, approximately 40,000; population in 1968, less than 4000. | Destruction of habitat and food supply; grossly excessive hunting. |
| Snow Leopard (*Panthera uncia*) | A cat of the high Himalayas (12,000 ft in summer). Its exceptionally beautiful gray-white fur is much sought after. Habits are poorly understood; not a true leopard. | Population in 1968, 400 ± 200, total for entire Himalayan range; totally protected in the U.S.S.R.; classified as "vermin" in Kashmir. | Excessive hunting for fur. (One of the few Indian animals not threatened by habitat destruction.) |
| Asiatic Cheetah (*Acinonyx jubatus venaticus*) | A medium-sized, spotted cat, resident of open savannas; fastest-running mammal; valuable fur. Tames readily but has not been bred in captivity. | *Extinct in India.* Perhaps a few hundred remain in other parts of Asia. | Destruction of habitat and food supply (blackbuck); excessive hunting. |
| Blackbuck (*Antilope cervicapra*) | A graceful and striking medium-sized antelope; males with long spirally twisted horns; celebrated in Indian mythology; the principal prey species for the cheetah. | Nearly extinct in most Indian states; very abundant 50 years ago. | Habitat destruction and competition with cattle; grossly excessive hunting. (Blackbucks were used as targets to sight-in rifles.) |
| Gaur (*Bos gaurus*) | The Indian bison; largest of the world's wild cattle; prefers high, grassy tablelands; travels in herds of 5–20; secretive. | Once fairly common; now much reduced in numbers. | Seriously afflicted by rinderpest and foot-and-mouth disease transmitted by native cattle. |
| Manipur Brow-Antlered Deer (*Cervus eldi eldi*) | A medium-sized deer with unusual, stately antlers; tends to wander great distances; lives in the floating swamp of Logtak Lake in | Declared extinct in 1951; rediscovered in 1952. Approximately 100 in 1968. May be increasing thanks to impenetrability of its habitat | Habitat destruction; poaching and wild dogs, especially during the unsettled conditions following World War II. |

Table 4-3   (Continued)

| Species | Description | Status | Cause of Decline |
|---|---|---|---|
| | Manipur State. | and vegetarian customs of nearby villagers. Manipur government taking steps to protect it. | |
| Great Indian Rhinoceros (*Rhinoceros unicornis*) | Largest of Asiatic rhinoceroses; primarily confined to reserves in India and Nepal; the subject of an unusually successful Indian conservation effort. | About 700 in India and Nepal; stable population, but still threatened by competition with cattle for food, and by cattle diseases. | Originally, habitat destruction; later, hunting. Much of the rhino's former habitat in west and northwest India is now desert because of bad agricultural practices. |
| Pigmy Hog (*Sus salvanius*) | A tiny wild pig; full-grown boars were less than 12 in. high; a nocturnal, forest animal of the Himalayan foothills. | *Possibly extinct*. Last seen in the winter of 1958-1959. | Habitat destruction. |
| Sloth Bear (*Melursus ursinus*) | A comical-looking, unaggressive bear that eats termites, grubs, and fruits, and which snores loudly when asleep. | Greatly reduced in numbers; has retreated into the remaining forests. | Habitat destruction. |
| Pink-Headed Duck (*Rhodonessa caryophyllacea*) | A unique and beautiful bird, perhaps related to American canvasback; confined to swampy jungle. | *Extinct*. A wild bird was last shot in 1935. The last captive specimen died in Britain in 1944. The Indian Government passed a law protecting the species in 1956. Was never common. | Drainage of swamp habitat; market hunting. |

stocks of wild animals (and occasionally plants) is the collecting of live specimens for the pet trade. A surprising variety of species are threatened, including such unlikely and unsuitable "pets" as sea turtles (which require facilities beyond the reach of nearly all reptile fanciers), ocelots (which after being declawed, castrated, and confined become pitiful caricatures of a superb animal), and monkeys (which are too destructive to be allowed to roam free around a house, too intelligent to be closely confined, and too fragile to survive the dietary and climatic abuse that is usually their lot in captivity).

The sale of wild animals as pets has become big business, especially in the United States. In June, 1968, the pet trade was described by William G. Conway (3), general director of the New York Zoological Society (which includes the Bronx Zoo and the New York Aquarium): "Although the exotic pet trade has tangible and intangible values it must be regulated. Many wild animal populations can withstand well-managed collecting but many rare forms cannot. Moreover, exceptionally delicate or highly specialized animals must not be sold as personal pets whether they are rare or common. The problem is one of cruelty as much as conservation. A few days ago, as I wandered through the pet department of a local five-and-ten-cent store, I happened upon a terrarium filled with 'common' horned lizards.

"The trade in horned lizards has been going on for decades. . . . The unforgivably immoral nature of this piece of commercialization is that horned lizards almost invariably starve to death after a few weeks in captivity. This tells us something about the character of the exotic pet trade for it is well known that horned lizards have highly specialized and poorly understood food and temperature requirements, which few pet buyers could hope to meet."

Among the rare and delicate species that are sold in New York pet stores, Conway has seen golden-headed quetzals, South American cocks-of-the-rock, equatorial barbets, Indonesian fairy bluebirds, South American hummingbirds, Saki monkeys, Malayan flying lizards, tamanduas (arboreal anteaters), three-toed sloths, uncommon species of parrots, and Texas tortoises. If such importations were unusual, it would be a matter for concern only in the case of those species whose total population size is of the order of a few hundred or thousand individuals. But the magnitude of the traffic in wild animals is staggering. In 1967 the U.S. Fish and Wildlife Service reported that among imports into the United States were 74,304 mammals, 203,189 birds (not including parrot-family birds and canaries), 405,134 reptiles, 137,697 amphibians, and 27,759,332 fish. When one adds to this the annual totals for other pet-loving countries like Great Britain and Germany, it is easy to see why species are threatened by the pet trade.

The wild animal import figures (for those countries that keep them) show only a fraction of the impact of this self-destructive industry because many, often most, and sometimes all wild animals in shipments transported from one country to another die during capture or en route. For example, incomplete figures for nine months of 1962 show that Ethiopia exported 40,000 birds. How many died during and immediately after capture but before export is not known; we can guess that the number is of the same order of magnitude as the 40,000 that survived to be counted. How many of the birds reached pet stores alive is also not known, but 20,000 is probably an overestimate.

The Amazon basin, usually thought of as an immense reservoir of wild country and wild species, has already been mentioned as an example of an area in which the pet trade has seriously eroded the native fauna. Endangered species and populations include jungle cats (see also "Fur Trade"), many kinds of rare monkeys and marmosets, alligatorlike caimen (sold as baby "alligators" in the United States), birds of many descriptions, a variety of small mammals, and tropical fish. According to Dr. Charles W. Quaintance (4) of Eastern Oregon College: "The native Indians who hunt the animals were reported to be penetrating deeper and deeper into the forest to secure their specimens which they sold daily to the honorary U.S. Consul at Leticia, Colombia, and he, in turn, shipped out great quantities of animals without any regard for their increasing scarcity." Other major ports of exit for Amazon animal shipments are Manaos, Brazil, and Iquitos, Peru.

It has been argued that maintenance of the pet trade is essential to the Indian economy of the Amazon region; however, it is doubtful whether any economy has, in the long run, benefited from an industry that operates by permanently destroying local resources. Whether one is referring to diamonds and gold in the Matto Grosso, to farmland in South Dakota, or to wildlife in the Amazon basin, the North and South American Indians have never profited from external exploitation, and it is the grossest hypocrisy to promote an unregulated exploitative trade on the grounds that it is in their behalf.

Zoos are an ancient institution in the civilized world, and their quality is judged by the strangeness of the animals they exhibit. Until 1967 many zoos competed for rare and endangered species. Although this undoubtedly resulted in saving a few species that could be bred in captivity, the high prices paid for rare animals also had the undesirable effect of subsidizing the legitimate or clandestine activities of wild animal collectors and dealers. The result was a vicious circle of diminishing populations, rising prices, and increasing pressure to collect more specimens. The circle was finally interrupted largely because of the conservation activities of Mrs. Barbara Harrisson, of Malaysia, who publicized the rapidly deteriorating status of the orangutan, *Pongo pygmaeus*, which is one of the four major types of great ape still existing in the world and among the closest relatives of man.

The great nineteenth-century naturalist and zoogeographer Alfred Russel Wallace supplied, unknowingly, all the reasons why the orangutan would be nearing extinction 100 years after the publication in 1869 of his book, *The Malay Archipelago, the Land of the Orang-Utan and the Bird of Paradise*. Wallace wrote: "It is very remarkable that an animal so large, so peculiar, and of such a high type of form as the Orang-Utan, should be confined to so limited a district—to two islands [Sumatra and Borneo]. . . . Now it seems to me probable, that a wide extent of unbroken and equally lofty virgin forest is necessary to the comfortable existence of these animals." In pointing out the orangutan's restricted range and highly specific ecological requirements, Wallace provided the key

Fig. 4-3  Young wild orangutan, Sarawak. (Courtesy Barbara Harrisson; © Sarawak Museum)

to its vulnerability. He also stated: "I have myself examined the bodies of seventeen freshly-killed orangs. . . .", thus foreshadowing the more extensive and less justifiable slaughter that was to follow. By 1966 the extensive destruction of habitat and the activities of animal collectors (including many members of the Indonesian Army) had reduced the total orangutan population to approximately 5000. The demand for baby orangs by pet dealers, medical institutions, and zoos increased steadily during the 1960s. Since the common method of collecting baby orangs involves shooting the mother, and since one in six infants survives this experience, it is easy to see why the continued existence of the species is in doubt.

Although it is now questionable whether orangutans will be able to survive in the wild, the publicity attending the plight of these shy, vegetarian animals has had two beneficial results. First, it was discovered by Mrs. Harrisson that Section 43, Title 18 of the United States Code states that: "Transportation of wildlife taken in violation of State, National, *or foreign laws* [author's italics] . . ." is a crime, and that a person convicted of this crime "shall be fined not more than $500 or imprisoned not more than six months, or both; and the wild animals or birds, or the dead bodies or parts thereof, or the eggs of such birds, shall be forfeited." With this law in the statute books of the major purchaser of orangutans, it remained only for Mrs. Harrisson to locate or secure passage of protective laws in each of the countries that exported the animals. With such "foreign laws" in effect, entry into the United States was automatically prohibited, and the major market was closed. Indonesia, Sarawak, and Sabah now have the necessary laws. They may possibly be too late to preserve the orang, but this important legal precedent provides the means for protecting other domestic and foreign wildlife.

Second, partly because of the efforts of Mrs. Harrisson and other conservationists, the American Association of Zoological Parks and Aquariums, meeting in Mexico City on March 14, 1967, took self-regulatory action to control the international traffic in endangered species. The voting member zoos agreed unanimously not to purchase, accept as a gift, sell, or trade any orangutans, monkey-eating eagles, Javan and Sumatran rhinoceroses, Galápagos and Aldabran giant tortoises, or any other rare species that may be added to the list by a two-thirds vote of the membership, unless the AAZPA Subcommittee on Endangered Species approves the specific case.

Medical institutions and medical researchers have never been particularly concerned about the sources of their experimental animals; the flourishing trade in stolen dogs and cats testifies to this in the United States. The demands of medical research are placing an increasingly heavy burden on wild stocks of certain animals — particularly primates. According to Conway, "In 1967, 65,526 wild primates, mostly for laboratory research, were imported into the United States." The yearly total has, on occasion, risen above 200,000. The consumption of wild primates for medical research now threatens many kinds of monkeys and most species of great apes, including the chimpanzee, the most numerous, whose total population is less than 250,000. Medical researchers are often thoughtlessly wasteful when working with wild animals, a habit that may be partly due to prior experiences with the inexhaustible supplies of laboratory rats and mice, and partly due to ignorance. Quaintance (4) reports that biologists at a wildlife conference in Colombia cited the case of a medical research team from the United States that killed over 400 monkeys, mostly howlers, in order to examine their aortas, but made no other use of the bodies. Nearly all species of monkeys and apes that are used in medical research will breed in captivity; however, few laboratories have assumed the responsibility of renewing the resource that they are so rapidly destroying.

Not all the abuse of research animal resources has occurred in strictly medical laboratories. At the Marine Biological Laboratories at Woods Hole, Massachusetts, sea urchin (*Arbacia*) eggs have been used for many years in a wide variety of biological experiments. The dead sea urchins are discarded after their eggs have been physically or chemically removed. This kind of careless waste of animals probably played a major role in the severe depletion of sea urchins, and other marine invertebrates, in the waters around Woods Hole (although there has been a recent recovery of sea urchin populations as investigators turn to other organisms). In contrast, the marine laboratory at Friday Harbor, Washington, usually obtains its sea urchin (*Strongylocentrotus*) eggs by allowing the captured animals to release them spontaneously into the water of the holding tanks. The sea urchins are then returned to the underwater area where they originated, and that area is left undisturbed for a year or more. There has never been a shortage of sea urchins at Friday Harbor.

Neither biomedical researchers nor anyone else will benefit from the extinction of the animals they need and use. Moreover, the exigencies of research do not justify an inadequate conservation policy because conservation and research are perfectly compatible if a little foresight and planning are exercised.

**HUNTING**

*Animal Products*

The per capita demand for many animal products has decreased in the twentieth century as a result of the development of industrial technology and subsequent manufacture of synthetic materials derived from wood, coal, and oil. In some cases, however, the favorable impact of this decrease on animal populations has been more than offset by the increase in human population and by the increased market for luxury items in some countries. Thus, although whale oil is no longer needed for lamps, whale meat is now used in some of the noncereal pet foods available in Europe. Two examples of animal species — the blue whale and the green turtle — that are currently nearing extinction because of exploitation by animal products industries are discussed in Chapters 5 and 8, respectively.

Among the various causes of species destruction, many of the animal products industries deserve special notice because they take advantage of scarcity of a species to increase demand and raise prices. Even in the early part of this century, when animal populations were much greater and human populations were smaller and poorer, short-lived fads for animal products brought several species to the verge of extinction. The craze for egret and ostrich feathers during the late 1800s and early 1900s nearly succeeded in wiping out a number of species of these once abundant birds. As Vinzenz Ziswiller has written in his excellent book, *Extinct and Vanishing Animals* (see Further Reading at end of this chapter): "When we consider that in the single year of 1912 more than 160 tons of ostrich feathers were sold in France alone, it becomes distressingly clear how close the African ostrich (*Struthio camelus*) came to falling a victim to women's whimsey. Fortunately, shortly before this fate was realized it became possible to meet the demand through ostrich farms, and in due time, much to the sorrow of the African ostrich-breeders, the fashions changed." Similarly, the American egret (*Casmerodius albus*) was saved just in time by the same change of fashion and by the actions of groups like the Audubon Society and of individuals like E. A. McIlhenny, who turned part of his vast Louisiana land holdings into a bird sanctuary where the egrets could be effectively protected and their habits studied.

Also saved in time by the death of a fad was the diamondback terrapin (*Malaclemys terrapin*), an inhabitant of Atlantic coastal salt marshes. The diamondback's northern and southern subspecies were relished by gourmets after the turn of the century. Dr. Archie Carr (5) writes: "Originally so abundant that eighteenth-century tidewater slaves once struck for relief from a diet too heavy in terrapin, the diamondback gradually found a place on the tables of the privileged, and during the roseate period that extended from the heyday of Diamond Jim Brady to the close of the First World War it came to be surrounded by an aura of superlative elegance as synthetic as a latest Paris fashion." In 1891 the total catch in the Chesapeake Bay area was estimated at 89,150 pounds valued at $20,559; by 1920 the total catch had fallen to 823 pounds worth $1000. In 1921 the attractive, 6-inch turtles were selling for as much as $90 a dozen in Savannah. As was the case with the ostrich, commercial breeding "farms" were established, but the real relief for the diamondbacks came when the fad expired during the Great Depression. Terrapin populations have now recovered slightly in some localities such as Connecticut and Maryland, but these animals came very close to extinction.

Diamondback Terrapin
*(Malaclemys terrapin)*
Average Size is 8 Inches

*Fig. 4-4    The diamondback terrapin, an inhabitant of salt marshes and tidal flats.*

At present, there are few species that can resist the fur and hide industries the way the egret resisted the feather hunters and the diamondback terrapin resisted the restaurant demand. Snow leopard furs are still being advertised and sold by some furriers, despite the fact that there are scarcely enough snow leopards left in all the Himalayas to provide 100 coats. New tiger coats are still on sale in the United States despite the fact that there are now less than 4000 Bengal tigers in India, and only about 500 tigers in all of southeast Asia, China, Siberia, and the Transcaspian region. Although space does not permit a discussion of all other cats endangered by the fur trade, virtually none of the large or showy varieties is safe at the time of this writing. For example, when the price paid to the hunter for an ocelot hide rose to $100 on the Costa Rican coast in 1967–1968, many of the able-bodied men stopped what they were doing, bought rolls of piano wire, and turned to setting choke-snares in the bush. In 1967 the United States Customs Department passed 115,458 ocelot skins alone. But cats are not the only animals used by the industry; the vicuña, a camel-like inhabitant of the Central Andean plateau, has fallen in numbers from 400,000 in 1957 to less than 10,000 in 1968. Its especially fine wool now commands a price of $25 per pound; one vicuña has one-third to one-half pound of wool. According to Dr. Peter Scott, a single British firm is importing 2 tons of vicuña wool a year. There is good evidence to indicate that the vicuña would respond well to wildlife management or semidomestication for commercial purposes, yet the Peruvian and Bolivian governments are only now begin-

*Fig. 4-5   Snow leopard. (R. Van Nostrand, National Audubon Society)*

*Fig. 4-6   Leopard head trophies in Nairobi, Kenya. (Loomis Dean, LIFE Magazine © Time Inc.)*

ning to explore this possibility. As is common practice in matters concerning the fur and the hide industries, commercially profitable conservation measures are rarely initiated before the wild resource has been exhausted.

Unlike the vogue for feathers or the fleeting popularity of certain furs, the public's desire for reptile leathers has been sustained, with minor ups and downs for many years. The greater part of the hunting pressure has fallen on the Nile crocodile, the South American caiman, and the American alligator. The situation of the Nile crocodile is illustrative of the problems facing all crocodilians. Dr. Hugh B. Cott (6) of Cambridge University's Museum of Zoology has studied the ecology of these animals and describes the difficulty of protecting them: "The main immediate threat to the crocodile's survival comes from the techniques now employed by professional hunters. Working at night in fast motor boats, these men easily locate their quarry in the beam of a powerful spot-light, approach at speed, shoot at point-blank range, and gaff the dying animal before it can sink. Against this form of attack the crocodile has virtually no defense . . . as the supply fails elsewhere, the crocodiles that remain hitherto preserved in reserves and national parks offer an irresistible attraction." In Uganda's Murchison Falls Park, Cott has recently found that poachers have reduced the once prodigious number of crocodiles to about 250 nesting females; overpopulation of storks, baboons, monitor lizards, hyenas and mongooses, the result of ecological imbalance, threatens the few eggs and young that are still produced (7). Unfortunately, the crocodiles that are killed by poachers are drawn almost entirely from the breeding population (Fig. 4-7).

The Nile crocodile is an important member of a major African ecosystem: As does the alligator (see Chapter 2), it benefits fishing as well as the tourist industry. But as Cott points out, the future of the species is in doubt if the hide industry continues to mine this resource like an exhaustible metal deposit rather than to crop the surplus in a regulated way so that the crocodile population can be maintained for future use. Although it is hardly necessary to repeat the justification for the conservation of species each time a new species is mentioned, Cott's statement on this subject is well reasoned and clear and deserves quotation: "Crocodiles essentially like the modern species existed in Jurassic times and were contemporaries of the dinosaurs. As the only remaining members of the archosaurian stock which have survived the age of reptiles, they are of quite exceptional scientific importance, not least from the indirect light which studies of anatomy, physiology, ecology and behaviour can throw upon the biology of ancestors long extinct. It would be a grave loss to science and research, and to posterity, if these saurians — which have survived for over a hundred million years — were now to be sacrificed to the demands of uninformed public opinion, and subordinated to a passing fashion in leather goods."

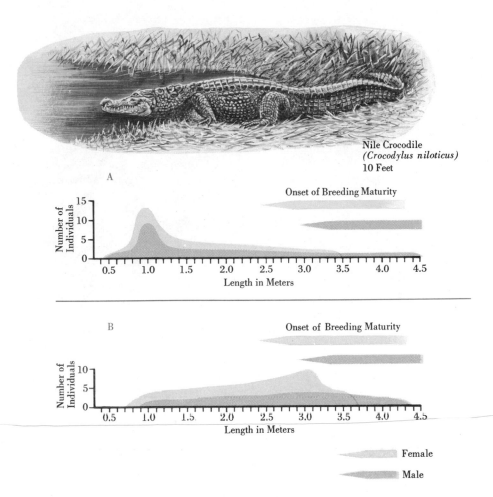

*Fig. 4-7  Comparison of length-frequency distribution of crocodiles shot: (A) in areas where hunters had already been at work (Luangwa Valley and Kafue Flats), and (B) in areas not previously exploited. (Modified after H. B. Cott, Trans. Zool. Society London 29 (4) (1961).)*

In the mid-1960s the leather trade began to process and sell (at very high prices) women's handbags and shoes made of sea turtle skin. Since a new market was created by advertising, this introduction of another source of reptile leather did nothing to relieve the hunting pressure on the crocodilian and lizard populations. Furthermore, the world populations of sea turtles of all species were already dangerously low, too low to support the demands of the reptile leather market. Evidently the industry saw this merely as an opportunity to make a quick profit in

**Fig. 4-8** *Piles of ridley sea turtle shells near a beach in Oaxaca State, Mexico. (Herbert M. Eder)*

a previously unexploited area—nothing more. The piles of hundreds of female Pacific ridley turtles (*Lepidochelys olivacea*) illegally killed on Mexican and Central American beaches still attest to this unscrupulous policy; in many cases, only the skin of the foreflippers is taken, while the carcasses amounting to tons of edible meat and thousands of fertile eggs — the future of the species — are left to rot in the sun.

***Game Hunting*** Hunting is an ancient human endeavor, probably as old as our species. There are still races and tribes of man who must hunt to live, but the vast majority of us — including virtually all the readers of this book — do not depend on a gun, a spear, or a bow to bring home dinner. Nevertheless, hunting survives and flourishes as a sport in all technologically advanced countries, particularly in the United States, which has, more than any other nation, glorified its recent frontier history.

If properly regulated, game hunting is primarily a conservation activity. It serves to control the population sizes of animals such as deer, squirrels, and rabbits that would tend to multiply excessively in the absence of their original predators. Hunting provides revenue — through the purchase of duck stamps, hunting licenses, and sales taxes on sports equipment—to run many governmental conservation activities. Most important, good hunters are familiar with natural environments, recognize both their unique value and precarious balance, and are often eager to work as a group to prevent them from being ruined. In an increasingly urban world, game hunters form an essential link between the natural earth and the constructed earth—two realms that can be separated only at the peril of the latter.

However, there remain abuses of hunting which threaten to cloud the image of the sport and to damage species. With a few exceptions, the hunting of "big game" is no longer a reasonable activity in the modern world; yet a handful of wealthy men are willing to risk causing the extinction of entire species for the sake of a few trophies. A notorious example of this befouling of an ancient sport is the hunting of polar bears in the state of Alaska. The bears are spotted by plane, and the "sportsman" is then landed at a convenient (and safe) spot to await the arrival of the bear, which may be driven into his gunsights by another plane. One result is a bearskin rug—to which a real hunter would be ashamed to lay claim; another is that the state of Alaska becomes richer by the few thousand dollars left behind by the free-spending tourist. The polar bear population in Alaska is rapidly dwindling to extinction (female polar bears breed only once every 3 years; hence the recuperative abilities of the population are low). Fortunately, both Canada and the Soviet Union have taken steps to protect the polar bear in their territories, but it is a national scandal that the people of the United States should permit the loss of one of their most exciting and magnificent native animals for lack of federal legislation to control the irresponsible actions of a single state.

Similar abuses of good hunting practice still occur in Africa, where big game is occasionally chased down and shot by hunters in planes, but an increasing number of persons on safari have discovered that after the thrill and danger of stalking a rhino in the traditional manner, the most rewarding shot may be one from a camera. For those who insist on a trophy, several African national parks and conservation departments issue restricted hunting licenses as a way of reducing local population surpluses of potentially destructive animals such as elephants.

In some countries where the army has considerable leisure time to spend in wilderness areas, and/or where the soldiers can contrive to keep their weapons after they leave the service, a new danger has arisen. No hunted species or natural community can withstand a heavy influx of armed men, especially if ammunition is free. Earlier in this chapter it was pointed out that the Indonesian Army in Sumatra constitutes a severe threat to the survival of the orangutan; similarly, in many Central and South American countries the soldiers and ex-soldiers hunt with submachine guns or semiautomatic weapons, and the damage is compounded by the fact that they generally shoot at anything that moves — even the smaller songbirds. Finally, according to the *New York Times* (September 13, 1968), "One of the biggest losers of the Vietnam war has been the elephant of the Central Highlands and northern provinces, which is frequently shot down by patrols and by machine-gun fire from helicopter. . . . Many South Vietnamese officials are concerned about what [they] call the indiscriminate shooting of elephants from the air." Other Vietnamese animals that have been killed or that have fled to Cambodia and Laos include deer, tigers, rhinoceroses, monkeys, wild boar, and many species of birds.

**PREDATOR CONTROL**    Predators are a component of virtually all ecosystems, and they include among their numbers the direct ancestors of man back to the time of the Australopithecine man-apes, and perhaps before. S. Eimerl and I. DeVore (8) have written: "It would be hard to exaggerate the importance of predation — or hunting — in the development of man. Together with bipedalism and the use of tools, hunting was the principal element which set him on the evolutionary path that was to lead, ultimately, to his position of dominance over all other animals." Despite his background, however, man has shown little fondness for other predators, regarding them, understandably, as competitors, and less understandably in the twentieth century, as dangerous, undesirable, and somehow unnatural. Although nearly all biologists, supported by a mass of good data, now advance the thesis that predators serve a necessary function in natural and seminatural communities, misguided attempts to exterminate these creatures are still going forward in many countries.

Predator control programs are generally based on two popular myths:

1. The myth that medium-sized and large predators are dangerous to man. Nearly all reports of wild animals attacking man without considerable provocation prove to be false (an exception is discussed in Chapter 8). According to John Hillaby (9), ". . . dispassionate travellers have stated that the big Labrador wolf has never been known to attack a man. In Sault Ste. Marie, the center of a region renowned for its blood-curdling wolf stories, the editor of the local paper offered $100 for authenticated accounts of wolf attacks. The cash is said to be still in the till." Similarly, the alligator is not nearly so fearsome as its reputation. Although reports of attacks by wild alligators date back to the time of the early explorers, it is curious that the "victims," if identified, always managed to escape unharmed. Alligators, as do other predators, have a

well-developed sense of what is the appropriate size and shape of their prey; they are not averse to nibbling on pet dachshunds, when available, but they do not attack people (captive, restrained, or semitame alligators that are used to being offered food are an exception). E. A. McIlhenny, the pioneer in the study of alligator behavior, recalled that when he was a boy in Louisiana the local swimming area was peacefully shared with a great many alligators of enormous size.

There are, of course, a number of marine predators, including some sharks, barracudas, and some groupers, whose reputation is partially deserved, and most large terrestrial predators like bears and tigers have been known to attack man. But man does not live in a marine environment, and the terrestrial attacks are so rare that they never justify the extirpation of a species.

2. The myth that predators are a threat to domestic livestock and wild game. As is the case with both other animals and man himself, the most dramatic, striking, and easily observable aggressive actions of predators are the ones that receive the most attention. Thus we hear about foxes and coyotes in South Dakota killing pheasants and snatching chickens from farms; we hear about snapping turtles in northeastern lakes striking at migratory ducks and smallmouth bass; and we hear about wolves in Canada eating caribou. All of these accounts are true, but it is essential not to pass judgment before some additional questions are answered in each case: First, does the predator keep the population level of its prey at an undesirably low level? Second, do the activities of the predator have any directly or indirectly beneficial effects?

Nearly all studies to date of predator-prey relationships support the idea that wild predators do *not* cause great reductions in the population density of prey species; in fact they seem to have little effect at all other than to check gross overpopulation (the converse is not always true; predator population size is closely controlled by the availability of prey, especially in simple ecosystems). This viewpoint was expressed by Dr. Paul Errington (see Further Reading at the end of this chapter), who made extensive investigations of the effects of predation on bobwhite quail and muskrat populations: ". . . the more a prey population is basically limited by some non-predatory feature of its environment, or by its own intolerance of crowding, the less it can be basically limited by predation. I do not say, and never have said, that predation cannot be a limiting factor with some populations; but with the living forms with which I am most familiar, I believe that the population effect of predation is often greatly overrated. . . ."

In South Dakota in 1966, when 409,757 acres of prime pheasant land were withdrawn from the soil bank program and mowed at the height of the nesting season, the resulting sharp drop in the pheasant population was naturally blamed on foxes and coyotes. Despite a vigorous program of predator control, the pheasant population has not fully recovered. The governor of South Dakota commissioned a group of scientists to study the situation, and they reported that "reduction of foxes in large areas has resulted in no significant change in the pheasant populations but has resulted in a sharp rise in rabbit and rodent populations." Evidently the populations of rabbits and rodents, high to begin with, were kept from an overpopulation crisis only by the predators, while the inroads of the foxes on the depleted pheasant population were small in comparison with the effects of habitat destruction. Similarly, no one but professional bounty hunters believes that the decline of the caribou can be attributed to the wolf. Before the days of uncontrolled hunting and poaching with modern weapons, both caribou and wolf populations were much greater.

Even the common American snapping turtle (*Chelydra serpentina*), which claims few friends other than customers of Philadelphia restaurants, does not deserve the abuse it receives from fishermen and duck hunters. Dr. Karl Lagler (*10*), who examined the stomach and colon contents of several hundred snapping turtles, stated: "It seems a conservative estimate that on the average not more than one game or pan fish is eaten per day by the individual snapping turtle." Nor was there any evidence that the snapping turtle was competing with game fish for the smaller "forage" fish that constitute the latter's food. Since a normal snapping turtle population approximates only two adult turtles per acre of water, Lagler came to the one sensible conclusion that: "Thus there need be little concern as to the adverse relations of snapping turtles to game fish populations in wild waters." The same statement might be made about ducks, which are caught by snapping turtles relatively infrequently, and are a minor item of the reptile's diet.

A number of beneficial effects of predators have been demonstrated or claimed. The most significant of these is certainly the widespread tendency of predators to prevent overpopulation of prey species. Numerous examples could be cited. These include many in which animals have been introduced into new areas where they have no natural predators — the most notorious instance being the importation of rabbits into Australia. Prey species have also shown disastrous population increases following "successful" predator control programs. The extermination of the wolf and the mountain lion in the Grand Canyon area resulted in a precipitous increase in the mule deer population from approximately 5000 in 1906 to 100,000 in 1924. This was followed by a massive, rapid die-off of most of the surplus population when the food supply gave out (see Chapter 6).

Another desirable effect of predators is pest control. Most predators regularly eat at least some animals that humans consider pests. The

**Fig. 4-9** *Mountain lion cornered by bounty hunters in Colorado. (Carl Iwasaki, LIFE Magazine)*

most common example is that of rodents; it is surprising to see how much of the diet of even large animals like wolves is composed of field mice and other small rodents. The discovery that foxes provided much of the natural rodent control in South Dakota is in accord with the results of many other studies of the effects of predators. For example, in the West Yellowstone area an uncontrolled increase in destructive rodent populations followed the use of cyanide bombs to eliminate coyotes. In at least one area, Colorado's Yampa Valley, enlightened ranchers halted a coyote extermination program in order to avoid these same consequences.

An indirect beneficial effect that has been attributed to predators is the maintenance of their prey species in a healthy condition. A number of biologists claim that, in addition to preventing overpopulation, predators improve the genetic fitness of their prey and increase the food and shelter resources available to the healthier animals by culling the weak and handicapped individuals from the prey population; wolf-caribou and wolf-moose interactions are usually cited as examples (*11*). Other indirect benefits have been observed. For example, on several islands off the west coast of Florida, a variety of herons and ibises nest in low trees in relatively unprotected locations. Here, their eggs and young are, in effect, guarded by unusually large numbers of poisonous water moccasins (*Ancistrodon piscivorous*), which cluster at the base of the trees and by their presence prevent the establishment on the island of other, more arboreal predators such as raccoons. The moccasins eat the occasional baby birds that fall out of the nest and any fish that may be dropped by the adult birds.

Although it is likely that many predators do exert some favorable effects on their prey, it is neither necessary nor desirable to rest the case against predator control on this argument. The idea that predators are "bad" and therefore should be controlled is a value judgment based on questionable philosphical grounds and contrary to scientific evidence. Predators do not harm the ecosystems in which they evolved, and are necessary, in one way or another, for the proper functioning of those ecosystems. It is not the predators but the massive predator control programs that should be eliminated.

Some of the motivation behind predator control programs is emotional, although it is hard to see how the occasional chicken-killing fox justifies the extermination of all foxes; and more important, much of the motivation is economic. The old Predator and Rodent Control Branch (now called the Division of Wildlife Services) of the U.S. Government had hundreds of employees and spent tens of millions of dollars on the killing of coyotes, beavers, badgers, bobcats, eagles, foxhounds, and anything else that happened upon their poisoned baits. Although there are indications of recent enlightenment among federal agencies that deal with predators, many state and local governments are still in the ecological dark ages. South Dakota, for example, spent $70,000 in one year (1967) on bounty payments, a large price to pay for nothing more than an increase in the populations of rats and mice.

*MUSEUM COLLECTING*   The hunting, by trapping or shooting, of specimens for museum collections sometimes constitutes an important drain on populations of endangered species. According to Conway (3): "A 1962 estimate of the number of mammal skins in some 307 public and private collections was 1,586,000. The American Museum of Natural History alone has nearly a million bird skins in its permanent collection." Fortunately, most contemporary vertebrates are already well represented in museum collections, and the analysis of existing material now occupies more time than collecting expeditions. When collections are made, they are generally made with more care than in the past, although occasional excesses do still occur.

By and large, the collection of museum specimens is more than justified by the scientific value of the collection. It is important, however, that museum scientists be aware of the population status of the species in which they are interested. Hopefully, if a responsible collecting policy is adopted by both individuals and institutions, we may never again witness depredations like the California Academy of Sciences' 1906 Galápagos expedition, in which, for example, 86 giant tortoises, constituting at least 40 percent of the living members of one species, were removed from the 3-mile wide Duncan Island.

*SUPERSTITION*    A wide variety of animals are hunted for superstitious reasons, in the belief that their fur, skin, bones, or other parts will have medicinal or magical powers (see Table 4-4). Although such beliefs occur among most of the human populations of the world, the demands of Chinese medicine have placed the greatest strain on threatened species. The Asiatic rhinoceroses have been particularly hard hit. According to Ziswiler (see Further Reading): "Chinese merchants gain huge profits by marketing the powdered rhinoceros horn as an aphrodisiac. Furthermore, goblets carved from rhino horn are supposedly able to detect poisoned drinks." There are now approximately 2 dozen Javanese, 100-170 Sumatran, and 740 Indian rhinos surviving in the wild. In the United States there are still Chinese families that treat their ailments with powdered tiger bone and rhinoceros horn, imported at considerable expense from the Chinese mainland via Hong Kong.

*ENDANGERED*    Plant species are threatened by many of the
*PLANT SPECIES*    same factors that menace animal species: The introduction of exotic competitors, herbivores and parasites, the practice of selective "hunting" as carried out by lumber and pharmaceutical companies and ornamental plant collectors, pollution, agricultural land improvement, and many other influences can lead to the diminution of particular plant populations. There are, of course, differences. Rarely are plants deliberately exterminated, and if they are, their lack of movement and usually high reproductive capacity makes it likely that some patches will be overlooked. Nevertheless, plant species can face extinction. There is little doubt that some have become extinct during recent times; but unless a plant is showy and its geographic distribution is sharply delineated, its passing may not be noticed.

Only a few perceptive naturalists have written about the disappearance of plants, and as the number of experienced naturalists dwindles, the writings are less frequent. Aldo Leopold(15), who died in 1948, was one such naturalist, and he described with special brilliance the vanishing plants and plant communities of the Midwest. "No living man

Table 4-4    **Some Animals Hunted for Superstitious Reasons**

| Species | Range | Estimated Population | Superstition |
|---|---|---|---|
| Somali Wild Ass *Equus asinus somalicus* | Ethiopia, Somali Republic | 200 in Ethiopia 10–12 in Somalia | Fat cures tuberculosis. |
| Javan Rhinoceros *Rhinoceros sondaicus* | Java | 25 | Every part of the body is used for medicinal purposes in south and east Asia. |
| Snub-Nosed Monkey *Rhinopithecus roxellanae* | Northwest China | Unknown, but very small | Fur used (formerly?) to prevent rheumatism. |
| Chinese Tiger *Panthera tigris amoyensis* | China | Unknown, but very small | Bones impart vitality and strength. |
| Barbary Hyaena *Hyaena hyaena barbara* | Morocco | 400–500 | Mane hairs used in black magic; brain has medicinal qualities. |
| Giant Armadillo *Periodontes giganteus* | Eastern South America | Unknown | Claws possess magical powers. |
| Shansi Sika (deer) *Cervus nippon grassianus* | Shansi region (China) | Unknown; probably extinct | Antler velvet has aphrodisiac properties. |
| West Indian Manatee (sea cow) *Trichechus manatus manatus* | Coasts and coastal rivers of Gulf of Mexico and Caribbean | Several thousand | Bones used as charms. |
| Imperial Woodpecker *Campephilus imperialis* | Sierra Madre (Mexico) | Unknown; probably almost extinct | Has medicinal value. |
| Hawaiian Crow *Corvus tropicus* | Mt. Hualalai (Hawaii) | 250 | Feathers once used for dressing idols. |
| Green Turtle *Chelonia mydas* | Pan-tropical | Unknown, but decreasing rapidly | Eggs thought to have aphrodisiac properties throughout Latin America. |

will see again the long-grass prairie, where a sea of prairie flowers lapped at the stirrups of the pioneer. We shall do well to find a forty here and there on which the prairie plants can be kept alive as species. There were a hundred such plants, many of exceptional beauty. Most of them are quite unknown to those who have inherited their domain."

Although as a group the plants of the world's grasslands may have suffered the heaviest casualties, other environments are losing plant species. In the eastern part of the United States several of the most beautiful native flowering plants have become extremely scarce. The fringed gentian (*Gentiana crinita*), an annual with tubular violet flowers composed of petals fringed at the ends, is an inhabitant of bogs and marshes. As the reckless and excessive drainage of wetlands continues, this plant is becoming nearly impossible to find. The situation is worsened by its being an annual; when an entire clump of its now unusual flowers is picked, it will not reappear in that place the next year. The trailing arbutus or Mayflower (*Epigaea repens*) is a low, short-stemmed plant with fragrant pink or white flowers. It grows in light shade and is a late successional or climax species. The trailing arbutus is very intolerant of soil disturbance and disappears rapidly in any area where man's activities are not strictly curtailed. In addition, because of its shape, it is difficult to pick the attractive flowers without damaging the plant or uprooting it entirely. A third endangered species, the pinxterflower or purple honeysuckle (*Rhododendron nudiflorum*) is a branched, 2 to 8-foot high shrub with pink-white flowers. It blooms in early spring before it and the surrounding deciduous trees have put out their leaves, and is thus easily spotted from a great distance by ornamental shrub hunters. Once extremely common, like the fringed gentian and the trailing arbutus, it is now encountered much less frequently in its natural setting. (Some states have passed laws to protect endangered plant species, and others have instituted propagation programs for their rare native plants.)

Selective lumbering can threaten tree species, especially in the tropical rain forests where artificial reseeding is difficult or impossible and where the high species diversity and thin soils mitigate against the establishment of tree farms (fortunately for the other species). In the North Patagonian Andes, for example, J. C. Lerman (12) found that conifers like *Fitzroya cupressoides* and *Araucaria araucana* (the monkey-puzzle tree), which frequently attain ages greater than 1000 years, have been endangered even in the absence of bulldozers and chain saws by "a few men working every summer with very simple tools and selecting the species and the specimens most suitable for their interests." In the rain forest, major damage to particular, valuable species can go unnoticed, and Lerman reported that "not only is it difficult to detect by aerial

**Fig. 4-10**   *Blue fringed gentian. (Jeanne White, National Audubon Society)*

inspection selective exploitation within thick rain forests, but it is impossible to evaluate the state of the remaining trees of the species and the damage done to its seedlings if they exist at all. In the air this *Fitzroya* probably appears as a 'green virgin forest,' as it does to the machete explorer until he begins to find stump after stump hidden by other replacing species."

As is the case with animal species, plants that have extremely restricted ranges are vulnerable to a variety of disturbing factors. On several of the Galápagos Islands, some floral species or subspecies and some floral communities of great interest to biologists may be lost because of excessive grazing by introduced goats. Unfortunately, in the Galápagos and elsewhere, the immense difficulty of preparing floral lists that are both up-to-date and taxonomically sound may prevent us from ever knowing what plants have become extinct because of our activities. There is not yet a world list of endangered plants to correspond to that of vanishing mammals and birds issued by the International Union for the Conservation of Nature. Such a list is badly needed.

*CHARACTERISTICS OF ENDANGERED SPECIES* Not all species are endangered at present; for example, fewer than 10 percent of all mammals are clearly faced with the threat of extinction. The percentages vary, however, from one taxonomic group to the next, and even at the level of orders we can see major survival differences (Table 4-5). Throughout this

*Fig. 4-11   Trailing arbutus. (Alvin E. Steffan, National Audubon Society)*

*Table 4-5*    **Number of Endangered Species and Genera in Selected Mammalian Orders**

| Order | No. of Endangered Species | No. of Species | Ratio | No. of Endangered Genera | No. of Genera | Ratio |
|---|---|---|---|---|---|---|
| Carnivora (cats, bears, weasels, etc.) | 31 | 232 | 0.13 | 22 | 72 | 0.31 |
| Perissodactyla (horses, rhinos, etc.) | 11 | 15 | 0.73 | 6 | 6 | 1.00 |
| Artiodactyla (deer, antelope, cattle, pigs, etc.) | 56 | 215 | 0.26 | 38 | 82 | 0.46 |
| Primates (lemurs, monkeys, etc.) | 31 | 180 | 0.17 | 24 | 74 | 0.32 |
| Marsupialia (kangaroos, opossums, etc.) | 31 | 245 | 0.13 | 27 | 80 | 0.34 |
| Cetacea (whales, porpoises, etc.) | 8 | 90 | 0.09 | 4 | 39 | 0.10 |
| baleen whales only | 8 | 11 | 0.73 | 4 | 6 | 0.67 |
| Insectivora[a] (shrews, moles, hedgehogs, etc.) | 4 | 311 | 0.01 | 4 | 64 | 0.06 |
| Pinnipedia (seals, walruses, etc.) | 10 | 31 | 0.32 | 7 | 20 | 0.35 |
| Sirenia (sea cows, dugongs, etc.) | 5 | 5 | 1.00 | 3 | 3 | 1.00 |
| Edentata (sloths, armadillos, anteaters, etc.) | 3 | 30 | 0.10 | 3 | 14 | 0.21 |

SOURCE: The data in this table were obtained from the *Red Data Book*, Vol. 1, compiled by Noel Simon (International Union for the Conservation of Nature), and from *Mammals of the World*, Vols. 1 and 2, by Ernest P. Walker (Johns Hopkins). "Endangered genera" refers to any genus containing one or more endangered species. Several orders, including the two largest — rodents and bats — were omitted.

[a] Since most insectivores are small and inconspicuous, the status of some endangered species may have gone unnoticed.

chapter we have been concerned with external environmental factors that endanger species. But because all species are not endangered equally, the differences must be determined by a set of species characteristics relevant to survival conditions in the modern world. When taken together, these factors determine the extinction potential of a species.

It is possible to analyze in a qualitative way those characteristics of animal species that can lower their survival potential. There are, of course, exceptions in every category, and interactions between categories may alter the results, but the parameters in the following list usually play a role in extinction.

| *Endangered* | *Safe* |
|---|---|
| Individuals of large size (cougar) | Individuals of small size (wildcat) |
| Predator (hawk) | Grazer, scavenger, insectivore, etc. (vulture) |
| Narrow habitat tolerance[a] (orangutan) | Wide habitat tolerance (chimpanzee) |
| Valuable fur, hide, oil, etc. (chinchilla) | Not a source of natural products and not exploited for research or pet purposes (gray squirrel) |
| Hunted for the market or hunted for sport where there is no effective game management (passenger pigeon) | Commonly hunted for sport in game management areas (mourning dove) |
| Has a restricted distribution: island, desert watercourse, bog, etc. (Bahamas parrot) | Has broad distribution (yellow-headed parrot) |
| Lives largely in international waters, or migrates across international boundaries (green sea turtle) | Has populations that remain largely within the territory(ies) of a specific country(ies) (loggerhead sea turtle) |
| Intolerant of the presence of man[b] (grizzly bear) | Tolerant of man (black bear) |
| Species reproduction in one or two vast aggregates (West Indian flamingo) | Reproduction by solitary pairs or in many small or medium sized aggregates (bitterns) |
| Long gestation period; one or two young per litter, and/or maternal care[c] (giant panda) | Short gestation period; more than two young per litter, and/or young become independent early and mature quickly (raccoon) |
| Has behavioral idiosyncracies that are nonadaptive today (redheaded woodpecker: flies in front of cars) | Has behavior patterns that are particularly adaptive today (burrowing owl: highly tolerant of noise and low-flying aircraft; lives near the runways of airports) |

[a] Especially for vanishing habitats like grasslands, virgin forests, swamps, etc.

[b] There is no way to predict what mixture of boldness versus shyness and aggression versus fear will place a species in one of these two categories.

[c] Dr. George C. Williams (13) has pointed out that "the maximization of individual reproductive success will seldom be achieved by unbridled fecundity." The litter sizes of pandas (1-2) and raccoons (1-7) have presumably been optimized according to the restraints imposed by their internal and external environments; under natural conditions

If one could assign a relative "point value" to each of the categories in the preceding list, it would be possible to sum the points for a given species and predict its chances of survival. Complex ecological situations do not lend themselves to such a simple quantitative approach, however; the best that can be done is to check our categories qualitatively against reality. In so doing, a picture of the hypothetical "most endangered animal" can be constructed. It turns out to be a large predator with a narrow habitat tolerance, long gestation period, and few young per litter. It is hunted for a natural product and/or for sport, but is not subject to efficient game management. It has a restricted distribution, but travels across international boundaries. It is intolerant of man, reproduces in aggregates, and has nonadaptive behavioral idiosyncracies. Although there probably is no such animal, this model, with one or two exceptions, comes very close to being a description of a polar bear. Conversely, if one "constructs" a species by taking the opposite extreme from each category (small, herbivorous, and so forth), one is left with a composite picture of the "typical" wild animal of the twenty-first century — some of the most familiar existing approximations would be the house sparrow, the gray squirrel, the Virginia opossum, and the Norway rat.

Species can be characterized in ways other than those listed above. Such parameters as size of home range, nocturnality versus diurnality, color, lifespan, or population size can play a role in determining the extinction potential of a species. But in the case of these and most other characteristics, the effects are so variable that generalization seems unwarranted. One partial exception can be noted. Ziswiler (see Further Reading) and others have suggested that there is a critical population size that varies from species to species. When the population of a given species falls below this point, the species is likely to become extinct even if accorded full protection. Classic examples of this phenomenon are the passenger pigeon and the heath hen.

The fate of the passenger pigeon is the most dramatic recorded example of extinction. Its population declined from several billion individuals in the late 1870s to zero in 1914, when the last survivor died in the Cincinnati Zoo. Evidently, the critical population size for this species was very high because the population continued to fall even though the market hunting ceased when there were still many thousands of

---

it would be absurd to declare that the reproductive fitness of the raccoon was greater than that of the panda. However, it seems likely (but would be difficult to prove) that the reproductive pattern of high fecundity and high mortality is better suited than the opposite pattern to resist the unnatural threat of civilized man. This would be especially true in the cases of those species faced with the direct and selective threat of hunting (as opposed to habitat destruction) where the removal of individuals from the population would, by decreasing intraspecies competition for food and shelter, decrease the usual mortality in the surviving large litters.

healthy birds left. Ziswiler suggests a variety of factors that may have played a role in determining the critical population size for this and other species. Some of his factors, paraphrased, are:

1. Population density too low for males to find females.
2. Local population density too low to stimulate courtship behavior.
3. Population density too low to overwhelm the large numbers of surviving predators and/or competitors.

We might add a fourth possibility: absolute population size too low to compensate normal losses due to disease, climatic changes, and natural disasters. This fourth factor is analogous to the Monte Carlo "gambler's ruin" problem, which states that even if the odds in a game of chance are fair, a player with a low amount of initial capital is likely to lose when, sooner or later, one of the customary fluctuations of fortune reduces his small assets to zero, thus ending the game. The American heath hen (*Tympanuchus cupido cupido*) is probably an example of a species that succumbed to "gambler's ruin."

In contrast to the passenger pigeon, there are a number of species, characterized in part by highly flexible behavior patterns and great mobility, that seem to have such a low critical population size that the concept has little importance. Perhaps the best example among mammals is the panther of eastern Canada (also known as mountain lion, puma, cougar), *Felis concolor couguar*. Although once believed to be extinct in northeastern North America, the eastern panther has recovered from a breeding nucleus of a very few individuals presumably overlooked in the forests of eastern New Brunswick and western Ontario, and has increased to the point where panthers have been sighted in all but two of the eastern Canadian provinces in recent years. This comeback, facilitated by the conversion of moose habitat into deer habitat by extensive pulpwood operations, is one of the rare examples of species survival aided by industrial expansion. If the eastern panther had had a critical population size comparable to that of the heath hen (a few hundred individuals), it would almost certainly have become extinct.

## FURTHER READING

Errington, Paul L., *Of Predation and Life*. Ames, Iowa: Iowa State University Press, 1967.

Fisher, James, Simon, Noel, and Vincent, Jack, *Wildlife in Danger*. New York: Viking Press, 1969.

Greenway, James C., Jr., *Extinct and Vanishing Birds of the World*. New York: Dover, 1967.

National Geographic Society, *Vanishing Peoples of the Earth*. Washington, D.C.: 1968.

Ziswiler, Vinzenz, *Extinct and Vanishing Animals*. New York: Springer-Verlag, 1967.

## REFERENCES

1.  Minckley, W. L., and Deacon, James E., *Science 159*, 1424 (1968).
2.  Schaller, George B., *Audubon 70* (3), 80 (1968).
3.  Conway, William G., *Animal Kingdom 73* (3), 18 (1968).
4.  Quaintance, Charles W., *Science 161*, 520 (1968).
5.  Carr, Archie, *Handbook of Turtles* (Cornell University Press, Ithaca, N.Y., 1952), 168.
6.  Cott, Hugh B., *Trans. Zool. Soc. London 29* (4), 211 (1961).
7.  *New Scientist*, Oct. 3, 1968, p. 9.
8.  Eimerl, S., and DeVore, I., *The Primates* (Time, Inc., New York, 1965), 180.
9.  Hillaby, John, *Animal Kingdom 70*, 143 (1967).
10.  Lagler, Karl, *Am. Midland Naturalist 29*, 257 (1943).
11.  *Am. Zoologist 7* (2), 233-278 (1967).
12.  Lerman, J. C., *Science 160*, 251 (1968).
13.  Williams, George C., *Adaptation and Natural Selection* (Princeton University Press, Princeton, N.J., 1966), 161.
14.  Talbot, Lee M., *A Look at Threatened Species* (published for the International Union for the Conservation of Nature by the Fauna Preservation Society, 1960).
15.  Leopold, Aldo, *A Sand County Almanac* (Oxford, New York, 1966).

chapter *5*

# Endangered Species: Case History—The Blue Whale

"*Wherefore, for all these things, we account the whale immortal in his species, however perishable in his individuality. He swam the seas before the continents broke water; he once swam over the site of the Tuileries, and Windsor Castle, and the Kremlin. In Noah's flood he despised Noah's Ark; and if ever the world is to be again flooded, like the Netherlands, to kill off its rats, then the eternal whale will still survive, and rearing upon the topmost crest of the equatorial flood, spout his frothed defiance to the skies.*"

*Herman Melville*, Moby-Dick

*CURRENT STATUS OF THE SPECIES* Blue whales, *Balaenoptera musculus*, are the largest animals that have ever lived on earth; they are 25 feet long at birth, are weaned at an average length of 53 feet when they are 7 months old, reach sexual maturity (females) at an approximate length of 78 feet when they are 5 years old, and have been known to attain lengths as great as 106 feet. One 83-foot male weighed 242,397 pounds. Their lifespan probably does not exceed 40 years. Blue whales live almost entirely on 2-inch euphausiid shrimp filtered from the water by the baleen plates that give them their name. They are migratory, usually spending 8 months of the year in the Antarctic Ocean eating the abundant krill, and staying for the rest of the year in warmer waters, nearly devoid of food, where the calves are born. The least gregarious of all whales in the family, Balaenopteridae, blue whales travel singly, or in groups of two or three. Nearly all their lives are spent in international waters, although they occasionally pass near the shores of Chile or South Africa during migrations.

Our knowledge of the size of the blue whale populations in past years is based on commercial whaling figures. Since the efficiency of catching methods, the number of whaling ships, the areas fished, the length of the fishing season, the minimum size requirement, and the reliability of the records have varied from year to year, the size of the annual blue whale catch is only an approximate indication of the true population size. Nevertheless, the trend is depressingly obvious, regardless of how the data are expressed (see Fig. 5-1). At the time of this writing it is doubtful whether there are as many as 300 blue whales left alive in all the waters of the southern hemisphere, and most authorities, fearing that the population has dropped below the critical level (see Chapter 4), predict that this greatest of animals in the history of the planet will be extinct within one or two decades.

**THE EXTERMINATION PROCESS**    There are three major reasons for the destruction of the blue whale by man:

1. The whales' tendency to concentrate in the Antarctic feeding grounds during the summer, allowing them to be caught in large numbers.

2. The exceptionally low reproductive potential of the species.

3. The existence of a ruthless and suicidal industry that has been able to thwart all meaningful attempts at regulation, and which has exploited the inability of all countries to give territorial protection to a creature of the high seas.

As can be seen in Fig. 5-1, virtually all whaling activities ceased during World War II. Yet the recovery of the blue whale population during this hiatus was negligible. Evidently the blue whale reproduces

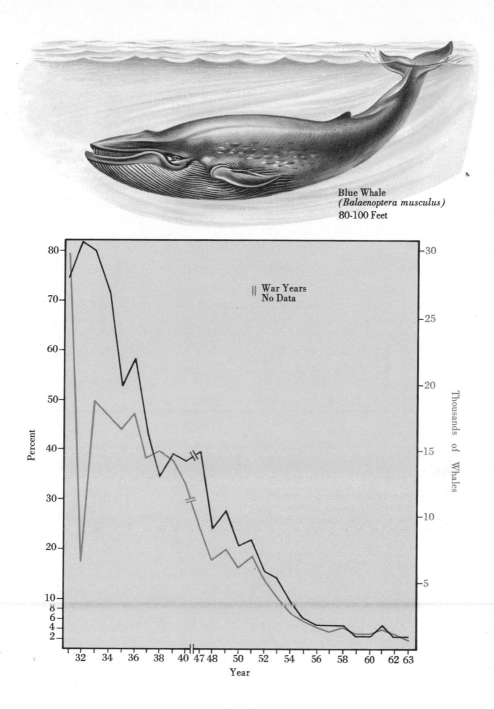

Blue Whale
(*Balaenoptera musculus*)
80-100 Feet

*Fig. 5-1* Decline of blue whale populations in Antarctic whaling areas, expressed as numbers of blue whales caught per year (blue line) and as captured blue whales as a percentage of all species of whales killed in Antarctic pelagic whaling (black line). (Modified from George L. Small, The Virtual Extinction of an Extraterritorial Pelagic Resource — The Blue Whale, *doctoral dissertation, Columbia University, 1968.*)

*Fig. 5-2   A 90-foot blue whale at the station of the Cia. Argentina de Pesca, Grytviken, South Georgia, October, 1925. The whale lies with its back upper- most, an unusual position for the cleaning operations. (© National Institute of Oceanography)*

itself very slowly, but this low biotic potential was not documented until 1950, when Dr. J. T. Ruud (*1*) and his colleagues in Norway discovered a method of determining the ages of blue whales by examining growth ridges on their baleen plates. When age was correlated with sexual ma- turity, it was found that female blue whales do not mature sexually until 4–7 years of age.

Moreover, a gestation period of approximately one year plus a 7- month nursing period for the single calf (during which the female does not become pregnant again), when correlated with the annual migration and feeding pattern, means that a female cannot bear more than one calf every two years—occasionally less often. In other words, as Dr. George Small (*2*) has pointed out, a female blue whale can have borne a maxi- mum of two offspring by age 10. This exceptionally low reproductive rate has made the population very vulnerable to intensive, indiscriminate hunting (see Chapter 4): For the past 20 years the average length of blue whales captured in the Antarctic has been less than 80 feet (approximately 6 years old), at which size the great majority of females are immature, recently matured, or pregnant with their first calf. Clearly, no population of like biotic potential could survive under these conditions.

Most of the information concerning the biotic potential and population structure of the blue whale was obtained after the species had become, for all practical purposes, commercially extinct. Small has calculated that by the time the Japanese had confirmed the age-maturity estimates of Ruud, in 1952, "95.2 per cent of all the blue whales to be taken in the history of Antarctic whaling had already been taken." (Blue whales are still being killed by "Chilean" whaling companies using leased Japanese vessels, but the small numbers taken, although catastrophic in terms of the survival of the species, are negligible when compared with past commercial catches.) In short, sustained-yield management of blue whale stocks based on accurate biological information was hardly possible until most of the whales were gone. This point is academic, however, for the whaling companies and the International Whaling Commission (which they effectively controlled) were uninterested in sustained-yield management. Whaling practices did not change after 1952; if anything, whaling intensified during the 1950s.

Because of their status as an exclusively international resource, blue whales could have been protected only by *all* whaling nations acting in concert. Yet with the exception of Norway, which instituted strong unilateral conservation measures pertaining to its own industry, the record of the member nations of the International Whaling Commission is a sickening testimonial to corporate and national greed, short-sightedness, and inertia. The Whaling Commission itself had neither inspection nor enforcement powers, and any of its majority decisions could, in effect, be vetoed by a single member nation.

Japan, whose commissioner to the Whaling Commission was, from 1951 to 1965, a representative of the Japanese whaling industry, was responsible for defeating nearly every attempt to limit the catch of blue whales in the Antarctic. The attitude of the Japanese whalers was summarized by Dr. N. R. Lillie in a letter reprinted in Dr. Small's dissertation (2): "The president of the largest Japanese whaling company, Mr. K. Nakabe of Taiyo Fishery Co., Ltd., was indeed difficult to deal with, insisting on breaking off all further discussions if I could not agree with him that there were plenty of whales left and that the killing could go on without restriction. The president of the third company, Kyokuyo Hogei, while not as extreme, was just as determined to go on with the killing until such time as the industry collapsed from the wiping out of the whales." During the critical period of the early 1960s, the Japanese even went so far as to insist on the existence of a separate species of "pygmy blue whale" in order to justify their continued catches of undersized animals in one of the Antarctic whaling zones.

The anticonservation attitude of most of the whaling nations cannot be explained in terms of the value of the blue whale catch after 1958. In 1960, according to Small, blue whales were responsible for only 2.52 percent of the total corporate income of Norwegian whaling companies. This had fallen to 0.06 percent by 1963. Although the Japanese whaling industry is more secretive than the Norwegian industry, the available income figures indicate that the blue whale was of no more commercial importance to these highly diversified corporations than to the Norwegians, who terminated all whaling operations in 1969.

If the value of the blue whale catch has been negligible at least since 1958, and if the stocks of other species of great whales are also nearing exhaustion, why have the whaling companies and nations been so reluctant to submit to sane regulation? After all, Japan, the Soviet Union, and the United States have managed, by international agreement, to regulate their equally exploitative fur industries with respect to the Pribilof Island fur seals. These fur seals are now probably more numerous than ever, despite a reasonable sustained annual yield of hides. The difference in whaling seems to depend on the high initial and maintenance costs of factory ships and their accompanying fast catcher boats. Small points out that: "The most important result of the large size and cost of such an operating unit is that fine adjustments in whaling capacity to changes in the stock of whales cannot be made, since a floating factory without its full fleet of catcher boats would be useless." Moreover, factory ships are not readily converted to other purposes, and must therefore be kept in whaling operations for at least 20 years in order to repay the original investment. Small concludes: "Thus an extreme rigidity, manifest by a determination to continue operations despite declining profits, characterizes the industry." As late as 1963 the Soviet Union purchased two factory ships from West Germany at a cost of $16 million each, a decision that bodes ill for whales, and, hopefully, for the state economic planner who made it.

*EPILOGUE – INCLUDING SOME HELPFUL HINTS FOR STATE ECONOMIC PLANNERS* The blue whale population has almost certainly been declining drastically since the 1930s, but whaling interests managed to interpret the data to mean that the species was in good condition right up to the time when it became commercially extinct in the 1960s. Recently, Dr. Kenneth E. F. Watt (3) of the University of California at Davis has formulated a set of warning signs or "symptoms" for use in determining when a population is being dangerously overhunted. The signs are as follows (all signs need not be present in any given case):

"1. A decreasing proportion of females pregnant.

2. A decreasing catch per unit effort.

3. A decreasing catch relative to the catch of related species.

4. A failure to increase in numbers rapidly after a respite from harvesting.

5. A change in productivity versus age curve [see Fig. 5-3], which, when interpreted using a fecundity versus age curve [see Fig. 5-4], shows that the ability of the population to replace the harvested individuals has been destroyed.

6. A change in survival versus age curve [see Fig. 5-5], which, when interpreted using a fecundity versus age curve, shows that the ability of the population to replace the harvested individuals has been destroyed."

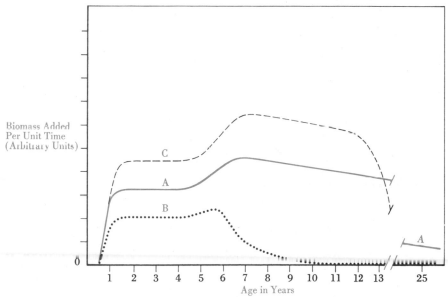

*Fig. 5-3  Hypothetical productivity-versus-age curves for the blue whale. Increase in weight per unit time is summed for all animals in each age class. Nursing calves less than seven months old (average age of weaning) are counted as biomass added to their mothers' weight. The increase in productivity from age 4½–7 years corresponds to the period of first pregnancy of maturing females. (A) Unexploited natural population, resource limited, and with many, old individuals. (B) Heavily overfished population with no chance to replenish harvested individuals (see age-versus-fecundity curve). Corresponds to current situation. (C) Population fished for sustained yield. Productivity of young whales is increased by removal of large, old individuals only. The average female in this population bears 2–3 calves before she is harvested (see age-versus-fecundity curve).*

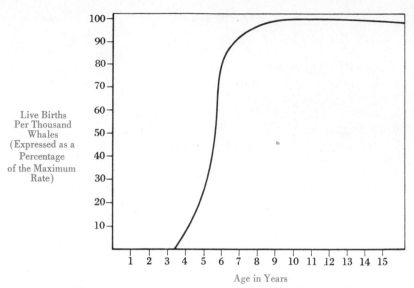

Fig. 5-4   *Hypothetical fecundity-versus-age curve for the blue whale. In-corporates information concerning age at sexual maturity (females), gestation period, nursing period, and inter-pregnancy recovery period. This curve shows maximum, theoretical fecundity per age class. It does not take into account such factors as decline in fecundity with age, or failure of some individuals to reproduce at the maximum rate, but the important initial portion of the curve is probably fairly accurate.*

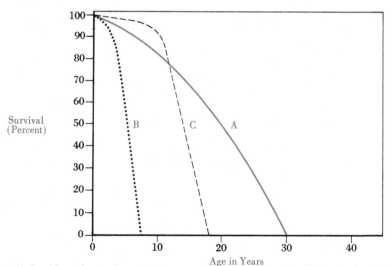

Fig. 5-5   *Hypothetical survival versus age curves for the blue whale. (Modi-fied after K. E. F. Watt,* Ecology and Resource Management, *McGraw-Hill, 1968.) Curves are theoretical and are the result of combining the scanty in-formation concerning blue whale survival with Watt's generalized survival curves for animal populations. (A) Unexploited population. (B) Over-Exploited population. Corresponds to current situation. This curve is based on the in-formation that in 1963 more than 80 percent of male and female blue whales killed in the Antarctic were sexually immature (Small, 1968). (C) Population fished for sustained yield. Decreased survival (removal) of old adults has increased the survival rate of juveniles and remaining adults.*

The blue whale thus represents a classical example of the results of excessive exploitation of an animal species by man. All six warning signs listed by Watt were clearly present in data available to the International Whaling Commission in the 1950s, and the theory and practice of game management were sufficiently well developed at that time so that the correct inferences could have been drawn. By ignoring these signs, the whalers added new information to our knowledge of the extinction process, but few biologists think the contribution was worth the price.

## FURTHER READING

Small, George, *The Blue Whale*, New York: Columbia University Press (in press).

## REFERENCES

1. Ruud, J. T., *Norsk Hvalfangst Tidende*, June, 1950, 245.
2. Small, George, *The Virtual Extinction of an Extraterritorial Pelagic Resource—The Blue Whale* (doctoral dissertation, Columbia University, 1968).
3. Watt, Kenneth E. F., *Ecology and Resource Management* (McGraw-Hill, New York, 1968).

# chapter 6

# The Preservation of Natural Communities

*"The world is a glorious bounty. There is more food than can be eaten if we would limit our numbers to those who can be cherished, there are more beautiful girls than can be dreamed of, more children than we can love, more laughter than can be endured, more wisdom than can be absorbed. Canvas and pigments lie in wait, stone, wood and metal are ready for sculpture, random noise is latent for symphonies, sites are gravid for cities, institutions lie in the wings ready to solve our most intractable problems, parables of moving power remain unformulated and yet, the world is finally unknowable."*

*Ian L. McHarg*, Design with Nature

**POPULATION CONTROL** The need for human "population control" is no longer a seriously debated question among scientists concerned with environmental quality; a review of the previous pages will show that

there is scarcely a single conservation problem that is not made worse —
or insoluble — by a rapidly increasing human population. Indeed, the
population control issue can fairly be said to be emerging (with some
exceptions) from its crusading phase and to be entering a period of
sophisticated analysis and self-criticism. As is so often the case of such
transitions, some of the clichés and slogans that helped make scientists
and laymen aware of the population crisis, are now being re-evaluated
by the advocates of population control.

Three concepts that were prevalent during the first phase of the
population control movement now seem to stand in the way of further
progress in this field. They are:

1. The Malthusian doctrine, which states that the principal danger
inherent in population increase is the potential exhaustion of world food
supplies.

2. The idea that population control can be effected primarily by
dissemination of birth control information and birth control devices.

3. The idea that the groups most in need of population control are
the lower classes of industrialized countries and the inhabitants of underdeveloped nations.

These three commonly accepted ideas will be considered in order.
First, it has been by no means proven that the human population is out-
growing its food supply, as Malthus predicted. The global potential for
food production was discussed in Chapter 2; suffice it to say that there is
no conclusive evidence that food production is currently lagging behind
the increase in population. It is true that local social, economic, and political problems that interfere with food production and distribution still
plague us (and threaten to worsen) and that because of high population
densities, greater numbers of people may die from famine than previously; but there is perhaps as much reason to believe that over-all world
nutrition will improve during the next 50 years as to believe that it will
deteriorate. Dr. Jean Mayer (1), professor of nutrition at Harvard University, has pointed out that "nothing is more dangerous for the cause of
formulating sound policy of population control than to approach the
problem in nineteenth century terms. . . ." In other words, by continuing to emphasize what may turn out to be a nonexistent inverse correlation between population and food, we run the risk, like the boy who
cried "wolf," of losing the confidence and co-operation of the public
when the other dangers of overpopulation are pointed out. Considering
the damage that the excessive numbers of people are *already* doing to
their environment and to each other, it would seem both worthwhile and
easy to develop a broad-based justification for the practice of population

control, emphasizing those dangers of population increase that are clear and present or inevitable.

The second idea, that the public will control its own population numbers if birth control information and devices are made available to everyone, has insufficient data to back it up. Dr. Judith Blake (2), of the University of California, Berkeley, has gathered and analyzed opinion poll data from several sources and has concluded that "for most Americans the 'family planning' approach, concentrating as it does on the distribution of contraceptive material and [information] services, is irrelevant, because they already know about efficient contraception and are already 'planning' their families." (Arguments against this controversial point of view have been summarized by Harkavy and co-workers (3), whose disagreement with Blake appears to concern the current methodology rather than the goals of population control.)

The real problem, according to Blake, is that Americans "want families of more than three children and thereby generate a growth rate far in excess of that required for population stability" (see Table 6-1).

*Table 6-1*    **Mean Number of Children Considered Ideal By Non-Catholic Women, According to Education and Economic Status, for Selected Years between 1943-1968**

| Date | Age Range | Level of Education[a] | | | Income or Economic status[b] | | | | Total Respondents | |
|------|-----------|-------|------|------|-----|-----|-----|-----|-----|------|
| | | College | High School | Grade School | 1 | 2 | 3 | 4 | X | N |
| 1943 | 20–34 | 2.8 | 2.6 | 2.6 | 2.9 | 2.7 | 2.7 | 2.5 | 2.7 | 1893 |
| 1952 | 21+ | 3.3 | 3.1 | 3.6 | 3.3 | | 3.3 | 3.3 | 3.3 | 723 |
| 1955[c] | 18–39 | 3.1 | 3.2 | 3.7 | 3.2 | 3.1 | 3.2 | 3.5 | 3.3 | 1905 |
| 1955[d] | 18–39 | 3.3 | 3.4 | 3.9 | 3.4 | 3.3 | 3.4 | 3.7 | 3.4 | 1905 |
| 1957 | 21+ | 3.4 | 3.2 | 3.6 | 3.3 | | 3.2 | 3.5 | 3.3 | 448 |
| 1959 | 21+ | 3.5 | 3.4 | 3.9 | 3.5 | | 3.5 | 3.6 | 3.5 | 472 |
| 1960[c] | 18–39 | 3.1 | 3.2 | 3.5 | 3.1 | 3.2 | 3.3 | 3.2 | 3.2 | 1728 |
| 1960[d] | 18–39 | 3.2 | 3.4 | 3.6 | 3.2 | 3.3 | 3.5 | 3.4 | 3.4 | 1728 |
| 1963 | 21+ | 3.2 | 3.4 | 3.5 | 3.3 | 3.3 | 3.5 | 3.5 | 3.4 | 483 |
| 1966 | 21+ | 3.1 | 3.3 | 3.7 | 3.2 | 3.2 | 3.4 | 3.7 | 3.3 | 374 |
| 1967 | 21+ | 3.1 | 3.3 | 3.4 | 3.3 | 3.2 | 3.1 | 3.4 | 3.3 | 488 |
| 1968 | 21+ | 3.2 | 3.3 | 3.7 | 3.2 | 3.0 | 3.4 | 3.6 | 3.3 | 539 |

SOURCE: Judith Blake, *Science 164*, 522 (1969). Copyright: American Association for the Advancement of Science, 1969.

[a] Level of education is measured by the highest grade completed.
[b] Levels 1 to 4 for economic status range in order from "high" to "low."
[c] Minimum ideal (results from coding range answers to the lowest figure).
[d] Maximum ideal (results from coding range answers to the highest figure).

The solution, therefore, is twofold: (1) establish in the public consciousness the acceptability of the idea of having few or no children, and (2), more important, take steps to abolish *existing* social and economic penalties for those who desire to deviate from the current reproductive norm. In particular, women, who constitute more than half our population, must be allowed to have a normal, healthy, and rewarding life in areas other than those relating to child care, and they must not be accused of avoiding "maternal responsibilities" if they choose this other life style. The tax laws of the United States seem similarly unresponsive to current needs. There is no reason why married couples should be allowed tax loopholes denied to single persons, nor is there any remaining justification for a federal child subsidy in the form of unlimited child-support exemptions from income tax.

The author of this book does not advocate that the existing birth control and family-planning programs be halted; they are vital short-term measures, and almost certainly account for part of the current decline of the birth rate in the United States. This decline, however, is only in the rate of increase; the population is still expanding rapidly, and if the population planners are to be successful in their goal of complete population stabilization, the existence of the pill, the intra-uterine device, and rapid male sterilization techniques cannot be used as means of avoiding confrontation with the long-range, motivational problems of population control.

The third idea, that the "excess" in "population excess" is contributed primarily by the poor and underprivileged members of society is the most palpably and demonstrably untrue of the population clichés, particularly for the United States; yet it is the most stubbornly rooted idea in both conservative and liberal political philosophies (for different reasons). It is the privileged who are consuming living space at a frightening rate while the poor crowd more to a room; it is the privileged who can afford "throwaway" containers of all sorts and who discard a 6-lb Sunday newspaper after one casual reading; it is the privileged who will not eat fish flour and who buy prime beef; it is the privileged who purchase the vast quantity of automobiles that spend their last days rusting in piles at the edges of highways or in once-productive salt marshes; it is the privileged who can attempt to shield themselves from the effects (rather than deal with the causes) of pollution and deforestation by means of zoning restrictions, resort vacations, and air conditioning; and it is, ironically, the privileged who will ultimately have the most difficult time adjusting to the limited carrying capacity of a finite planet. Although assigning blame is not a very productive activity, the question of who is damaging the earth more—the rich or the poor—will no doubt be raised by some. Of the various possibilities, the conclusion that seems to make the most sense is that in poor countries the poor are at fault; in rich countries, it is the rich. The difference between the two is that the poor degrade their environment directly while the rich use technology and can thus indirectly achieve the same effect with fewer numbers.

The percentage of "privileged" varies greatly from country to country. In the United States it includes a considerable majority of the population, but in Haiti, where people occasionally venture 75 miles through open sea in small boats to scavenge broken crockery, odd bits of scrap metal, and empty bottles on a neighboring island, an enterprising person could learn the names of most of the country's privileged families. But regardless of the amount and distribution of national wealth, it is not the point of this discussion to prove that population control should proceed at the expense of any one economic or social class. Rather, if we desire the ratio of privileged to underprivileged to increase, and if the life-style implication of "privileged" is to remain unchanged, then the current rate of destruction of nonrenewable resources makes necessary a reduction in total world population, a reduction shared proportionately by all segments of that population. The only reasonable alternative that would not necessitate a reduction in population would have to involve a re-evaluation and modification of the privileged variety of life-style in order to bring it more into accord with the real needs of man and nature. This subject will be discussed further in the last chapter.

## POLLUTION CONTROL

### Introduction

Pollution, like usury and child labor, is a good thing to be against in the last third of the twentieth century. One journal published by the American Chemical Society (*Environmental Science and Technology*) now features a 180-page "Pollution Control Directory," which lists among other things more than 800 corporations supplying pollution control equipment or services. A national pollution control exposition, trying to enlist new industrial exhibitors, advertised: ". . . your pollution control products will be exposed to 4,000 bona fide buyers — all under one roof."

Unfortunately, along with this popular burst of enthusiasm has come the fairly widespread belief — even among biologists — that pollution control is entirely a question of economics: Is manufacturer A willing to pay the price of a water purification apparatus? Is manufacturer B willing to invest in the research and equipment necessary to retool his assembly line to produce a less polluting product? If modern technology were simple, this simplistic assumption might be correct, but it is not. Certainly, economic factors are implicated in most pollution problems, but in some cases the implementation of the solution to one pollution problem also serves to generate new ones. For example, the burning of

# "It Says Here We're Winning The Space Race"

***Fig. 6-1*** *(© 1969 Herblock; courtesy The Washington Post)*

fossil fuels for the production of electric power accelerates the "green-house effect" (see Chapter 2) through the release of carbon dioxide, and usually increases the concentration of sulfur-containing air pollutants. The installation of atomic power plants solves both major problems, but in return there are the new or increased dangers of (1) the accidental release of radioactive pollutants, (2) explosion (very unlikely), and (3) thermal pollution (likely, increasingly widespread and serious). If one tries instead the use of low-sulfur heating oils (as is New York City), the $SO_2$ air pollution is greatly reduced, but the $CO_2$ production is unchanged, and if the additional refinery facilities needed to remove sulfur from Venezuelan oil are unavailable, the source of the oil changes to Nigeria-Biafra, where the occurrence of naturally low-sulfur oil was a central issue in a terrible war. On this cautionary note we turn to an examination of some present and future solutions of the problems of pollution.

*Amelioration*   Much of the money now expended on pollution control is used to treat existing pollutants in such a way that they become less injurious to the environment, rather than to alter the source of the pollution. Although this involves a continuing or long-term expense for treatment facilities, it offers the short-term economic advantage of allowing production to continue; moreover, it does not require costly revamping of industrial equipment and processes.

Some of the recent treatment facilities are extremely efficient. An example is provided by a curious new way of dealing with suspended solids in fast-flowing streams. In watersheds where extensive land-clearing and building construction operations are under way, great quantities of raw, exposed earth are washed into streams during storms. One result is that silt rapidly accumulates in lakes and ponds, smothering the bottom-dwelling plants and animals, driving away game fish, and making the water shallower (see Chapter 2). This problem is particularly severe in the Rock Creek-Mill Creek watershed near Washington, D.C., where 5 or 6 ft of loosely packed silt can accumulate in a lake or pond in a few years.

Ideally, we would outlaw all building practices that lead to erosion; or failing that, we would have some way of preventing exposed dirt from washing away. But since neither alternative seems practical at the moment, the next best approach, an ameliorative one, is to cause the colloidal, suspended solids in streams to settle out in predetermined settling ponds before they reach recreational lakes. In order to achieve this, the Dow Chemical Company has developed a polymeric flocculant (Purifloc C-31) that, when added in low concentrations to streams, causes the suspended particles of dirt to clump together in large aggregates. The resulting flocs settle quickly to the bottom as soon as they reach nonturbulent water. If settling ponds are strategically located upstream from lakes, very little silt reaches the lakes, even during storms, provided the proper amount of flocculant has been added upstream.

In a pilot study of the system, a stream flow-monitoring station was installed at Mill Creek above Lake Needwood. When the flow rate increased significantly, flocculant was automatically added in the appropriate amount. M. F. Katzer and J. W. Pollack (16), who headed the research team at Mill Creek, reported that during one major storm the maximum rate of removal of solids by flocculation was 3700 pounds per minute. During the 10-hour period when flocculant was added, an estimated 145 tons of solids were deposited, mostly in the stream itself and

*Fig. 6-2  Flocculant addition facility at Rock Creek, Md. Pipe releases chemical automatically according to stream flow rate. (Courtesy Dow Chemical Co.)*

in the settling pond. This operation required 50 gallons of chemical. During a similar storm, a control study (without flocculant) indicated that nearly ten times as much solid material was reaching the settling pond still in suspension; much of this was subsequently carried on into Lake Needwood.

If the flocculation system works, it could be of great use in protecting lakes from silt "pollution"; and the settling ponds can provide an abundance of high grade landfill (an estimated 15,000 cubic yards per year at Mill Creek-Needwood). Against these prospective benefits must be weighed the potential hazards, none of which has been experimentally evaluated:

1. It will be necessary to determine whether there is any biological damage to the stream flora and fauna because of settling of flocculated material prior to the settling ponds. This is particularly important because the bottom-dwelling organisms of fast streams generally need a clean sandy or gravelly substrate.

2. Although the flocculant is described as "nontoxic" and "biodegradable," this will have to be proved during continuous field trials over several years.

3. The fate of the flocculated silt after degradation of the flocculant will have to be ascertained. This pertains especially to silt originally deposited in running water upstream from the settling ponds.

4. The local authority managing the project must have a realistic plan for preventing the settling ponds, with their occasional power scoops and dirt-handling equipment, from becoming regional eyesores.

Forms of ameliorative pollution control are so numerous that there is no room here for a complete list. Among the more promising stop-gap measures are the use of abandoned strip mines for the disposal of trash, the use of compaction techniques to turn garbage and other solid wastes into construction materials, and the use of deep wells for the disposal of heavily polluted waste water. Again, most methods have their risks and side effects. Strip mines can be used for trash disposal only after engineers have studied their drainage patterns and only if an experienced bulldozer operator is available. Even then, a hastily prepared public may react unfavorably to such projects, unaware that the mine, when filled, will be available as parkland. Deep-well injection is associated with still more serious hazards: If the underground geologic formations are of the wrong kind (see Fig. 6-3), if the well is improperly made, or if the waste is disposed of at incorrect pressures, polluted water may escape from the deep formations and contaminate usable, subsurface water supplies; or, in some areas, the water may open fissures, allowing slippage along rock faults and increasing the danger of earthquake. For example,

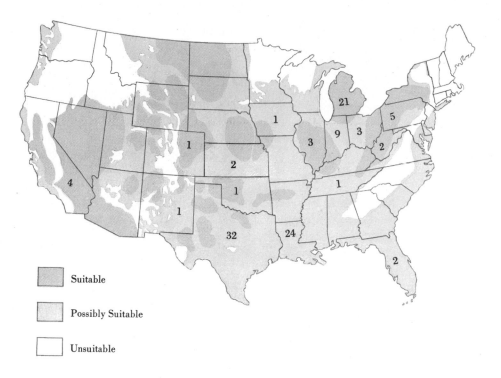

*Fig. 6-3 Areas of the United States suitable for deep well waste injection systems. Numbers indicate the number of wells already in existence. (Modified after* Environmental Science and Technology 2 *(6) (1968).)*

an increase in the number of earthquakes in the region of Denver, Colorado, has been attributed to deep-well waste disposal by the Army (*17*).

No ameliorative pollution control method should be put into practice until the ultimate fate of the pollutant or pollutant by-product has been analyzed. There are, in the last analysis, only three places where pollutants can go: the soil, air, or water. Until a pollutant has been traced — in whatever form it may be — to one of these final resting places, and the consequences of all steps along the route have been examined, a "pollution control system" has not been thoroughly evaluated.

**Prevention**　Preventing pollution is usually preferable to treating it later; in fact, some pollutants (like cyanide, heavy metals, arsenic, and selenium in municipal sewage systems) are virtually impossible to deal with once they have left the source and have become diluted in air or water or absorbed by the soil. As in the case of ameliorative control, there are a variety of problems associated with the prevention of pollution. These seem to fall into loose but recognizable categories:

1. The technological problem of the recirculation of waste materials within a factory so that they can be re-used in early steps of the same process, or used at various stages of other processes (for example, the carbon-containing wastes of the paper and other industries can occasionally serve as low-grade fuels).

2. The problem of pollution exchange, in which the prevention of one kind of pollution is achieved by increasing another kind of pollution.

3. The problem of the unwillingness or inability of the public, when faced with manufacturers and consumers who pollute because it is profitable or convenient, to cope with the situation via legislation or a change in life style.

The problem of "pollution exchange" is encountered in the prevention of thermal pollution of lakes and rivers by power plants. Most power plants scheduled to start operations during the 1970s are at least ten times as large in terms of megawatt output as pre-World War II units. Since the nuclear plants require 40 percent more cooling water than fossil-fuel plants of the same power output, the cooling burden to be placed on fresh-water streams and lakes in the United States will be excessive. In order to prevent thermal pollution, a number of power companies have turned to the use of cooling towers, which are air-cooled by forced draft. Because air has a far lower heat capacity than water, the towers must be enormous, and huge volumes of air must circulate rapidly through them. This, in turn, creates at least two more specific pollution problems:

1. Because of their size, the towers are an aesthetic blight on the landscape.

2. The heated air effluent has a low-moisture holding ability, which in certain climates results in fog and mist that may affect the surrounding area. Here, as in other cases of pollution exchange, a value judgment involving both aesthetic and material considerations may be necessary. From the biological viewpoint, the cooling towers, despite their pollution drawbacks (and despite high cost) seem in most cases clearly preferable to the thermal pollution of natural waters.

Some pollution seems curiously unnecessary, since there are perfectly acceptable alternatives to it. In cases of this sort, one often finds that the polluting activity is creating profit for some sector of industry and that the public is ineffective in defining the problem, in assigning blame, and in enforcing alternatives. An example is provided by "throwaway" beverage containers.

According to A. J. Darnay, Jr. (*4*) of the Midwest Research Institute, production of nonreturnable bottles and cans (for beer and soft drinks) increased from 10 billion units in 1958 to 25.6 billion units in 1966, and if the trend is allowed to continue, will reach 58 billion units in 1976. Although these containers do not contribute substantially to air and water pollution, they are nondegradable and thus disfigure the landscape if they are discarded carelessly or consume needed trash disposal space when they find their way into refuse collection systems. Deposit-return bottles do not present this problem, and they are only a small inconvenience to the consumer, who may not even want to pay the extra cost of the throwaways. Yet throwaway containers are rapidly displacing returnable containers from the market. The average returnable bottle is sold and refilled 20 times before it breaks; therefore, for each deposit-return bottle, 20 throwaways must be manufactured and ultimately discarded.

This is one of the few areas of pollution control where economics seems to be the only major determinant of the situation. In a larger sense, the American economy is geared to the pattern of virgin materials to finished products to consumption to waste of finished products. Frequently the consumer is given no choice but to go along with this cycle: Many products have to be discarded when they break because they are manufactured so that they cannot be repaired (for example, electric fixtures molded in plastic). Repair and re-use of manufactured items at the expense of new production is usually unprofitable in the United States (as is the reclamation of raw materials from trash). Existing economic priorities and values evolved at a time when technology was relatively underdeveloped and there were vast resources available to support a small population. Times have changed, and a waste economy is no longer appropriate.

It is difficult for some people to understand why minority interest groups in a democracy find it so easy to make life unpleasant for the majority. Every day the majority of Americans are bothered or even made ill by automobile exhaust fumes, despite the fact that there is an alternative. The external combustion steam engine is thought to be safe, quiet, inexpensive to produce, and economical to drive and maintain; it allegedly performs well and does not pollute the atmosphere with lead and carbon monoxide. Yet the automobile industry, unwilling to pay for a complete retooling, is resisting even discussion of a possible change. Although the superiority of the steam car is widely claimed except in Detroit, and although New York, Los Angeles, and other urban areas now experience more than a dozen days a year when the air is unfit to breathe, the public and the government that represents it seem powerless to bring about the necessary crash program of research and development.

Part of the problem has been characterized by Garrett Hardin (5) as "the tragedy of the commons," where the "commons" refers to elements of our environment such as air, which we think of as belonging to no one, and those of our activities such as reproduction, which we think of as subject to no one's control. As Hardin points out, in the absence of coercion the rational individual (or industry) places himself at an intolerable competitive disadvantage if he heeds his conscience and stops exploiting the commons. "The rational man finds that his share of the cost of the wastes he discharges into the commons is less than the cost of purifying his wastes before releasing them." In other words, the tragedy of the commons is that our system pits short-term self-interest (private interest) against long-term self-interest (public interest) in an impossible struggle.

This dilemma goes far toward explaining why the public has been powerless to influence pollution control by advertising campaigns, individual and group protest, and moral condemnation. All but the saints among us are polluters, and nothing short of completely removing threatened areas from the realm of the commons — that is, by instituting coercive control over everyone's access to air, land, and water — is likely to prevent us from destroying our environment and each other. Whether, in the long run, this represents a net loss or a gain in personal freedom is not yet clear, but the need to survive has made the question academic, for certain freedoms now endanger survival. That is why the last decades of the twentieth century will probably be characterized by increasing governmental control over individual activities that were once considered beyond the scope of mass regulation, activities that many of us will be loath to give up.

*INDUSTRIAL ACCIDENT CONTROL*  The complexity of the problem of industrial accident control is reflected in the measures necessary to prevent or reduce the danger of oil spills at sea. As was the case with routine pollution control, the measures fall into the categories of amelioration and prevention.

Ameliorative procedures that have been proposed center on the need for contingency plans, more research on oil-clearance methods, and an unscrambling of the international legal confusion concerning inquiry and liability in the event of accident. In the United States, contingency plans were prepared following a presidential memorandum in 1968; however, the apparent confusion that surrounded the clean-up efforts after the oil-well leak in California's Santa Barbara Channel in 1969, testifies to the need for further action. Detergents were used despite the Plymouth Laboratory's previous findings (see Smith, Further

Reading at end of this chapter) that "the more efficacious the detergent, the more toxic it is." Adequate contingency planning should include provision for depots near all major waterways, where oil booms, straw, powdered chalk, steam-cleaning equipment, and other safe oil removal aids can be stored for emergency use. Transportation and storage facilities for the recovered oil are also necessary. Local officials responsible for navigation, harbors, and beaches must be trained in the methods of coping with oil spills. Research on oil removal and disposal techniques should be intensified and should be concerned with finding nontoxic substitutes for the volatile aromatic fractions of existing detergents. More work is also needed on methods of sinking oil at sea and of removing oil-sand crusts from beaches without causing erosion. Finally, the Intergovernmental Maritime Consultative Organization (IMCO), an agency of the United Nations, has set up a legal committee to help define the legal rights of coastal states, assignment of liability, participants in investigations, insurance requirements for tankers, and regulations concerning the movement of salvage equipment when oil spills occur at sea.

The accidental discharge of oil into marine or fresh waters could be greatly reduced by improvement in navigation aids, by improvement in vessel design, and by passage of tough laws delineating the responsibilities of ship companies and offshore oil-well owners in observing safety precautions. The IMCO subcommittee on safety of navigation is concerned with (1) sea lanes, (2) navigational equipment, (3) shore guidance, (4) speed restrictions, (5) periodic equipment checks, (6) officer and crew training, (7) use of automatic pilots, (8) indentification and charting of hazards, and (9) reinforcement of lookout systems. There is great room for improvement in all these categories. According to *Environmental Science and Technology*, (*2*, 512, 1968), U.S. regulations "do not require vessels to carry sailing directions, Notices to Mariners, and tide tables." Nor are charts of the locations of the more than 7000 oil wells and 1800 miles of pipeline in the Gulf of Mexico available to mariners.

Although the tankers that are being constructed today are reasonably well designed, cargo transfer, deballasting, tank draining, and bilge draining features could be further improved to minimize oil losses. The question of size is also important: Supertankers of more than 200,000 tons deadweight capacity may represent so great a damage potential (and so small an economic advantage) that their construction is unwarranted. Some companies, such as Shell International Marine, Ltd., have stated that they see no advantage in exceeding this size limit, but a year after the sinking of the *Torrey Canyon*, Gulf Oil Corporation was continuing with plans to have six 300,000-ton tankers built in Japanese shipyards.

There are obviously many other kinds of industrial accidents besides the spilling of oil into waterways, but few are more complicated to control or have such widespread effects; and some of the lessons learned here have general applicability. Hindsight is cheap, but both the *Torrey Canyon* and Santa Barbara Channel accidents might have been avoided if there had been some standard compulsory procedure for estimating the accident potential before operations had begun. Too often we ignore the environmental hazards associated with technological and/or economic "progress." Existing safety regulations and codes never seem to cover the entire scope of industrial operations from raw materials to the distribution (and use) of finished products, nor do they provide the public with meaningful opportunities to examine and delay projects. In an age when every big city is destined to be surrounded by nuclear reactors, and when environmental poisons are produced and shipped in 300,000-ton quantities, these problems need both thought and action to prevent catastrophes.

***PROTECTION OF NATURAL COMMUNITIES*** One way to preserve natural communities is to insulate them from the adverse influences of population and technology by according them some sort of protected status. Before briefly considering several of the ways of doing this, however, it is necessary to introduce a word of warning. Officially designated parks, monuments, and wildlife refuges are not necessarily protected. Many government agencies have high priority rights of eminent domain, and some, like the Atomic Energy Commission and the Department of Defense, exercise these rights in an atmosphere of comparative secrecy. In 1965, for example, these two agencies detonated an underground atomic explosion on Amchitka Island in the middle of the Aleutian Islands National Wildlife Refuge, and subsequently announced and began to carry out plans for five more atomic explosions. This island, one of the last abodes of the sea otter, was thus converted from a wildlife refuge to an atomic proving ground without benefit of democratic review and in spite of the protests of Alaska's Governor Walter J. Hickel (later Secretary of the Interior). Nearly all "protected" land is under continual challenge by a variety of interests like Disney Productions with its proposed resort in the Mineral King National Game Refuge (to be serviced via a proposed superhighway cut through Sequoia National Park), like the Kennecott Corporation with its proposed open-pit copper mine near Image Lake in the middle of the Glacier Peak Wilderness Area, or like Columbia University with its attempted nibbles at the irreplaceable public park land of Manhattan Island.

*Fig. 6-4   Image Lake, Glacier Peak Wilderness Area, Wash. (Philip Hyde)*

There is ample precedent for the creation of new national parks, additions to existing national parks, and designations of wilderness areas by acts of Congress, and since these processes are subject to the same pressures already described, there is no need for elaboration. There are, however, new and exciting opportunities to protect natural communities at the municipal and county level, particularly in suburban areas where the need is greatest. Increasingly, the problems of conserving natural communities, of designing livable residences, and of providing outdoor recreation facilities have been drawing together. Leadership in this last great attempt to provide a healthful and healthy environment for the urban American has fortunately passed into the hands of a small group of unusually practical and creative men. Names like Ian McHarg, Phillip H. Lewis, Jr., William H. Whyte, and Charles E. Little are not known to the majority of city and suburb dwellers, who are nevertheless already greatly in their debt.

Every piece of accessible land, public or private, within 50–100 miles of all major cities is in danger of being used for residential or commercial construction by 1985 (see Chapter 2). Thousands of suburban and semirural communities, which were created to provide former city dwellers with peaceful and natural surroundings in which to relax after a hectic day in the city, are being turned into "development slums." The tired commuter often fights traffic in the evening to come "home" to an environment in which surface area consists of 30 percent asphalt, 30 percent rooftop, 30 percent lawn, and less than 10 percent of the kinds of woods and meadows that once made the area beautiful. In addition, the suburbanite must pay exorbitant property taxes so that his municipality can afford to cope with the flooding and erosion caused by the destruction of marshes, swamps, and forests; with the necessity of supplying water, police and fire protection, and waste removal services; and with the overwhelming costs of schools.

Contrary to popular belief, the addition of new residential property to the tax rolls, particularly in development blocs, rarely helps the community economically. Although tax returns increase, the cost of services to be borne by the entire community increases more. Charles E. Little (6), recounts the story of Closter, New Jersey, which in 1965 wanted to acquire seven parcels of land totaling 80 acres, to be set aside for limited recreational purposes. Acquisition costs were approximately $500,000, and some residents wondered if the town might not be better off by letting the owners sell their property to residential builders. At this point Mayor James E. Carson carried out some calculations: Assuming that the 80 acres could accommodate 160 houses, these houses in turn would produce approximately 200 children to be educated at $720 per pupil per year, for an annual total of $144,000. Additional garbage collection, police services, fire protection, lighting, and other services would cost about $12,000 annually. Thus the total annual increase in municipal costs would be $156,000. Tax returns from these proposed new residences would amount to approximately $100,000, leaving a $56,000 annual deficit to be shared by all residents in the form of permanently increased taxes. On the other hand, if the community bought the land for parks—even assuming no federal or state aid (which they have received)—the land would be completely paid for in 10 years, at approximately the same annual cost but with no subsequent expenses except for nominal maintenance costs.

Ecological balances are too delicate and land is too expensive for conservation to proceed in a haphazard way. Conservation and development must be planned together, and with equal care. Professor Ian McHarg (7), of the Department of Landscape Architecture and Regional Planning of the University of Pennsylvania, has formulated the following set of criteria for selecting "open space" in the Philadelphia metropolitan area:

1. Surface water and waterfront land should be used only for functions that cannot occur elsewhere, including harbors and water-using industries. McHarg estimates that this would consume only 1 percent of

the river area around Philadelphia, leaving the remainder for forestry, agriculture, recreation, and open space adjacent to housing.

2. The wastes entering streams should be regulated according to the ability of the waterway to absorb pollutants without seriously altering the aquatic flora and fauna.

3. Marshes must be protected from drainage or filling in order to serve as wildlife reservoirs and flood storage areas.

4. Flood plains that are under water once every 50 years or more should be closed to all residential and commercial building construction. Recreational, agricultural, and open-space uses and related functions are excepted.

5. Ground water resources, or aquifers, must be protected by careful management of deep-well injection, sewage disposal, rate of water withdrawal, and similar practices.

6. Good soil is an irreplaceable asset, slow to form, and like many complex living systems, easily killed. The best agricultural land should be used as such, and not be permitted to be developed for other purposes.

7. Steep slopes (12° or more) erode rapidly when their natural cover is disturbed. This in turn causes siltation of waterways, flooding, failure to replenish aquifers, and destruction of terrestrial and aquatic habitats. Steep slopes should remain completely untouched if unforested, and sparsely developed (less than one house per 3 acres) if forested.

8. Forests and woodlands, which are "the major regulators of equilibrium in the water system," which "exercise a profound effect upon climate," and which are "a prime scenic and recreational resource," should be used for forestry, water catchment areas, airsheds, recreation, and cluster housing restricted to an over-all density of one house per acre or less.

Professor McHarg claims that if these guide lines were followed in the 3500-sq mile area of Greater Philadelphia, studies indicate that there would be no added economic burden on the population and that development could proceed normally without upsetting the local ecology or destroying the natural beauty of the region.

Philip H. Lewis, Jr. (8), project director of the monumental Upper Mississippi River Comprehensive Basin Study (Department of Interior), has formulated a different but equally useful set of guide lines for determining which land should be conserved. Lewis and his associates, with the cooperation of conservationists, county agents, and the general public, prepared a "Resource Value Point System" in which hundreds of natural and cultural features of the landscape were characterized and were assigned values in terms of their relative importance to recreation

# WATER RESOURCES

## Natural Resources

Waterfalls
Bathing Beaches
Natural Springs, Artesian
　Flows
Canoe Routes
Wild Rice Areas
Exceptional Islands
Fish Habitat
Chasms
Trout
Catfish

## Man-Made Resources

Swimming Facilities
Boating Facilities, Ramps

Boating Areas
Harbors of Refuge
Campsites
Fish Hatcheries
Mill Ponds
Reservoirs

# WETLAND RESOURCES

Exceptional Wetlands
Wildlife Observation
Wildlife Hunting
Wildlife Preserves

State Forests (Existing,
　Potential)

# TOPOGRAPHIC RESOURCES

Unique Geological
　Formations

Caves
Exceptional Glacial Remains
Mineral Ore Outcroppings
Ski Trails
Hiking
Picnic Areas
Nature Camps

# HISTORICAL AND CULTURAL RESOURCES

## Man-Made Resources

Blacksmith Shops
Bridges (Covered, etc.)
Trading Posts
Old Forts
Battlefields
Historical Markers
Museums
Modern Mines
Ghost Towns
Theaters

# VEGETATION RESOURCES

## Natural Resources

Virgin Stands (Timber)
Rare Remnants
Wildflowers
Orchards

## Man-Made Resources

Fire Trails and Breaks

# ARCHEOLOGICAL RESOURCES

## Man-Made Resources

Quartzite
Quarry Flint
Copper
Campsite
Cornfield
Trail
Historic Village Sites
Historic Cemetery
Burial Ground

# WILDLIFE

## Natural Resource

Bear
Wolf

Deer
Pheasant
Beaver
Mink
Ducks
Geese
Swans
Eagles
Great Horned Owls
Ospreys
Falcons
Cranes

# VISUAL QUALITY OF SPACE

Rural Regional "Spatial"
　Classification

Enclosed partly by vegetation,
　partly by topography
Enclosed by solid and open
　vegetation
Enclosed by open vegetation
Enclosed by open topography

# TOURIST SERVICE FACILITIES

Accommodations
Hospital
Water

(*Above*) *Some of the natural and man-made resources inventoried in the Wisconsin study. When plotted on maps, 85–90% of the natural and cultural features identified in the field were found to lie within the environmental corridor pattern (see text).*

Fig. 6-5 (*Below*) *Environmental quality inventory map for Iowa-Missouri-Illinois tri-state area, showing a high correlation between locations of natural and man-made resources and locations of waterways. 1: Bathing beaches; 2: Wild rice areas; 3: Chasms; 4: Outstanding soil and farm conservation projects; 5: Rare remnants of natural vegetation; 6: Wild flowers; 7: Existing or potential state parks; 8: Historical homes; 9: Songbirds; 10: Red and gray fox; 11: Prairie chicken; 12: Falcons; 13: Accommodations. (From P. H. Lewis, Jr. et al., Regional Design for Human Impact. Kaukauna, Wisc.; Thomas, 1969).*

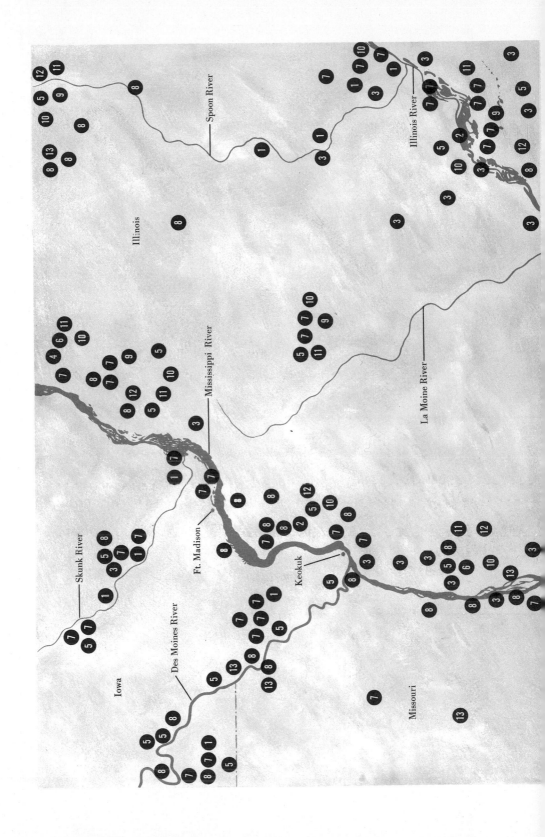

and maintenance of environmental quality. These features were then located and charted for a number of areas in the Mississippi Basin and Great Lakes region. According to Lewis, the most striking finding was that 85–90 percent of all identified natural and cultural features could be seen to lie within "environmental corridors" that coincided with topographic corridors delineated by waterways and associated ridges (Fig. 6-5).

Thus, both McHarg and Lewis agree that the key to land acquisition in any regional conservation program is the distribution of water. Only after this has been carefully studied can conservationists and planners decide what land ought to be preserved as open space. If environmental corridors are maintained intact, or nearly so, the result is a network of park land and scenic areas readily accessible to nearly all the population, and which frequently extend, as in the case of Washington's Rock Creek Park, into the heart of the central city.

Once it has been decided what land to acquire, there is the problem of gaining title or control. Few counties or municipalities can readily afford to spend vast sums on land, yet the land must be acquired. In recent years, in response to this need, a number of organizations and individuals have devised and publicized a whole catalogue of ways in which local governments can acquire land without going bankrupt or alienating large segments of the community. The America the Beautiful Fund of the Natural Area Council, Inc., publishes a pamphlet series called *Aims*, in which such topics as land trusts, grants-in-aid, environmental manpower needs, and even tree-moving machinery are discussed. The Open Space Action Institute, Inc., has published several reports, including *Challenge of the Land* by Little(6), a short, practical, and extremely well-written manual "for municipal officials and civic leaders" who want to know the whole range of basic land acquisition techniques, including the political and legal pitfalls that must be avoided. *The Last Landscape* by Whyte (see Further Reading at end of the chapter) is a somewhat more theoretical but equally valuable book on the same theme, and there are many others.

A complete account of all current methods of land protection would fill a lengthy volume, but a few of the more common ones can be briefly described. First, direct acquisition by purchase can be financed by bond issues and/or assisted by federal or state grants. Sources of federal funds include the Department of Agriculture's "Greenspan" program for purchase of agricultural land to be dedicated to conservation or recreation purposes, or Public Law 566 which provides money for constructing small dams and associated recreation areas. The Department of Commerce may pay up to 75 percent of the cost of parks in certain areas. The Department of the Interior administers conservation funds through its Bureau of Outdoor Recreation. The Open Space Program of the Department of Housing and Urban Development can give matching funds for land purchase. Even the Department of Defense* and the Department of Health, Education and Welfare can assist in safeguarding land for conservation. In the case of direct land purchase by local governments, the problem seems not to be one of financing, but of presenting the case to the public in a forthright and professional manner.

Second, there is the technique known as "cluster development," in which a residential builder agrees to cluster new homes on smaller-than-normal lots so that part of his tract can be set aside for recreational purposes. This concept works well only if the local government can decide which acreage should be set aside and if that acreage is both legally and financially protected in perpetuity. On occasion, cluster development has been used by unscrupulous developers to crowd an excessive number of people on their land. This is easily avoided by alert city officials; well-managed cluster developments make attractive and viable communities.

Third, many private owners of large tracts of land are willing to donate part of their land to municipalities or to conservation organizations. There are a variety of perfectly valid motivations involved, including tax relief, enchancement of the value of their remaining land (because it is now next to a park), and philanthropy. The Open Space Action Institute estimates that there are approximately 10,000 private owners of "significant open land" in the New York metropolitan region, and a special landowner program has been designed to advise them of the advantages of land donation.

Fourth, there are "easements" in which the owner of land agrees to give permanent protection to some natural feature of his land without surrendering actual ownership. This method has not been very popular, but it has worked well in some cases. In central Florida, the Audubon Society has been able, through the cooperation of many cattle ranchers, to protect bald eagle nesting trees scattered over tens of thousands of acres.

Fifth, municipal zoning such as Westport, Connecticut's Design Development District (DDD), can be used, cautiously, to bring commercial offices and light industry into residential areas, provided attractive structures are built and a significant amount of the company land is set aside as permanent open space. In such an arrangement the participating company benefits by having a good environment for its employees in a setting that will not deteriorate; and the town benefits by both adding to its tax revenues and protecting part of its natural landscape.

*Some of the finest urban and rural landscapes left in the United States are located within the confines of military installations. The Presidio of San Francisco and Fort Lewis in the State of Washington are examples. A few bases now have conservation officers or base agronomists.

Sixth, tracts of land may be purchased by the Nature Conservancy or by similar, nonprofit, conservation organizations for donation or sale to local, state, or federal agencies as parks, or for protection as private wildlife preserves.

*MANAGEMENT OF NATURAL COMMUNITIES*

*Characterization of the Community*

Before a natural community can be managed, its principal elements and their principal interactions must be known. At the least, a managed community should be characterized with respect to species composition, population sizes, and history of fluctuations of these two variables, whenever possible. Errors, false assumptions, and oversimplifications in the evaluation of community attributes can result in mismanagement and loss of natural features and economic values that should have been preserved.

The following discussion applies primarily to wildlife refuges, national parks and forests, wilderness areas, and other large tracts of land. With the exception of ecologically unusual and fragile communities like the ancient holly forest on Sandy Hook, New Jersey, most small and open space parcels of land are best managed by limiting recreational and related uses to a reasonable level and by interfering with natural processes only when there is no alternative.

An example of the management problems that stem from application of ecological theory based on conjecture rather than on factual data was described in 1964 by Dr. Hugh Raup(9) of the Harvard Forest. The Harvard Forest project was started in 1908; its development plan at that time was based on the prevailing assumption that the "primeval" forests of the pre-Colonial era had been rich and productive and that the surviving forests of twentieth-century New England were sorry remnants of the original forest, still suffering the consequences of early depredations by the European colonists. A guiding corollary of this assumption was that, with proper management, the Harvard Forest could be restored to its former productivity and that it would pay for itself while serving as a model of sustained-yield forestry.

According to Raup the experiment was a complete failure. He says: "At the end of half a century the Harvard Forest, as a demonstration of sustained yield, was a sorry spectacle. It had almost no annual income, and it had lost two-thirds of its capital, due almost entirely to external causes over which it had no control, and which had been unpredictable." Although the economic reasons for this failure are not entirely relevant here, there is a strong indication (as Raup suggests) that the original productivity assumptions based on the conception of a rich, primeval American forest were wrong and that this in turn generated misleading estimates of both the potential productivity of the Harvard Forest and the demand for its lumber on the open market.

Using a variety of methods (many available in 1908), including examination of early historical accounts of the landscape, studies of soils, and analyses of tree ages versus species distribution in existing forests, Raup and his associates have concluded that the pre-Colonial forests were very similar in many respects to those relatively undisturbed forests existing today.* "Our natural vegetation in America, even before the coming of Europeans, seems to have lived in a continuing state of major readjustment. Its history of disaster (such as wind and fire) had atomized it, and this I conceive to be one of the greatest blessings we received when we inherited it."

Thus, in the first decades of this century, the lack of attention to the ecological history of the Harvard Forest community led to two serious management mistakes: first, an overestimate of future productivity; and second, a mistaken emphasis on long-range planning because of the false premise on which some of the early foresters based their understanding of American forest ecosystems. Of course economic return is not the yardstick by which we measure all management efforts in protected areas; nevertheless, the lesson is plain. Ecology was not then and is not yet a fully predictive science; community management, to be successful, must strive to base itself on the maximum amount of ecological data, be responsive to change, not be unduly influenced by rigid ecological theories and models, and must utilize the best historical information available.

**Culling, Pruning,**
**and Manipulation**
Good management of natural communities is not synonomous with blanket protection of all species. Occasionally, populations of some species must be thinned to protect the rest of the community. This is especially true in the case of vertebrate herbivores, now that large predators have been virtually eliminated from most communities. Population regulation techniques can be applied for either or both of two purposes: (1) To keep particular animal or plant populations at peak productivity for economic gain; (2) To maintain populations at optimum size for the good health of the community. Except when dealing with pests, the procedure in the two cases is often the same: Populations must be kept at less than their maximum possible density. Optimum population

---

*For example, the picture of a damaged forest slowly recovering from Colonial depredations is contradicted by Raup's data gathered from another northeastern forest: "Individual old trees ranging in age up to 300 years were found throughout the forest. . . . Wherever found they matched the species and growth forms around them, thus suggesting that neither the trees nor the sites had changed much during their lifetimes."

densities vary with the species and community, and their determination is a complex process. At a simpler level, many of the changes that occur in population density can be described by the sigmoid (S-shaped) population-growth curve (see Fig. 6-6), which plays an important role in the practice of ecological management.

A classic example of the need for active intervention is provided by the history of the Kaibab deer herd (see Chapter 4). These deer, living on the forested rim of the Grand Canyon in northern Arizona, numbered 4000 in 1906, when a game preserve was established and hunting was forbidden. By 1924 the population had increased to 100,000 and the Kaibab National Forest was in danger of destruction by overbrowsing. But the population-growth curve hardly had time to enter a stationary phase. During the next 6 years, 80,000 deer starved to death while officials debated, and the crisis ended. It can, of course, be argued that the need for active management would never have occurred if an early pre-

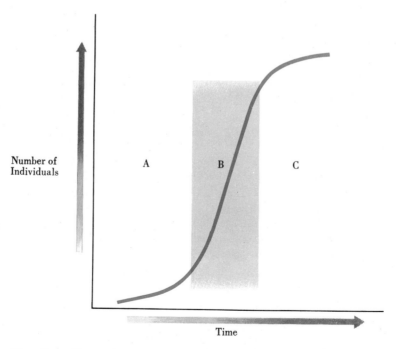

**Fig. 6-6** *Sigmoid population growth curve. (A) Initial lag phase. Underutilization of food and shelter resources, danger of population extinction. (B) Exponential growth phase. Maximum productivity, optimum utilization of resources. (C) Plateau or stationary phase. Low productivity, high morbidity and mortality, overutilization and destruction of food and shelter resources.*

dator (wolf, bear, mountain lion) elimination program had not upset the equilibrium in the first place. This is probably true, but the point is academic. One would have to go far today to find a natural community unaffected by modern man, and especially to find one in which the predator level in the food pyramid remains intact.

There are numerous additional examples of the dangers of just passive protection of wildlife. In 1968 the Advisory Board on Wildlife Management, chaired by Dr. A. Starker Leopold (*10*), recommended to the Secretary of the Interior that: "The (National Wildlife) refuge system as a whole should be designed and managed to spread migratory waterfowl as evenly as possible throughout the flyways. Excessive concentration, such as the gathering of Canada geese at Horicon Refuge in Wisconsin, should be avoided or rectified to reduce danger of overkill, crop depredations, and epizootic disease. . . . Reducing the intensity of the feeding program would seem to be an initial step in this process, along with regulated hunting on the refuge itself and possible drawdown of water levels."

The extreme form of population control is population elimination. In some kinds of management, particularly for economic gain, simplification of ecosystems by selective elimination of species is practiced. Occasionally this is necessary. It is difficult, for example, to see how wheat could be economically grown and harvested if it were interspersed with other plants in a seminatural prairie community. Nevertheless, there is debate on the value of many oversimplified communities, including such important ones as single-species tree farms and cattle and sheep ranches.

It was pointed out in Chapter 2 that ecologists like Margalef base their ecological theories on the idea that high species diversity generates stability in a natural community. If one accepts the idea, then it follows that anything that greatly reduces species diversity will induce excessive and possibly ruinous population fluctuations in the remaining species of the community. Conservation policy is clearly delineated within this conceptual framework.

This is a controversial area of theoretical ecology (see Slobodkin, Further Reading at the end of this chapter), but for practical purposes it seems best to follow the advice of F. Fraser Darling(*11*), a pioneer in wildlife management and conservation: "We are beginning to see that where there are definite limitations in the environment, such as hard and fast wet and dry seasons, combined with permeable young volcanic soils or senile lateritic earths as in many parts of Africa, it is better to take stock of how the country gets along with its natural communities. . . . Simplification in such conditions produces rapid loss of efficiency in biological activity. . . ."

"[An] example of projected simplification is in the tropical forests where one school of foresters advises removal of 'weed' trees and encouragement of denser stands of the desirable timber trees. To speak of 'weed' trees in the beautiful intricacy of the oldest life form on the planet is sheer arrogance. It is of the very nature of the tropical forest with its thousands of tree species, and characteristic low densities of any one species, to preserve variety and thereby resist change. This community resistance to change is the strength and immunity of the biome to organic catastrophe."

Another example of the consequences of altering the species composition of natural communities is provided by the substitution of domestic cattle for the savanna herbivores of much of Africa south of the Sahara. The wild ungulates of the African savanna are an extremely diverse group, including scores of species from several mammalian orders, and ranging in size from the 11.5-pound dik-dik to the 11,500-pound elephant. These different species occupy a wide variety of feeding niches, and are therefore not all in competition with each other for food. Unfortunately, conventional European concepts of range management were, until recently, widely adopted in Africa; in vast areas the wild ungulates were removed and replaced with large numbers of cattle, sheep, and goats, all existing on grasses and low plants and unable to use much of the local vegetation for food. In a short time, the original carrying capacity* of many areas was exceeded, plant cover disappeared, carrying capacity declined, livestock died, and dust bowls or baked clay crusts (the hallmark of ecological mismanagement) left thousands of square miles unfit for any human endeavor.

On the other hand, if the native ungulates are kept as part of the community and regularly harvested for meat and other animal products, the results are a much greater total productivity than that provided by cattle, sheep, and goats, without destruction of the habitat (see Table 6-2). The meat of most wild ungulates, if cured properly, tastes like beef. As much as 25–50 percent of the total populations of several ungulate species can be harvested annually without a decline in yield. In addition, Talbot and associates(12) report that many of Africa's hoofed wild animals offer possibilities for domestication, although, curiously, this has not been done in Africa since the Neolithic period. If estimates are correct, 20 percent or more of the African continent that is unfit for other enterprises could be used for "game ranching," thus both conserving and benefiting from the unique character of the savanna community.

---

*Lee M. Talbot, *et al.* (12), authorities on African community management, define the carrying capacity of an area as "the number of animals of a given size which can be supported for a given period of time by the vegetation growing in that area without adversely affecting the vegetation production."

**Fig. 6-7** *Overgrazing and drought contributed to the deterioration of this rangeland in Frio County, Texas. (U.S.D.A.—Soil Conservation Service)*

**Table 6-2** **Year-Long Standing Crop (Biomass) of Domestic Livestock and Wild Ungulates Relative to Carrying Capacity in Equivalent East African Rangelands**

| Type of Range | Animals | Year-Long Standing Crop (lb/sq mile) | (kg/hectare) | Stocking Rate Relative to Carrying Capacity |
|---|---|---|---|---|
| Acacia savanna | Cattle, goats, sheep | 11,200–16,000 | 19.6–28.0 | Over |
| Acacia savanna | Wild ungulates | 37,400–90,000 | 65.5–157.6 | At or under |
| Moderately managed grass savanna[a] | Cattle | 21,300–32,000 | 37.3–56.0 | At or slightly over |
| Acacia-commiphora bushland | Sheep, goats | 2,100–8,000 | 3.7–13.5 | At or over |
| Acacia-commiphora bushland | Wild ungulates | 30,000 | 52.5 | At or under |

SOURCE: L. M. Talbot, *Publ. I.U.C.N.* N.S., No. 1 (1963) 328.

[a] Provision of water, fencing, some brush control, dipping, and other disease control.

*Fig. 6-8  Mixed herd of wildebeests and zebras on healthy rangeland, Lake Manyara, Tanzania. Cattle egrets accompany the herd. (Marc and Evelyne Bernheim, Rapho Guillumette)*

There are other wildlife management tools besides the ax or gun; one of the best ways of shaping and manipulating natural communities is by the careful use of fire. Fire is an important component of many ecosystems (see Chapter 3, The Pacific Coast Redwood Communities), and a number of species like longleaf pine (*Pinus palustris*) and sand pine (*Pinus clausa*), in the southeastern United States, are especially adapted to resist it and to profit by its competition-reducing effects. Sand pine, for example, rarely drops its seed cones until they are released by the heat of a strong fire. Even if the parent tree is killed, a new crop of seedlings will quickly spring up in the ashes.

Complete fire protection over a long period of time may cause a drastic change in the local community. One Florida live oak hammock experimentally shielded from fire since 1936 has been studied by Dr. Albert Laessle (*13*) of the University of Florida (see Fig. 6-9) since 1939. Although the live oaks still are dropping thousands of viable acorns, these are not sprouting. Longleaf pines in an adjacent fire-protected area are also not reproducing themselves. In the absence of fire, fire-intolerant trees like the laurel oak (*Quercus laurifolia*) are invading the region. Other trees like the swamp maple (*Rufacer rubrum*) and the swamp red bay (*Tamala pubescens*), normally confined to bayheads or swamps, have appeared; evidently they usually inhabit wet areas not because of a great need for water but because of their lack of resistance to fire. If fire protection is continued, the old community will have completely disappeared in a few decades.

Fire is often far more useful than complete fire prevention in ecosystem management. Foresters have known for many years that carefully controlled annual burning in some pine tree farms removes undesirable shrubby vegetation and helps prevent more serious fire from occurring. Some quail hunters in the southern states have refined burning methods to a fine art in order to provide ideal vegetation for maximum bird populations and good hunting. Fire may be even more important in the management of savannas and grasslands. Dr. Paul C. Lemon(14) of the State University of New York at Albany studied the effects of annual burning on the Nyika Plateau grassland of Malawi, where fires are common. He found that the forage grasses in areas that were burned yearly were much more abundant than in unburned areas, and that the herbaceous legumes that are essential for soil nitrogen metabolism were more numerous after burning. Lemon concluded: "The welfare of herbaceous legumes . . . and of the entire grassland ecosystem may very well depend upon periodic fires. . . . Thus, where it is desirable to encourage the large grazing animals, it seems wise to plan a regimen of regular, if conservative, burning." In other studies it has been found that occasional (but not too frequent) prairie fires are needed to release mineral nutrients that otherwise would remain trapped and unavailable in organic debris.

It should be clear to readers of this section that active intervention is often necessary to preserve natural communities. Nevertheless, this is one of the most difficult aspects of conservation. Nobody can predict, even with sophisticated models and the help of computers, all the results of community management. With the establishment of the migratory waterfowl refuges in the upper Mississippi Valley, most Canada geese stopped migrating to their former wintering grounds south of Illinois. More depressing illustrations of the problems of wildlife management could be cited, but there is no need—the moral is evident: Cautious manipulation of ecosystems should always be accompanied and followed by prolonged observation of the flora and fauna; and when in serious doubt, the wisest management is none at all.

***Size of
Managed Areas***    It is a truism to say that protected areas should always be large enough to serve their prime recreational, economic, or wilderness function without deterioration of the natural community. Two acres of protected land near Perth, Australia, are quite sufficient to conserve all

**Fig. 6-9a**  *Live oak hammock, Florida Conservation Reserve, Welaka, Florida, May, 1942. Fire protection had been in effect since 1935. Note the small amount of Spanish moss. The ground cover is mostly myrtle oak. (Dr. Albert Laessle)*

living individuals of the rare species of sidenecked turtle, *Pseudemydura umbrina*. On the other hand, a 500-acre wilderness area with no visitors would be too small if its purpose was to provide refuge for a wolf pack. A 1200-square mile national park is also too small if it receives more than 2 million visitors in a season.

In the case of the hypothetical wolf refuge, the only alternatives would be to enlarge it or to change its prime function. In the case of the national park (Yosemite), enlarging it would be costly and would not solve the basic problem. If we wish to keep the park worth visiting, the total number of visitors will have to be reduced. This could be accomplished in several ways, but the method of advance reservations adopted by the Park Service seems far preferable to financial exclusion based on a high admissions fee. A workable plan to limit automobile traffic without penalizing campers should also be devised. Any such plan consistent with maintenance of park values and standards will not involve building new roads, which would be both inadequate to handle the steadily increasing traffic (new roads attract new traffic) and extremely

*Fig. 6-9b   Same location, October, 1956, still protected from fire. In addition to the great increase in Spanish moss, note the increase in height of the myrtle oaks; laurel oaks are now evident to the right and left of center. (Dr. Albert Laessle)*

destructive of wildlife. Instead, relatively unobtrusive transportation systems, like monorails, offer the best hope for handling park crowds without obliterating what the people come to see(15).

All national parks that successfully contain large wild animals in a self-perpetuating community maintain their integrity by virtue of established or informal usage zones. In Yellowstone Park, only a few percent of the park area is developed for auto-bound visitors (this part is grossly overcrowded), and the remainder — accessible to hikers — serves as much-needed shelter, forage, and breeding space for the park's celebrated animal populations. There are also large forested areas adjacent to the park.

As another example, Nairobi National Park is 5 miles from Kenya's largest city, yet it contains lions, rhinos, giraffes, and many other large mammals as well as over 400 species of birds. The future existence of this small park is linked in part to the continued free access of its animals to the adjoining few hundred square miles of Masai territory

*Fig. 6-10 (left) Yosemite Valley and Domes, 1899. (Library of Congress)*

*Fig. 6-10 (right) Yosemite Valley traffic jam, 1963. (National Park Service)*

that have in the past been open to them. This kind of zonation, where areas of heavy use border on recovery areas with few visitors, allows respectable numbers of people to enjoy natural communities without destroying them.

The dismal failure of the government's "multiple use" policy, as evidenced in places like Alaska's Admiralty Island (see Chapter 8), also testifies to the need for clear management priorities and usage zonation when dealing with unspoiled ecosystems. The "multiple use" policy, set forth in Public Law 86-517, urges that National Forest land be used for a variety of purposes simultaneously; thus one area may conceivably be supposed to satisfy mineral, lumber, recreation, and wilderness interests at the same time. Needless to say, first wilderness and then recreation disappear under these conditions.

## FURTHER READING

*Cleaning Our Environment: The Chemical Basis for Action.* Washington, D.C., American Chemical Society, 1969.

Cox, George W., *Readings in Conservation Ecology.* New York: Appleton-Century-Crofts, 1969.

Darling, F. Fraser and John P. Milton, eds., *Future Environments of North America.* Garden City, N.Y.: Natural History Press, 1966.

Hardin, Garrett, *Population, Evolution, and Birth Control.* San Francisco: Freeman, 1969.

Mayda, Jaro, *Environment and Resources — From Conservation to Ecomanagement.* Rio Piedras: University of Puerto Rico Law School, 1968.

McHarg, Ian L., *Design with Nature.* Garden City, N.Y.: Natural History Press, 1969.

Mumford, Lewis, *The City in History.* New York: Harcourt, Brace and World, 1961.

Slobodkin, Lawrence B., "Aspects of the Future of Ecology." *BioScience*, 16, January, 1968.

Smith, J. E., ed., *'Torrey Canyon' Pollution and Marine Life.* Cambridge: Cambridge University Press, 1968.

Whyte, William H., *The Last Landscape.* Garden City, N.Y.: Doubleday, 1968.

## REFERENCES

1.  Mayer, Jean, *Daedalus 93* (3), 830 (Summer, 1964).
2.  Blake, Judith, *Science 164,* 522 (1969).
3.  Harkavy, O., Jaffe, F. S., and Wishik, S. M., *Science 165,* 367 (1969).
4.  Darnay, Arsen J., Jr., *Environmental Science and Technology 3,* 328 (1969).
5.  Hardin, Garrett, *Science 162,* 1243 (1968).

6.  Little, Charles E., *Challenge of the Land* (Open Space Action Institute, New York, 1968), 83.

7.  McHarg, Ian, in *Taming Megalopolis 1*, Eldredge, H. W., ed. (Doubleday, Anchor Books, Garden City, N.Y., 1967), 540.

8.  Lewis, Philip H., Jr., *Regional Design for Human Impact* (Thomas, Kaukauna, Wisconsin, 1969).

9.  Raup, Hugh M., *British Ecological Society Jubilee Symposium*, a supplement of *J. Ecology 52* and *J. Animal Ecology 33* (Blackwell, Oxford, 1964), 19.

10.  Leopold, A. Starker, *et al.*, *Audubon 70* (3), 8 (1968).

11.  Darling, F. Fraser, *British Ecological Society Jubilee Symposium* (Chapter 6, Ref. 9), 39.

12.  Talbot, Lee M., *et al.*, *The Meat Production Potential of Wild Animals in Africa* (Commonwealth Agricultural Bureaux Technical Communication No. 16, Farnham Royal, England, 1965).

13.  Laessle, Albert, *Quart. J. Fla. Acad. Sci. 21* (1), 101 (1958).

14.  Lemon, Paul C., *Ecology 49*, 316 (1968).

15.  Carter, Luther J., *Science 161*, 770 (1968).

16.  Katzer, Melvin F., and Pollack, James W., *Environmental Science and Technology 2*, 341 (1968).

17.  Evans, David M., and Bradford, Albert, *Environment 11* (8), 2 (1969).

# chapter 7

# Analogues of
# Natural
# Communities

"But in a sense I do remember different seasons, because all my memories are bound up with things to eat, which varied at different times of the year. Especially the things you used to find in the hedges. In July there were dewberries — but they're very rare — and the blackberries were getting red enough to eat. In September there were sloes and hazel-nuts. The best hazel-nuts were always out of reach. Later on there were beech-nuts and crab-apples. Then there were the kind of minor foods that you used to eat when there was nothing better going. Haws — but they're not much good — and hips, which have a nice sharp taste if you clean the hairs out of them. Angelica is good in early summer, especially when you're thirsty, and so are the stems of various grasses. Then there's sorrel, which is good with bread and butter, and pig-nuts, and a kind of wood shamrock which has a sour taste. Even plantain seeds are better than nothing when you're a long way from home and very hungry."

George Orwell, Coming Up for Air

*HEDGEROWS,*
*WINDBREAKS,*
*RAILROAD EMBANK-*
*MENTS, AND*
*HIGHWAY MARGINS*

Not all of man's interactions with nature have been senseless or destructive. Upon occasion people have intentionally or accidentally reshuffled and rearranged the elements of natural communities, making use of evolved relationships between species, and have come up with stable new communities, well suited to coexist with man. Such communities, in a sense man-made as well as man-maintained, can provide some of the values of the original, free-living wildlife of a region.

One of the best examples of a man-dependent community of great beauty and of great ecologic and economic value is the English hedgerow, which was described by Charles S. Elton (1) as "the last really big remaining nature reserve we have in Britain, except for the wild moors and lakes of our northern mountains and the seas around us." These hedges, unlike the American imitation, are not rows of trimmed shrubs of a single species used to delineate the margins of suburban lots. Rather they are complex mixtures of trees, shrubs, flowering and simple plants, small mammals, song birds, and a host of invertebrates. They run along country roads and lanes, border fields, and occasionally extend into urban areas. To many people, they are the essence of England, the most memorable and distinctive feature of its countryside, although they are a relatively recent addition, largely coming into being since the time of Shakespeare. Karel Čapek (2), the great Czech author, wrote in *Letters from England*: "I have been down in Surrey, and up in Essex; I have wandered along roads lined with quickset hedges, sheer quickset hedges which make England the real England, for they enclose, but do not oppress. . . ."

In addition to the aesthetic value of the hedges, they make other contributions to the quality of English life. Hedgerows serve as a reservoir for the vanishing fauna of England, and they preserve plant species that would otherwise have disappeared, to the detriment of local ecosystems. According to Elton, one-fifth of Britain's homegrown timber comes from hedges; they act as windbreaks, thus retarding evaporation from fields, and they provide shady areas for domestic animals and for hikers. Elton also points out that hedges are a reservoir for spiders and other natural enemies of insects and mites that prey on crops. But mainly they are a joy to walk along for anybody who belongs on earth.

In the United States, the closest approximation to English hedgerows is the windbreaks that have been planted in the plains states since the dust storms of the 1930s. Under the aegis of the Forest Service's Shelterbelt Program, more than 18,000 miles of windbreaks were started between 1934 and 1941. These tree belts soon acquire a characteristic associated flora, which, in turn, provides a habitat for small animals.

*Fig. 7-1   Hedgerows on minor road from Samford Spinney to Ward Bridge, South Devon, England. (Douglas P. Wilson)*

Railroad embankments have always been a rich source of wild-flowers and a haven for rare plant species. Aldo Leopold (6) wrote in *A Sand County Almanac*: "The outstanding conservator of the prairie flora, ironically enough, knows little and cares less about such frivolities: it is the railroad with its fenced right-of-way. Many of these railroad fences were erected before the prairie had been plowed. Within these linear reservations, oblivious of cinders, soot, and annual clean-up fires, the prairie flora still splashes its calendar of colors, from pink shooting star in May to blue aster in October." Many railroads now spray herbicides to keep plants from overgrowing the tracks. From the point of view of the ecologist, mechanical cutting confined to the immediate strip along the tracks would be better, even though it may be somewhat more expensive.

Superhighways in the United States have traditionally been land-scaped with showy trees or planted with grass; but highway architects are beginning to learn how to encourage the more desirable elements of the local wildlife to become established along highway borders. Components of early successional stages grow best on the exposed soils along road shoulders; these include (in the eastern United States) pine, yellow poplar, sweet gum, tulip, and birch. The small residents of these communities, such as rabbits and birds, may occasionally be killed by cars, but are rarely dangerous to traffic. Unusual problems are encountered in the maintenance of roadside communities; for example, trees, grasses, and legumes must, in the north, be selected for resistance to the effects of salts (NaCl, CaCl₂) spread to combat ice during wintertime. Such complications are generally trivial, however, and the extra trouble is a small price to pay for the absence of billboards and of concrete dyed to look like grass.

*ARTIFICIAL REEFS*   Most of the great commercial fisheries of the world are located in the colder oceans, where currents upwelling from the benthos recycle mineral nutrients, which are the foundation of all food chains. By contrast, the south temperate and tropical seas are frequently poor in marine life except in shallow coastal waters. Here the intricate structures of coral reefs provide a substrate for marine plants and animals and support the most elaborate natural communities to be found in the sea. Unlike the northern fisheries, which are composed of a small number of species, the reef communities contain hundreds of species of fish and a vast assortment of invertebrate and algal forms. Where there are no reefs, the warmer waters of the continental shelf region harbor a relatively sparse fish fauna.

Divers have known for many years that sunken ships attract a number of reef fishes. In Japan, for several centuries fishermen have carried this process a step further by deliberately placing rocks in the sea in order to provide a surface of attachment for kelp and other algae, and thus to supply food and shelter for fish and crayfish. The success of this technique inspired numerous studies of artificial reef communities. Since 1955 at least nine states and the Virgin Islands have sponsored or encouraged research programs to determine the best construction materials and building methods for artificial reefs. Hawaii and California have been particularly active, and on the east coast the Bureau of Sport Fisheries and Wildlife's Atlantic Marine Laboratory at Sandy Hook, New Jersey, has teams of divers and marine biologists observing artificial reefs in both temperate and tropical waters.

Artificial reefs perform two services exceedingly well: They establish good sport fishing in areas where there was none before, and they provide a constructive way of getting rid of an assortment of junk that only clutters up the environment while on land. An artificial reef in the Gulf of Mexico near Galveston, Texas, had the effect of "bringing" good fishing grounds 16 miles closer to the city. In less than 60 days after the reef was made, red snapper, grouper, and sand trout took up residence in the damaged concrete pipe sections that formed the reef. Alabama, in studying its man-made reefs in the Gulf has found that not only do individual red snappers become permanent residents of the artificial reefs, but also that they attain a greater average size than inhabitants of near-by, natural formations.

Materials used in reef construction include such unlovely items as old automobile tires, chipped building blocks, worn-out ships, broken or damaged concrete pipe, empty oyster shells, old wooden streetcars, building rubble, and stripped used-car bodies. Special concrete "fish houses" seem to be no more attractive to fish than a properly made reef built out of junk. The reefs must be located on a fairly firm bottom and in water sufficiently shallow to transmit light for photosynthesis. Light-weight items should be strung together by cable. The reef components should preferably be of varying size and arranged in such a way as to provide crevices and deep passageways for all sizes of fish. High-profile

*Fig. 7-2  Kelp bass swimming inside a car only a few hours after it was "planted" in an artificial reef near San Diego, Cal. A diver from the state Fish and Game Department takes notes. (Gene Daniels, Black Star)*

reefs are better than low ones. The reef should be accurately charted and provided with buoy markers. When periodic biological observations of the reef community are planned, the site should be studied for at least a year before the reef is laid down. Permits for artificial reef construction in the United States coastal waters are issued by the Army Corps of Engineers (3).

It is difficult to prove that artificial reefs "make" more fish rather than serve as a gathering point for fish that would otherwise be diffusely scattered. Nevertheless, since artificial reefs do cause an increase in primary productivity because of their attached algae, it seems likely that some associated fish populations must increase in size. Regardless of which alternative is true in any particular case, these analogues of natural communities are likely to become increasingly important in future years, especially as other human activities — pollution, dredging, filling, overfishing, and similar depredations — begin to threaten the supply of marine fish.

### NATURE IN THE CITY

". . . in Babylon [the United States] there is not really a scarcity of goods, and there is, objectively, no real reason why there can't be people's parks, because the land is available and the wherewithal to build such parks is there in abundance. . . . These two questions [the Breakfast for Children Program of Oakland and the People's Park of Berkeley] pose the basic problem that radicals have to deal with in Babylon; ultimately, they both pose precisely the same question. It is only because they start from such divergent sources that they give the appearance of being worlds apart. One springs from needs that are obvious and basic, and people can relate to them on that basis, while the other springs from an area that we are not accustomed to looking upon as basic to survival. People can readily relate to the need to eat breakfast, but it is possible that they cannot see the need for a park."

Eldridge Cleaver, *On Meeting the Needs of the People* (7)

All large cities contain a surprising amount of wildlife, but with a few notable exceptions it is not well integrated into any complex community. Books have been written about the flora and fauna of metropolitan London, Paris, San Francisco, and New York, and sightings of wild animals are common. Although the giant alligators and caimen of New York's sewer system are mythical, the author is personally acquainted with one 30–40 pound snapping turtle that lives secretly, and presumably happily, within walking distance of the State House in a major United States city. The wolves, mountain lions, bears, and salmon that were part of the Manhattan ecosystem prior to its purchase by the Dutch in 1624 are gone, but the red fox, opposum (a new resident), flying squirrel, gray squirrel, muskrat, raccoon, several species of bats, and a host of birds remain (4).

The most successful nondomesticated species in the city are those whose niches in the wild pre-adapted them behaviorally and physically for life in the human community. These include plants like *Ailanthus* (tree-of-heaven), an introduced species from China, which is an early successional colonizer of disrupted soils and which is tolerant of air pollution. Also included are the Norway rat, cockroaches, the rock dove or common pigeon, and the house sparrow. The large size of the urban niche and the paucity of predators have most likely made these animals far more common than they ever were in prehistoric times.

Rats and cockroaches are hardly a good advertisement for the desirability of wildlife (although to millions of ghetto dwellers they represent "nature"); to find a pleasant analogue of a natural community, one must turn away from the creatures that have found a place in the crannies of the human community, and look at the city park. Except in those cases where an unspoiled "environmental corridor" has been allowed to penetrate into the inner city, city parks are a highly artificial community. This is not an implied value judgment; city parks are deemed successful not in the extent to which they duplicate nature, but in the extent to which they promote an interface where the urban population can come in contact with some selected salutary features of the natural world. As Jane Jacobs (5) has pointed out in *The Death and Life of Great American Cities*, open space in the city is not automatically a good thing; a park and the human community around it must be planned and modified with each other in mind: "City parks are not abstractions, or automatic repositories of virtue or uplift, any more than sidewalks are abstractions. They mean nothing [when] divorced from their practical, tangible uses, and hence they mean nothing [when] divorced from the tangible effects on them—for good or for ill—of the city districts and uses touching them." The ideal city park is one in which the biological needs of trees, shrubs, birds, and other creatures have been satisfied in a way compatible with a maximum diversity of human use. It is difficult to imagine a more challenging problem in wildlife management.

• • •

As the human population continues to increase we will turn increasingly for recreation and food to analogues and models of natural communities. In so doing, it is frighteningly easy to forget the real thing—human beings have an extraordinary ability to adapt to inferior environmental conditions. But submerged tires are not the same as a coral reef, and Central Park is not a wilderness area. It would be folly to base all land policy on the doctrine of efficiency; things that have no "use"—like wilderness—may yet have great value. The defect in the

Fig. 7-3 Ailanthus
(tree-of-heaven) grow-
ing in Manhattan.
(Holt photo by John
King)

Fig. 7-4 "The Ram-
ble," Central Park,
New York City (look-
ing westward). (Holt
photo by John King)

systems analysis, cost-benefit approach to complex issues like the fate of natural communities is that we cannot analyze all significant variables; nor do we really know what our future needs and hence our future priorities will be. Under these circumstances a dual program of preserving some natural communities in all their diversity and adapting others to meet current requirements is the only policy that makes sense now and which maximizes the alternatives available to our descendants.

## FURTHER READING

Bardach, John E., "Aquaculture." *Science 161*, 1098, 1968.

Bennett, George W. *Management of Artificial Lakes and Ponds*. New York: Reinhold, 1962.

Bureau of Sport Fisheries and Wildlife (U.S. Department of the Interior), *Man and Nature in the City*. Washington, D.C.: Government Printing Office, 1968.

Geertz, Clifford, *Agricultural Involution: The Processes of Ecological Change in Indonesia*. Berkeley: University of California Press, 1968.

Kieran, John, *A Natural History of New York City*. Boston: Houghton Mifflin, 1959.

## REFERENCES

1. Elton, Charles S., *The Ecology of Invasions by Animals and Plants* (Methuen, London, 1958), 155.
2. Čapek, Karel, *Letters From England* (Geoffrey Bles, London, 1925).
3. Unger, Iris, *Artificial Reefs—a Review*, adapted by E. C. Bolster from a senior thesis for the Department of Conservation of Natural Resources, Barnard College, Columbia University (American Littoral Society Special Publication No. 4, Highlands, New Jersey, 1966).
4. Arbib, R. S., Jr., *et al.*, *Enjoying Birds Around New York City* (Houghton Mifflin, Boston, 1966). Bull, John, *Birds of the New York Area* (Harper & Row, New York, 1964). Rublowsky, John, *Nature in the City* (Basic Books, New York, 1967).
5. Jacobs, Jane, *The Death and Life of Great American Cities* (Vintage, New York, 1961), 111.
6. Leopold, Aldo, *A Sand County Almanac* (Oxford, New York, 1966), 48.
7. Cleaver, Eldridge, *Ramparts 8* (3), 34 (1969).

# The Preservation of Species

***INFORMATION*** There are so many
***AND DECISIONS*** local populations of
specific kinds of animals and plants going
out of existence in our time that not all can
be saved. Conservation resources are
strained everywhere, and politicians and
philanthropists, whose continued support is
needed, soon tire of perpetual alarms. In
biblical days, species conservation evidently had a high priority. Noah was instructed: "And of every living thing of all
flesh, two of every sort shalt thou bring into
the ark, to keep them alive with thee; they
shall be male and female" (*Genesis*, 6:19).
Today, however, there is no ark, and conservationists must decide which threatened
populations they will try to preserve and
which they must of necessity leave to their

fate. Two kinds of biological information are needed in order to make these conservation decisions. It is necessary to know what fraction of the total gene pool is threatened, and it is essential to be familiar with the behavior and natural history of the species.

In their discussion of the endangered fishes of the southwestern United States (see Chapter 4), Minckley and Deacon (*1*) state that the inclusion in an endangered species list of "peripheral" species ("those represented in a given state or county by an isolated or remnant population peripheral to the main body of the gene pool") "seems unwarranted." On the other hand, when small, isolated populations constitute the majority or entirety of a gene pool, as in the case of many of the native fishes of the Southwest, there is justification for acting to conserve them.* If these species are inconspicuous and of no obvious economic significance, it is probably best to group them in some category that has meaning to the layman — such as "Arizona's endangered desert fish" — rather than to try to enlist public support for them species by species. Finally, there can be no set rules for making conservation decisions in difficult, borderline situations involving races or subspecies, as for example, the case of the red wolf and coyote (see Chapter 4). Here, each case should be argued on its own merits.

Some species are far more difficult to protect than others because they are forced by their unique behavior and physiology to occupy some inflexible niche that is particularly vulnerable to the activities of man. The ivory-billed woodpecker is an especially good example of this kind of species. The ivory-bill (*Campephilus principalis*), the largest woodpecker in North America and second largest in the world, formerly inhabited swampy and low-lying forests throughout the southeastern United States. James T. Tanner (*2*), author of the best modern account of the bird, has written: "Its large size, striking coloration, ivory-white bill, and curious voice have impressed nearly everyone who has seen it . . . and I, myself, have been impressed by the bird's striking and graceful appearance and the energy and strength of its actions and attitudes." From the early days of this country the ivory-bill has been considered one of the most spectacular of American animals, numerous articles have been written about it, and conservationists have maintained an interest in it; yet for all of this, its decline has been steady. The last fully authenticated sighting of an ivory-bill in the United States was in northern Florida in 1950; a dozen or more individuals of a slightly smaller race survive in the wildest mountain forests of Oriente Province, Cuba.

There is little doubt that the ivory-bill, never a common bird, fell victim to its own specialized habitat requirements. Although it inhabits

---

*It is important to preserve peripheral species when they are part of an isolated and locally unusual community whose scientific, educational, and aesthetic value is high. This holds true even though the peripheral species may be common somewhere else in the world.

*Fig. 8-1    Male ivory-billed woodpecker returning to its nest to relieve the female, Singer Tract, La., April, 1935. (A. A. Allen, National Audubon Society)*

different kinds of forests containing a variety of tree species, all of these forests have one thing in common: They have virgin timber with old trees. The ivory-bill feeds on wood-boring insects that invade large dead trees — young, growing trees do not harbor such insects. Because of these food needs, ivory-bills are far-ranging, seeking out the occasional suitable tree among its healthy neighbors, or looking for local patches of forest where fire or flood has recently killed a large number of trees in one place. The birds rarely come near the ground and therefore do not normally take advantage of insects that may inhabit logging debris. Tanner estimates that a minimum of $2\frac{1}{2}$–3 square miles of prime, untouched habitat is needed to support one pair of ivory-bills.

Throughout the twentieth century there has been a steady loss of virgin forest in the Southeast as lumber companies have turned one area after another into comparatively sterile, single-species tree farms or have abandoned the clear-cut land for cultivation or disuse. By the mid-1930s the best forest that Tanner could find with a reasonable ivory-bill population, and suitable for conservation efforts, was the giant Singer Tract in Madison Parish, Louisiana, which also contained wolves, panthers, and black bears. Still, despite its obvious suitability as a National Wildlife Refuge, the Singer Tract was completely and recklessly lumbered within a few short years of the publication of Tanner's book.

What kind of conservation effort would be needed now to save the ivory-bill, should remnant populations be uncovered in the United States?* Although the bird is adapted to exist at very low population densities, there would have to be enough individuals left to preserve a semblance of genetic variety. Twenty-five pairs would probably be an absolute minimum figure. This, in turn, would represent a minimum land commitment of 75 contiguous square miles of mature, lowlands forest, with a surrounding buffer zone of intermediate-quality habitat. Management techniques such as selective cutting of healthy timber and deliberate killing of certain trees in the buffer zone might increase the carrying capacity of the reserve. The entire tract would have to be fully patrolled for poachers. But even if all these provisions could be satisfied, few biologists would be willing to predict the ivory-bill's chances of survival. The probability of allocation of public funds for an ivory-bill wilderness region would thus seem very small, unless other independent reasons for protection of the area could be cited.

It would be hard to find an example of an animal more difficult to protect than the ivory-billed woodpecker, but the conservation literature is filled with accounts of other species whose behavior creates similar problems for conservationists.† Clearly, it is difficult to formulate a plan of protection for any creature unless its natural history is known and its environmental niche has been well characterized.

Other kinds of species characteristics may complicate conservation efforts. If a plant or animal is considered injurious or dangerous to man, there is usually an effort made to eradicate it, regardless of its aesthetic, ecological, or historical value and regardless of its present real impact on the human community. If economic or other interests stand to benefit indirectly from the eradication, the anticonservation pressures may be strong. Elton (5) reports that automobile manufacturers in England advocate the destruction of hedges and that one chemical herbicide company, lobbying for the spraying of roadside meadows, included

---

*In recent years there have been unconfirmed reports of sightings of ivory-bills from both Texas and Florida, but the likelihood of its survival is not great.

†One animal that might be even harder to manage on reserves than the ivory-bill is the Siberian tiger. Dr. F. E. Warburton (personal communication) estimates that a single pair of Siberian tigers, with cubs, needs at least 500 square miles of woodland to meet daily food requirements.

the wild rose in its list of weeds to be eliminated (the Nature Conservancy thought differently).

Occasionally an otherwise valuable wild animal does pose a real threat to man. On the morning of August 13, 1967, within a matter of several hours, two 19-year-old girls camping in different areas of Glacier National Park were killed by grizzly bears. Although there have been previous attacks by bears (mostly by the more common black bears), both in and out of national parks, this grim incident focused attention on the problem. No one will ever know why the first two human killings by grizzly bears in the long history of Glacier National Park took place on the same day; there are, of course, numerous theories. Certainly the nightly feeding of bears at the Granite Park Chalet, the lack of proper garbage incineration facilities, and the building of a campground in the middle of a traditional grizzly foraging area did not help create an environment in which humans and bears could mix safely (3).

Park officials and conservationists are now faced with the need to make a decision about the future management of grizzly bears. One alternative is extermination, at least in areas visited by human beings. Most rational and informed people reject this idea. After the Glacier Park incidents, some angry park visitors demanded to know whether the park was being run for people or for bears—a legitimate question, but double-edged when so many thousands of people visit Glacier Park in order to have the privilege of seeing dangerous wild animals in the setting of their native mountains.

Conflicts between people and grizzlies can be prevented if proper species management techniques are employed. The major principle of such management is to avoid letting bear and human territories overlap when there is likely to be heavy use by either side. The government agencies that administer our parks and forests have been guilty of near criminal ineptitude in failing to come to grips with this elementary safety requirement. Instead of installing incinerators that are capable of making garbage unpalatable to bears, the personnel of national parks and monuments are instructed to capture persistent garbage-seeking bears and transport them elsewhere. Most return promptly, or others take their place. One national monument in Alaska attracts tourists with a brochure that features a photograph of ten brown bears fishing for salmon in a river, thus forcing the overworked rangers to devote much time and effort to keeping new visitors away from this dangerous spot (which is also outside park boundaries). A safe observation post equipped with wide-field telescopes would eliminate much of the risk in this case. The Park Service has the right to demand that tourists who wish to use remote trails and campsites meet some minimum standard of fitness and experience. This criterion should be enforced. The new policy (adopted after the Glacier National Park killings) of closing any trail or campsite where there has been a bear incident, pending investigation by ranger-naturalists, is sensible and should not be relaxed.

The Forest Service of the Department of Agriculture, in its insistence on "multiple use," is in the process of needlessly generating some of the same kinds of species conservation problems in the national forests that are now encountered in the national parks. Admiralty Island, in Alaska's Tongass National Forest, is approximately the size of Yellowstone National Park and is probably the richest wilderness area left in North America. It contains 67 streams used by all five species of Pacific salmon and four kinds of trout. There are high densities of mink, otter, beaver, marten, waterfowl, and many other wild animals. There are more bald eagles than in all other 49 states combined. And there are 800–1000 grizzly (brown) bears. There are also at least 265,000 acres of good commercial timber land, much of which has been leased for clear-cut logging, in the best "multiple use" (see Chapter 6) tradition.

According to reports from visitors to Admiralty, logging operations have already resulted in erosion along stream banks, with the loss of salmon runs. Garbage is allegedly sprinkled along logging roads, and illegal hunting of grizzly bears is flourishing. In the light of these accusa-

*Fig. 8-2    Alaskan brown bear (grizzly) with salmon. (Leonard Lee Rue, National Audubon Society)*

tions, the reply of the Forest Service that only one-third of the island will be logged and that the forest renewal cycle is only 100 years is not convincing.

The one-third of the island that will be logged contains the best forests. Moreover, although the spruce may grow back in 100 years, the contracts negotiated with the lumber companies call for completion of cutting in 50 years or less. In other words, either the lumber firms will cease their Admiralty operations in 50 years or, more likely, they will exert pressure to be allowed to cut in adjacent areas that are now considered commercially unprofitable.

The grizzly bear is not a species that can tolerate multiple use (nor, in this case, is the bald eagle, which does not nest in saplings, or the salmon, which will not spawn in silt-polluted waters). The Forest Service regulations to protect grizzlies and other wildlife on Admiralty, however stringent and well-meaning, are often unenforceable. As the island is exposed to more and more people its bear population will dwindle; in the process there may be more incidents like the ones in Glacier National Park. Priority, not multiple use, is what the grizzly needs. The value, to man, of knowing that we have enough humanity left to save a few small places for other creatures cannot be translated into economic terms. It has been argued that hunting* on Admiralty would bring more revenue to the state than the pulpwood operations, some of which are foreign-owned. In addition to being economically dubious, this kind of conservation argument is unwise. Short-term economics almost always favor exploitation. The bears of Admiralty Island will be preserved only if the Forest Service decides that in this specific case a population of undisturbed grizzlies is more important to the people of the United States than another commercial timber tract. If they decide otherwise, the euphemism of "multiple use" will fool only the uninformed.

**THE ROLE OF ZOOS**  As open space vanishes and habitats disap-
**AND COMMERCIAL**  pear, zoos have been increasingly called
**ANIMAL FARMS**  upon to preserve homeless species that will
breed in captivity. Special facilities, like the
Patuxent National Wildlife Center in Maryland, have research programs that are designed to promote the breeding of endangered species and their ultimate reintroduction to their native habitat. Such programs are only now beginning, but some pilot studies already appear promising.

The masked bobwhite quail (*Colinus viginianus ridgwayi*) was formerly a resident of the southwestern tall grass and mesquite plains

---

*Well-regulated hunting by parties on foot would probably not deplete any of the island's big game populations.

from Sonora, Mexico, to southern Arizona east of the Baboquivari Mountains. As overgrazing by domestic cattle destroyed its habitat, its range contracted, and it is now found only in a small area of southern Sonora. An early attempt to establish the quail on a 640-acre, seeded reserve west of Tucson met with limited success because of vandalism and winter losses. Two other preservation efforts may be more promising. In one, interested parties from Arizona and Mexico have set aside land and provided a cattle fence to protect a remnant quail population in Sonora. Also, in anticipation that a suitable habitat could be found and maintained in Arizona, a breeding colony of masked quail was started at the Patuxent center. At the request of Senator Mundt of South Dakota, Seymour and James Levy of Tucson provided four pairs of birds, which have now produced a great many offspring that are destined for return to their proper habitat. These quail are the first of a series of native American species to be released in a suitably protected part of their original range after restoration of safe population levels at Patuxent.

Even when species can be bred in captivity, there may be unexpected problems associated with their release, particularly when the captive population is small and the period of captivity extends over several generations of the animal or plant species. Inbreeding in a small population usually increases the frequency of homozygosity of harmful recessive alleles. When these cause lethal or serious alterations of phenotype, the affected individual will be removed from the breeding pool; but when the phenotypic change is small, it may not reduce reproductive fitness in the supportive and nonselective environment of a zoo. The result is a population less well equipped to deal with the vicissitudes of a wild existence after release. Still more dangerous is the possibility that the complex behavioral adaptations appropriate to the wild may disappear through genetic change combined with lack of selective pressure in zoos. Cave animals frequently show a loss or reduction of eyes and pigment, not necessarily because these features would be disadvantageous in caves but because random, normally deleterious mutations that affect the pigment and eye-forming systems go unchallenged by natural selection. This loss of genetically maintained pattern or structure in the absence of reinforcing feedback is roughly analogous to the increase in entropy (energy unavailable for work) that is seen in isolated physical systems. One can imagine, for example, a small population of a species of captive migratory bird losing its capacity or motivation to migrate after several generations in cages. This tendency might be greatly accelerated if it were advantageous to a caged bird not to become restless in the normal way at migration time.

Another genetic hazard of "zoo banks," different from the two mentioned in the preceding paragraph, is the reduction of genetic variability associated with small, inbred populations. One great advantage of the diploid state is that rare recessives can "hide" in genotypes, ready to become more common through selection should an environmental change favor the phenotype that they represent. When homozygosity increases, this advantage disappears. Economic botanists have long pointed out that highly inbred plants are often less resistant to epidemic disease than are their more variable wild forebears. [For an explanation of the genetic terminology and concepts used in this section, see Levine (6)].

Despite these considerations, it appears that unless there is deliberate selection for some trait, or unless there is consistent brother-sister mating in zoo populations, considerable genetic variability is maintained and genetic change is slow. The Syrian hamsters kept as pets in the United States are derived from a single pair, yet they show great variability in size and coat color. Mutation has evidently restored a great deal of variation that may have been lost. More to the point is the case of the European bison (*Bison bonasus*), whose last wild population was destroyed in Poland's Bialowieza Forest during World War I. Subsequently re-established from a very small number of captive individuals, the Bialowieza herd is thriving, and breeding is proceeding normally. Although there is no way of preventing subtle behavioral and physiological alterations in captive populations, the occurrence and significance of these theoretical results of changes in gene frequencies remain to be tested. The alternative to "zoo bank" preservation of remnant populations — that is, no preservation at all — will certainly be worse in the great majority of cases.

There is no point in returning a zoo-maintained population to its former habitat unless that habitat has been placed under protection in the interim. If this proves impossible, there is always the option of establishing the population in a suitable environment outside its original range. Generally this is a bad idea (see Chapter 2); the majority of exotic introductions are probably harmful. Nevertheless, under certain conditions they can be considered if:

1. The exotic species has a low reproductive potential or if it is a big game species that could be easily controlled or removed by hunting, if necessary.

2. The species usually maintains a low population density and/or has a relatively minor impact on its ecosystem.

3. There are no obvious competitor species native to the area of introduction.

4. The area of introduction already has a relatively impoverished flora and fauna.

Not all these conditions need be satisfied; introductions are largely a matter of biological common sense. Few could object, for example, to an attempt to save the tiny, attractive, and endangered American bog turtle (*Clemmys muhlenbergi*) by trying to establish it in bogs of southern Ireland, but no one in his right mind would protect the endangered brown hyena (*Hyaena brunnea*) by releasing it in New Mexico.

Commercial wild-animal farms have the capability of relieving much of the economic pressure on rare species, *provided they can supply their animal products more cheaply than the exploiters of wild populations are able to do*. This has happened with the ostrich, the mink, and others; it could help the alligator, the vicuña, and even some of the spotted cats. Animal farming, however, is a risky and difficult operation. At best, as with domestic animals like cows and chickens, there is the possibility of epidemic disease and other disasters. With wild animals there are additional complications related to peculiarities in their behavior, nutrition, and life cycle.

**Case History — The Green Turtle**   Of all the wild animals that are currently being commercially farmed, perhaps the most difficult to raise are sea turtles. Of the various kinds of sea turtle, the green, or "soup," turtle (*Chelonia mydas*) is the most valuable to man. An adult green turtle weighing 150–400 pounds, provides a large quantity of edible meat, eggs in the case of females, leather for shoes and handbags, calipee (cartilage) for clear turtle soup, fat for oil, and a shell for the tourist trade. However, its potential value to man is far greater than the profit now being realized. There are vast underwater beds of turtle grass and related plants in the shallow parts of tropical oceans, but as Dr. John Randall (4) has claimed: "At the present time, the utilization of the sea grasses as food by animals, particularly those of economic importance to man, is negligible." The green turtle and the manatee (sea cow) are the only large, edible animals that feed on these grasses, but the manatee, in addition to being more coastal in its distribution, has a low reproductive potential. This leaves the green turtle as the *only* grazing animal of economic importance that can take advantage of the earth's underwater "grasslands." Before discussing some of the problems of turtle farming, both the life cycle and pattern of exploitation will be described.

Green turtles are strictly marine in nature; only the females leave the water, briefly, at nesting time. The hatchlings, born on tropical beaches, emerge from their nests at night, scramble to the ocean, and disappear in the surf. Until they reach an age of approximately 6 months or more, their whereabouts and habits are unknown. Since tagging of adults has revealed that green turtle nesting beaches and feeding grounds are usually widely separated (by as much as 1500 miles), we assume that during their first months, the young turtles are moving toward the areas that will be their feeding grounds, most likely carried passively by the currents. In captivity, young green turtles are carnivorous for the first 6–8 months; we can therefore guess that their food source while floating on the surface of the open sea is small invertebrates like the ones associated with the large, floating patches of sargassum seaweed. When the turtles arrive at their shallow-water feeding grounds, they become herbivorous and begin to eat underwater turtle grass (*Thalassia*). It is at this point that they begin to achieve the bulk of their weight and size.

After reaching maturity, in 5–7 years, both males and females return to their birthplace to mate and nest. The females lay approximately 100 eggs at 12-day intervals four or five times during a summer. They then swim back to their feeding grounds (the males leave earlier). This cycle is repeated at 2- or 3-year intervals. It is not known how long green turtles live; if they are like their distant relatives, the giant land tortoises, they may live more than 100 years. Once they are full-grown, only sharks are likely to injure them; such injuries are probably not common.

Green turtles are easily overexploited because of their habit of congregating at specific beaches to nest. Although widely dispersed at different feeding grounds, all green turtles of the western Caribbean and Gulf of Mexico, for example, return to one beach, Tortuguero, Costa Rica, at breeding time. Similarly, nearly all green turtles that feed in coastal waters off the bulge of Brazil are born and nest at Ascension Island in the mid-Atlantic. At the great majority of nesting beaches there is no protection for the species, and the rapidly expanding populations of coastal peoples take virtually all the eggs. (A few turtle beaches, such as Tortuguero, are now partially protected — most are not.) The nesting females are also killed, sometimes for their meat, but more often for their valuable and easily portable calipee and hide. Since the nesting process lasts more than an hour, and since sea turtles leave an enormous track in the sand, a few poachers on a beach at night can easily find and kill every turtle that comes out of the sea to nest. But there is little more safety for the turtles in the water. Harpooners in small boats are active near the nesting beaches, and if a turtle manages to return to its feeding ground, fishermen with nets await it there. During the past 400 years the green turtle populations of the warmer oceans have been reduced from tens of millions to a few thousand individuals.

The two main problems facing a commercial turtle farmer can be deduced from a knowledge of the life history of *Chelonia*. During their early, carnivorous phase the small green turtles can be fed ground or chopped fish (inexpensive "trash fish" species can be used) or an assortment of commercial animal foods made from animal products. When the turtles weigh several pounds, after 6–8 months of age, they are willing to eat vegetable food. Although they will continue to eat ground fish indefinitely, it is totally uneconomical to raise livestock on animal products. The easiest way to provide vegetable food is to fence a sizable, shallow water area that contains a good stand of turtle grass. This, in turn, creates additional problems. Underwater fencing is expensive, difficult to maintain, and easily damaged by storms. Sea turtles kept in this kind of enclosure are likely, sooner or later, to escape. If an enclosed bay is fenced across a narrow neck, the fence acquires a heavy growth of seaweed that impedes the tidal flow necessary to keep the bay water (with its dense animal population) clean and also necessary to prevent the area from filling up with silt washed off the land by rain. Furthermore, a few thousand rapidly growing green turtles will soon denude even a moderately large area of its turtle grass. Land-grown vegetable foods could be used, and this would obviate the necessity of having unusually large pens. However, it is not known whether any nutritionally acceptable crop could be grown in the sandy, salty soils found near most tropi-

*Fig. 8-3  Mr. Samuel Nixon, game warden, holding a three-year-old, 60 pound green turtle raised at the Caribbean Conservation Corporation's experimental turtle farm, Great Inagua, Bahamas. Turtles are still sexually immature at this age. (David W. Ehrenfeld)*

cal places that would be otherwise suitable for raising green turtles. Machines to harvest and collect turtle grass are another possibility now in the developmental stage.

The second problem that must be solved is the matter of replenishing the supply of young turtles. No existing rookery can tolerate the annual loss of thousands of eggs or hatchlings for commercial farms. It has been argued that since the natural mortality of the tiny hatchlings must approach 99 percent, the eggs taken can be "replaced" by the release of a few hundred, pen-raised yearlings a year later. In a sense this is true, but since there is no evidence that these herbivorous yearlings are motivated or physiologically equipped to travel safely to the feeding grounds a year late, nor is there evidence that they are still capable of "learning" the route if necessary, these released turtles cannot be considered an acceptable substitute for the thousands that were taken.

Of course it is conceivable that green turtles could be bred at a turtle farm and the wild populations left alone. However, even if we avoid the still unanswered questions of whether green turtles will breed in captivity and whether the females will use the beaches provided as nesting sites, there is still an overwhelming difficulty facing the turtle farmer. He will need, at the very least, 20,000 eggs per year, the produce of approximately 50 females. Since the turtles will probably nest only every 2 or 3 years, this means a total of nearly 150 females will have to be kept on hand. Another 25–50 adult males will be required. In other words, any turtle farmer who does not intend to parasitize natural nesting grounds will have to keep and maintain more than 60,000 lbs of adult sea turtles. Clearly, the only easy solution to this problem (and a possible solution to the problem of feeding the young turtles) is to turn them loose on turtle grass flats near the farm and hope that they will stay. (Marked turtles escaping from commercial pens in Key West, Florida, have been known to return to their own Nicaraguan feeding grounds.) If this is done, new difficulties will be encountered. Will the turtles nest on nearby beaches? How can the turtles and nests be protected from poachers? How can the young turtles be harvested economically?

When we add to everything already mentioned the usual hazards of disease, egg and infant mortality, hurricanes, and other dangers, the labors of Hercules seem easy in comparison to turtle farming. However, turtle farming may yet have some promise if the young-adults and adults can be induced to stay and eventually to breed near the farm without being penned, and if the projects can free themselves from dependence on natural nesting grounds. Even if turtle farms fail commercially, they may still prove useful on a government- or foundation-subsidized basis as a way of circumventing the usual high hatchling mortality associated with the first 6 months of life in the wild. In this case the turtle farm would be increasing the world population of green turtles by releasing healthy, 6-month-old animals in large numbers, but would not necessarily be able to harvest enough adults to pay for operations during the first one or two decades.

The problem of green turtle conservation is extremely complex; it involves economics, international law, national policy, local customs, and the physiology and behavior of the animal itself. Consequently, no single approach is likely to resolve the difficulty. In such a situation, one is wise to consider all the conservation alternatives. Turtle farming has been attempted by various individuals and groups for at least a half-century, with no great commercial success (although the first large-scale project with adequate financial backing did not begin until 1968). There are, however, other ways of conserving sea turtles. Between 1960 and 1968, Dr. Archie Carr (see Further Reading at the end of this chapter), director of the Caribbean Conservation Corporation, airlifted a total of several hundred thousand Costa Rican hatchlings to protected former nesting beaches in many Caribbean countries. The U.S. Navy provided an amphibious plane and crew for these operations, and the Costa Rican Government has protected part of the Tortuguero nesting beach. It is perhaps too early to tell whether nesting colonies have been re-established in any of the transplantation sites, although there has been a marked increase in young-adult green turtles seen in Florida Bay near an Everglades Park beach where Costa Rican turtles were released. In Sarawak, Professor Tom Harrisson has helped develop another kind of conservation technique: The nesting beaches there are controlled by a Turtles Board, which fully protects the females and conserves a portion of the eggs in a hatchery. Nevertheless, the Sarawak green turtle population is declining, in part because of excessive hunting of adult turtles throughout the South China Sea. At several South American nesting beaches, Dr. Peter Pritchard, with financial assistance from the World Wildlife Fund, has introduced a modified version of the egg-protection scheme employed at Sarawak. Instead of setting aside a small fraction of the eggs, nearly all are "purchased" from the natives at the nesting beach. This highly successful conservation venture not only protects the eggs, but allows the local Indian populations to be economically independent of turtle meat and eggs as a source of food. Unfortunately, egg purchasing is too costly to be continued indefinitely at any locality; it is strictly a stopgap procedure.

Turtle farming, transplantation of eggs and hatchlings, and egg protection will probably be inadequate by themselves to reverse the effects of overexploitation. International agreements will be needed to prevent the extinction of the species. Any such agreements, to be effective, will have to regulate all activities pertaining to the taking of turtles (and eggs), including fishing in international waters. A large number of governments will have to participate, and enforcement will be difficult.

**Fig. 8-4** *Turtle nesting beach, Tortuguero, Costa Rica. A solitary female green turtle returns to the sea in the early morning after a late night's nesting emergence. This beach is protected, but elsewhere the huge tracks of these ponderous creatures enable poachers to find them quickly, usually before they have had a chance to lay their eggs. (David W. Ehrenfeld)*

Enforcement, however, might be unnecessary if the provisions of the agreement could be extended to limit manufacture, distribution, and sale of turtle products, especially in the consumer nations, the United States, Great Britain, West Germany, and Japan. In the world of economically valuable but endangered species it is demand, ultimately, that is the arbiter of supply, and the relationship is always inverse.

It is probably unfair to the topic of wild-animal farming to pick an illustrative example that is so complex and problem-ridden and then to confuse the issue with mention of other kinds of conservation techniques. In fact it would have been easier to write a brief description of an ostrich farm. But the kind of conservation victory represented by ostrich farms, although real and worthwhile, is misleading because it is out of context. The context of conservation is the sum of man's activities in the world, and in the light of this context, the saving of a species by inclusion in a refuge or by propagation in a zoo or animal farm seems sadly transitory in these times. Unless conservation operates at a global level with full involvement in all aspects of the conduct of human life, it will be an anachronistic and unsuccessful endeavor. This matter is considered more fully in the final chapter.

## FURTHER READING

Carr, Archie, *So Excellent a Fishe—A Natural History of Sea Turtles.* Garden City, N.Y.: Natural History Press, 1967.

Conway, William G., "Zoos: Their Changing Roles." *Science 163*, 48, 1969.

Hediger, H., *Wild Animals in Captivity.* New York: Dover, 1964.

Leopold, Aldo, *Game Management.* New York: Scribner's, 1933.

Watt, Kenneth E. F., *Ecology and Resource Management.* New York: McGraw-Hill, 1968.

## REFERENCES

1.  Minckley, W. L., and Deacon, James E., *Science 159*, 1424 (1968).
2.  Tanner, James T., *The Ivory-billed Woodpecker* (Dover, New York, 1966).
3.  Olsen, Jack, *Sports Illustrated 30*, 36 (1969).
4.  Randall, John E., *Ecology 46*, 255 (1965).
5.  Elton, Charles S., *The Ecology of Invasions by Animals and Plants* (Methuen, London, 1958), 156.
6.  Levine, Robert P., *Genetics*, 2d ed. (Holt, Rinehart and Winston, New York, 1968).

# chapter 9

# *Conclusions*

***THE DANGERS*** Because of our extensive alteration of the physical world and our failure to conserve the communities and species that constitute our biological environment, mankind is now confronted by a number of general ecological crises, each capable of having global effects in the near future.

***The Buffer Effect*** Buffers are defined chemically as solutions of a weak acid or base and its salt, which resist the changes in hydrogen ion concentration that would ordinarily occur upon further addition of acids or bases (see Fig. 9-1). It is a characteristic of buffers that they work well in one particular portion of the pH range, but that at the extremes of this zone any further addition of hydroxyl or hydrogen ions results in rapid changes of pH, as if the buffer weren't there. All chemistry students are aware of how easy it is to shoot past the pH indicator end point during a titration, after having added scores of drops of acid or base with no great change in the color of the solution.

Certain physical and biological systems in the natural world act in a way that is roughly analogous to one property of buffer solutions. They can tolerate a reasonable amount of manipulation or abuse without showing much evidence of serious damage, but when the limits of their ability to buffer external influences is exceeded, they deteriorate rapidly. Unlike buffer solutions, however, this deterioration may be irreversible. Several examples follow.

Populations of many organisms are adapted to survive fairly large fluctuations in their number of individuals, but for some of these populations there is a critical point (see Chapter 4). When the number of individuals falls below this critical level, intraspecies relationships are markedly altered and the population decline continues to extinction.

Soils are also capable of adjusting to a wide variety of physical and biotic fluctuations. However, when bad agricultural or building practices or improper lumbering operations occur, the soil may give way. Erosion and chemical changes of soils can be self-accelerating processes, particularly in the tropics (see Chapter 2), and these changes may occur with comparative speed after several years of mismanagement.

Finally, the organic pollution of lakes offers another example of the buffer effect (see Chapter 2). Pollution with organic wastes first causes gradual eutrophication in lakes that have a large volume of water to dilute the pollutants. This is usually characterized by an increase in diatoms, algal flagellates, and bacteria, with a corresponding increase in ciliates and other zooplankton that consume these organisms. Although the species composition of the community may change, there are still many fish, invertebrates, and other organisms living in the lake. But if pollution continues or increases, there eventually comes a time when the microflora characteristic of early pollution is replaced by green algae like *Chlorella* and by blue-green algae like *Microcystis*, neither of which will support a large zooplankton population. As the zooplankton population dwindles, some kinds of fish — at the other end of the food chain — also become scarce. Meanwhile, the algae pile up against the leeward shore in rotting masses, the toxins of the blue-green algae kill farm animals, birds, and still more fish, and the deoxygenation caused by the algal decay further reduces the flora and fauna of the lake. Here, again, although pollution may have been going on for years with no gross effects, these final changes, irreversible in the course of a lifetime, often occur with drastic suddenness.

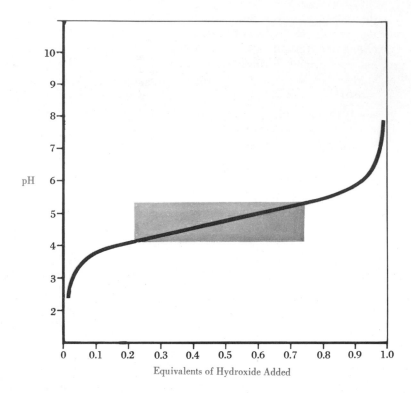

*Fig. 9-1* *Titration curve for acetic acid. An acetic acid-acetate ion solution has its maximum buffering ability when it is at a pH of 4.75. Effective buffer zone (gray area) extends from approximately pH 4.25 to pH 5.25. Note the abrupt change in pH that occurs at either end of the buffer range when hydroxyl (or hydrogen) ions are added.*

There is no way of telling with certainty how significant the buffer effect will turn out to be with respect to global environmental parameters. We do not know, for example, how the oceans, upon which we depend for food and for oxygen renewal, will respond to a continued influx of waste materials, whether there will be signs of change that will warn us to stop in time, or whether we will be lulled to catastrophe by the false promise of an infinite capacity to absorb pollutants. If the latter is a more accurate representation of the true situation, conventional pollution-monitoring systems will be of little use, and only a fundamental breakthrough in our understanding of oceanic ecosystems will enable us to predict the danger point.

**Hidden Relationships and Unforeseen Ramifications**

"Oh, a sleeping drunkard
Up in Central Park,
And a lion-hunter
In the jungle dark,
And a Chinese dentist,
And a British queen—
All fit together
In the same machine.
Nice, nice, very nice;
Nice, nice, very nice;
Nice, nice, very nice—
So many different people
In the same device."

Kurt Vonnegut, Jr., *Cat's Cradle**

In 1958, Dr. LaMont Cole (*1*) coined the word "ecosphere." By this he meant "the largest possible ecosystem: namely, the sum total of life on earth together with the global environment and the earth's total resources." His reason for inventing this word was that it describes a functional entity, a unit, whose myriad, interdependent elements, including the inorganic environment, are bound together in part by photosynthesis, respiration, and other fundamental metabolic activities of plants and animals.

In any such functional unit it is impossible to isolate and contain the effects of a major change in one of the components. Readjustments take place throughout the system, and there may be no way of knowing what these will be. Flood control in California mountains may destroy coastal plain redwood communities (see Chapter 3). On a grander scale, the continued use of combustion engines and fossil fuels by an expanding population, and the continued destruction of forests and green space may, via the "greenhouse effect," cause worldwide climatic changes and the flooding of coastal cities (see Chapter 2).

Another example of unforeseen ramifications of disturbances in ecosystems concerns the destruction of Pacific coral reefs by the sea star, *Acanthaster planci*. Dr. Richard H. Chesher (*2*) of the University of Guam has reported that, since 1967, large sections of the reefs around Guam, Palau, Truk, Rota, Johnston Island, Wake, and other islands, as well as parts of the Great Barrier Reef of Australia, have been killed by this predatory starfish. The situation is serious, for when the reef is gone, the islands lose both their fisheries and their main protection against wave erosion. Although the reasons for the sudden proliferation of starfish can only be guessed at, Chesher points out that the larvae of the starfish are normally eaten by the filter-feeding corals, resulting presumably in a natural equilibrium. But when man kills reefs by blasting and dredging, the larvae are provided with fresh, safe surfaces on which to settle. When in turn they mature, they kill adjacent reef areas, produce more successful larvae, and the population of starfish spirals out of control. (Another theory postulates the destruction of starfish predators by insecticides.)

On the positive side, the encouragement and growth of Rocky Mountain beaver populations has been found to smooth the annual fluctuations in the run-off of water to the southwestern desert below. The effects of beaver dams and ponds on stream flow are easy to comprehend, but this is a doubly exceptional example: Changes in one part of the ecosphere often have unforeseen or remote ramifications, and these are rarely as beneficial to the environment of man and nature as beaver dams. The few examples listed above are of situations we think we understand; the ones we do not recognize may prove the greater danger.

### The Irreversible Loss of Diversity

The many factors that tend to reduce the diversity of the earth's species and natural communities have been discussed throughout this book; it is the consequences of loss of diversity that concern us here. Some individuals would prefer a simpler planet. As late as 1967, an American corporation advertised that the conversion of virgin forests to tree farms was in part a public service because "most virgin forests are already doomed. They're waging a constant, losing battle against disease, insects and wildlife. . . . But when [we cut] a stand of trees, it's like gardening on a grand scale. New seedlings are planted and grown under the best possible conditions. Excess undergrowth is thinned. Protective sprays and fertilizers are applied. The result is a healthier, more abundant forest." What they did not add is that the forest, if it replaced a diverse hardwood stand, is also very monotonous, that it supports an impoverished fauna of animals and birds, that nobody knows whether it will last more than three or four cycles, and that it is suspect by many ecologists of being potentially susceptible, like the banana plantations of Central America, to uncontrollable parasitic infestations. It has, in short, all the potential hazards of any truncated, oversimplified ecosystem (see Chapter 6).

What the proponents of simplification fail to comprehend is the ominous uncertainty of their schemes. Forest ecosystems cannot be freeze-dried or stored on microfilm to be reconstituted in case of emergency. What if tree farms begin to fail in the twenty-first century, and there are no sizable natural forest communities left in some of the climatic and soil regions? The prospect of vast blighted zones choked with weeds and scarred by erosion is more than a Wellsian fantasy. In the marshes, the prairies, the deserts, and even the oceans, as well as the forests, the specter of the irrevocable loss of the diversity that stabilizes the ecosphere and makes it habitable, threatens all species, including man.

• • •

The thread that unites the three dangers enumerated above is the lack of scientific predictability of outcome that characterizes all our interactions with ecosystems. There is danger only because of our ecological ignorance. In a more restricted context, Hugh Raup (3) has given the best advice for dealing with these realities of existence: "I propose that we should plan ahead only so far as we can see with some degree of precision, and then readjust our plans at frequent intervals. We can be assured that there will never be enough facts available to give these plans any finality, and that we shall always be making judgments based upon probabilities. At every point of decision we will make use of whatever knowledge and measurement of value we can acquire, testing each for relevance to the point at issue as it relates to the frame of reference existing at the time." If we add two injunctions — (1) to conserve variety in order to preserve the options available to future generations, and (2) to place the burden of justification on those who advocate disruptive actions — we have acceptable guide lines for management of the natural amenities of our planet.

### THE SOURCES OF THE PROBLEM

When conservation programs go awry and conservation policies are blocked, it is an exercise in paranoia to search for scapegoats — there are so many of them everywhere. Yet only by identifying the sources of the problem is it possible to devise solutions. The principal causes of conservation failure are described below.

### The Economics of Perpetual Expansion

The economic success of modern nations is often judged and possibly dictated by their growth rates. When the Gross National Product goes up a little, economists fidget and smile reassuringly, but when it goes up more, they laugh. The Gross National Product is the monetary value of goods and services produced by a country in one year. If it goes up, that usually means more goods produced or more services rendered, or both. This in turn means an increase in the consumption of raw materials or, in some cases, an increase in the population (that provides and accepts services), or both. In Communist countries there are similar measures of economic health that are based on the value of goods and services produced.

How long can economic expansion continue, and is there any theoretical limit to economic growth? Obviously, the response will vary for different countries, but in general the answers seem to be: Economic expansion cannot continue indefinitely if it happens in the traditional way, and it will be limited by exhaustion of mineral resources or destruction of the environment (including destruction by war or war production)—whichever comes first. Of these two limiting factors, the first is at least approachable.

Dr. Walter R. Hibbard, Jr. (4), formerly of the U.S. Bureau of Mines, has warned: "The needed materials which can be recovered by known methods at reasonable cost from the earth's crust are limited, whereas their rates of exploitation and use obviously are not. This situation cannot continue." It is true that we have not yet started to mine our wastes, but even if we are able to recover large quantities of iron from assorted scrap, some metals, such as silver and mercury, are largely nonreclaimable. One-third of our silver, for example, is used (and therefore lost) in the manufacture of photographic films and papers. Nevertheless, it does seem that by economies and substitutions combined with new prospecting and mining techniques we ought to be able to postpone the inevitable raw materials crisis at least until the end of the twentieth century.

In the case of environmental destruction, the period of grace seems shorter and the prospects more gloomy. Economic expansion is too closely linked to the growth of population and technology. The only way man can avoid wrecking his environment is to find out how many people and machines the earth can support in something approaching an equilibrium condition, and then limit their numbers to these calculated levels. But it is entirely possible that this would mean, even now, a gradual reduction in the earth's population and a cutback in certain industries. Clearly, until we can uncouple the concept (and reality) of economic health from the process of economic expansion, until we can disassociate "progress" from "growth," there will be no effective conservation.

*Local Political Systems and Practices*　Today, many political decisions affecting conservation interests are made at the levels of municipal, county, or state governments; these decisions involve zoning regulations, local pollution control ordinances, park policies, waste disposal, and similar actions. It is, however, at the local level that government seems most inadequate and incompetent to deal with conservation problems. Too often the quality of local government is poor, with cumbersome, archaic charters, conflicting and inadequate laws, uncertain financial and political ties with higher governmental agencies, and a kaleidoscopic procession of uneducated, lackluster officials often drawn from the most exploitative segment of society and heavily in debt for campaign expenses. Problems are judged only according to the business ethic—if no orthodox solution is forthcoming, decisions are postponed until the time of the next administration. The disposition of land is decided by realtors; the regulation of industry is managed by industrialists. It was funny when Dickens lampooned it a century ago; it is far from funny now.

The trend toward use of trained professional "city managers" is an encouraging sign of change in local government; some of these managers have shown themselves to be remarkably resistant to traditional political pressures. Even more desirable would be the social and economic upgrading of local political offices. Why shouldn't the mayor of a city with a population of 50,000 individuals be as well paid and socially esteemed as the president of a medium-sized corporation? If part-time county commissioners were paid the same $100 per day fee that is given to expert industrial consultants, more experts in government might serve, part-time, as county commissioners. The increase in salaries could hardly cost more than the current price of bad government.

### Collective Interests

"The world is *not* so governed from above that private and social interest always coincide. It is *not* so managed here below that in practice they coincide. It is *not* a correct deduction from the Principles of Economics that enlightened self-interest always operates in the public interest. Nor is it true that self-interest generally *is* enlightened; more often individuals acting separately to promote their own ends are too ignorant or too weak to attain even these."

John Maynard Keynes, *The End of Laissez-Faire*

The greatest barrier to the implementation of a strong and unified conservation policy is the difficulty of protecting those parts of the public domain that have traditionally been exploited by private interests. Both Keynes and later Hardin (see Chapter 6) have explained that there is no logically consistent reason why an individual, corporation, or nation acting in self-interest should voluntarily abstain from exploiting the public domain even when the result will be certain destruction of the valuable features of that domain. Hardin, in fact, goes somewhat farther in "The Tragedy of the Commons" by asserting that it is usually damaging to private interests (at least in the short run) to act for the collective good insofar as the commons are concerned. Of the many examples of this paradox given in previous chapters, the extermination of the blue whale and self-extermination of the whaling industry is the most striking (see Chapter 5).

If private interests cannot be expected to protect the public domain, then external regulation by public agencies, governments, or international authorities is needed. If that regulation is effective, the commons will be managed to provide the maximum *sustained* yield of natural products, which in turn will ultimately maximize the sum total of the profits for the various interests that rely on the commons. This concept, simple in theory, is difficult to put into practice.

In a book entitled, *The Common Wealth in Ocean Fisheries* (8), Francis T. Christy, Jr., and Anthony Scott examine three suggested methods of protecting overexploited fisheries:

1. Sacrifice the freedom of the seas and assign exclusive fishing rights for a specific area to a particular nation or consortium of nations.

2. Allow free entry into all fishing areas, but establish some absolute quota or limit to the catch of each nation.

3. Internationalize the fishery, with all the details concerning which vessels will be allowed to fish, and which methods and equipment will be used being regulated by the control authority, and with the only "rights" of the member nations being to a proportionate share in the catch or to an equity in the profits of the fishery.

Each protection scheme has its limitations; moreover, there are a large number of possible permutations and combinations of the three, and therefore Christy and Scott wisely refrain from advocating any one in particular. Nevertheless, from the restricted point of view of the problem of the commons, it does seem possible to make some value judgments.

The first method, exclusive use, only transfers the public domain problem to a smaller stage, as various interests compete within each assigned territory. Even if there is regulation by individual nations, it is likely to be piecemeal; in the oceans, this makes little biological sense.

The second method, the quota system, is theoretically attractive, but is easily crippled by international political and economic squabbles. In this case the difficulty is that the absolute size of the catch itself is subject to international negotiation as each country, in competition with its fellows, argues for a larger quota. Countries that have quotas too small to enable them to fish at a profit may have to abandon their rights to the fishery, sell their quota at a loss to some other country, or may elect to ignore the quota altogether. The whaling treaty is an example of the latter.

The third method, internationalization, may be the best of the three. Here the participating nations can fight over the size of their proportionate share in the fishery without affecting the actual fishery management decisions. This is a flexible system, permitting rapid adjustments to ecological change. It is also efficient, as the fishing authority would be free to buy its labor and capital in the cheapest markets and to bargain effectively for the highest price for its products. The Pribilof Island seal treaty is an example.

All "solutions" to the problem of public domain involve subdividing and apportioning the commons in some way. When the commons refers to some kind of natural resource, it is probably sufficient to separate the functions of resource management and distribution of profits, as in the case of an internationalized fishery. When the commons refers, however, not to a material resource but to a previously unregulated activity such as adding to the world's stock of children, the hazard to collective interests is equally great, but the remedies are much farther away.

**The Adaptability**   In the preface to his book, *Ulendo* (see Fur-
**of Homo Sapiens**   ther Reading at end of this chapter), Archie
Carr writes: ". . . the way the world is changing, how do we know what will seem pleasant to people a thousand years from now? . . . People can be made not just to live shoulder-to-shoulder in tiers, but to enjoy living that way." Adaptability to changing environments is a useful quality in a nomadic and curious creature like man, but it can be a deadly trap when the changing environments are themselves man-made. It can lead to acceptance of deteriorating living conditions, to a breakdown, in effect, of the feedback that is essential for maintenance of environmental quality control.

The essence of the problem was stated by Dr. Francis N. Ratcliffe (5), writing in *The Australian Quarterly*: ". . . The changes which conservationists worry about, and which the practice of conservation is designed to prevent, take place a little too slowly for the ordinary man to appreciate, although horribly fast in terms of historical time. Most people find it hard to conjure up a detailed picture of a situation or scene as it was ten years before; and yet one must be able to do this in order to appreciate the extent and nature of progressive change. Steady deterioration, in fact, tends to be accepted uncritically." This problem is at its worst in the urban New World, where nothing seems to last long enough to become a permanent part of the public image of the countryside because nothing is valued so much as newness. Claude Lévi-Strauss (6) has pointed out that the "cycle of evolution" of large American cities is very rapid, but this is now also true of all areas within a distance of one-to-two hours' drive from a large city. Change is expected and accepted;

the fact that so much change, from the central city to the national park, is for the worse, is only recorded as a vague awareness or a confused recollection by the majority of people.

The way to make people aware of slow deterioration is to keep some of the former landscapes around for comparison. In Boston, it may have been the contrast between the greatness of Louisberg Square and Faneuil Hall, on the one hand, and the drab "modern" office buildings in Scollay Square on the other, that made the city fathers accept an unconventional plan for the superb new City Hall built in the late 1960s. In Maine, the existence of a squalid horror like Route 1 south of Belfast, side-by-side with the unrivaled scenery of Acadia and Baxter Parks may help conservationists argue against hasty commercialization.

Perhaps county or district conservators, skilled in photography, would be of use, particularly if they were provided with attractive, centrally located exhibit halls in which to show the history of the area. Certainly, the officials of the Sierra Club must have had something like this in mind when they began to publish their magnificent photographic records of vanishing landscapes.

### The Shortage of Ecologists

The science of ecology, which is the foundation of biological conservation, suffers from both a shortage of trained personnel and an inadequate commitment of national resources and priorities. In 1968 there were slightly more than 3000 members of the Ecological Society of America and approximately 2500 ecology students in all stages of training for the Ph.D. The shortage of ecology teachers weakens existing ecology training programs. A few universities, like Cornell, can muster 40 or 50 faculty members qualified to train graduate students in ecology and evolutionary biology, and some, such as the University of Michigan and Yale, are well known for the excellence of their training in practical conservation, but there are other major universities that do not offer a single graduate course in ecology.

At the national level we find that the Department of the Interior is supposed to represent the interests of mining, oil, and power companies at the same time that it is guarding the ecological health of the nation — an impossible task. Clearly, a separate and powerful department or institute of ecology is essential. Ecologists are not among the principal scientific advisors to the President and are not strongly represented in the National Academy of Sciences. Consequently, scientific research and development priorities and allocations of funds are decided by industrial and defense-connected physicists and chemists, and by biologists whose primary interest and knowledge lie in the areas of medical and biochemical research. (Recent presidential and congressional efforts to form a cabinet-level council on ecology and a Council of Ecological Advisers, respectively, may herald a change in this situation.)

The key to obtaining an increase in both the number of ecologists and their national influence lies in the realm of popular, secondary school, and college education. Ecologists, with the exception of Aldo Leopold and a very few others, have largely ignored these areas in the past while concentrating on graduate education. The growth since 1960 of a cadre of energetic and skilled ecologist-educators, including scientists like Paul Ehrlich, Archie Carr, LaMont Cole, Barry Commoner, Eugene Odum, and Charles Wurster, is the most promising sign that in the near future ecology will be able to supply the large numbers of researchers, consultants, and teachers that are so urgently needed.

*Rationalization* People have a remarkable ability to avoid
*and Denial* confronting unpleasant facts, and the prob-
lems of conservation are very unpleasant. History has conspired in a number of countries to aid and abet these processes of rationalization and denial.

*The Big Country Mystique* In the United States, the Soviet Union, Australia, and all other large industrialized nations that have recently had a frontier, there is a myth. The myth goes something like this: "This is a big country with a lot of open space in it. The people are all crowded together in the cities, but if you fly across the country by jet you see nothing but trees and empty land. There's plenty of room for more people, more houses, more factories and businesses if we spread them out properly. Even if we make a few mistakes, there is always more land."

This widespread misconception, which Ratcliffe (5) terms the "Big Country Mystique," is as outmoded as butter churns and flintlock rifles, but it stubbornly persists. The amount of unpopulated open space left is greatly exaggerated; the amount of unruined, unpopulated space is far less. Things have changed since the days of the frontier. Not only does suburban sprawl fill the interstices between many cities, but as one might expect, the best sites for cities already have cities on them. There is no need, however, to rest the case on this argument. The amount of unpopulated open space left is irrelevant. The ecological resources of all developed countries are already strained to the breaking point. They can hardly be strained less by an added burden of people and their accoutrements, no matter what the spatial arrangements of new population centers may be.

*Scientism and the Cult of Science* "Ah, my child, if you wish to overturn the world by striving to set a little more happiness in it, you have only to remain in your laboratory here, for human happiness can only spring from the furnace of the scientist."

Emile Zola, *Paris*

"Students are beginning to doubt that Galileo, Watt, and Edison have contributed as much and as lastingly to human advancement and happiness as Socrates, Lao-tze, and Francis of Assisi."

René Dubos, *So Human An Animal*

When the Big Country Mystique fails and the ecological facts of life threaten to push their way into the public consciousness, there is always someone who tries to frighten them back with the specter of science. Scientism, the belief that the methods of science can be used to solve all problems, including those of the humanities and social sciences, has waxed strong since the days of Zola, fed by the great twentieth-century discoveries in physics, chemistry, and biology. With respect to conservation, scientism is expressed as the optimistic faith that the most challenging problems concerning population control, pollution, exhaustion of resources, food production, protection of species, and similar questions will be overcome by scientific-technologic discoveries or applications yet to be made. Among scientists, some of whom believe in scientism, this faith is occasionally sustained by the idea that if the public and big business wanted to, they could easily extricate the country from its ecological predicament by spending large sums of money on appropriate technological research and development.

Apart from the philosophical objections to scientism and its corollaries (7), one way to counter this kind of argument is to point out that in scientific terms, the bulk of the data would not appear to support the hypothesis. Science has a long history of creating ecological problems; its record for solutions that do not in themselves generate more problems is less than impressive. It is a strange kind of self-deception that enables a person to stand among the high-powered automobiles, chemical insecticides, thermonuclear bombs, napalm, and nerve gas and look to science for salvation. Science does have a major role to play in the future of conservation; some aspects of that role have been indicated in this book. Nevertheless, science will need careful guidance and supervision from other disciplines; and even given the best of circumstances, the outcome of its efforts will remain for some time beyond the reach of scientific prediction.

### The Good Life   "In wildness is the preservation of the world."

Henry David Thoreau, *Walking*

A reverence for the natural world was one of the first signs of man's humanity and an important feature of early societies. Throughout the Old and New Stone Ages this attitude flourished, and it was made a vital part of the great Mediterranean and Oriental civilizations that followed. In Greece, before the Roman conquests, the land was alive with spirits; every grove was filled with the presence of protective deities, every stream and mountain was personified and respected by the people who lived nearby. But the rise of western Christianity, with its Judeo-Christian doctrine of an exclusive relationship between man and God, largely put an end to this special regard for nature; in so doing it set the stage for the global ecological crises that threaten to culminate in our century.

The dominant theme of Occidental culture is embodied in the word "progress," a concept that has been remarkably sacrosanct until now. One trouble with progress, apart from its effects on the ecosphere, is paradoxically, its animal mindlessness; in the excitement of change there is neither time nor apparent need to do what humans are uniquely capable of — to make plans for the future. Progress discourages independent speculation about goals and meanings. There is never time to ask the question, "What do we want?" except in the most immediate and material sense. Yet this question must be asked at this time — and answered — if it is not already too late. Either nationally or internationally the world's peoples will have to define what the good life is, and then must reconcile this ideal with the closest approximation that the earth can provide on a sustained basis.

In any consideration of the good life we must first evaluate the prevailing Western ethic. Lynn White, Jr. (see Further Reading at end of this chapter) has stated the problem well: "I personally doubt that disastrous ecologic backlash can be avoided simply by applying to our problems more science and more technology. . . . Both our present science and our present technology are so tinctured with orthodox Christian arrogance toward nature that no solution for our ecologic crisis can be expected from them alone. Since the roots of our trouble are so largely religious, the remedy must also be essentially religious, whether we call it that or not. We must rethink and refeel our nature and destiny. The profoundly religious, but heretical, sense of the primitive Franciscans for the spiritual autonomy of all parts of nature may point a direction."

Ironically, the nations best suited to grapple with the problem of the good life are those that we refer to as "underdeveloped." Most of these poorer nations still have the chance to control technology before it masters them, and many of them, such as India, China, and Indonesia, still have at least the remnants of cultural and religious traditions that teach man to live in peace with nature. But even though we may have more difficulty, the industrialized countries, especially the United States, will have to move toward the same goal, for the sake of everyone who lives on the planet.

The only justification of the Western ideal of progress has been that it promotes man's comfort and well-being, but if we look dispassionately at the results of a century of progress, we find nearly all men anxious and alone. Technology, masquerading as an end rather than a means, has unnecessarily moved man away from nature, and in so doing has moved him away from himself. Even if there were no ecologic crises, conservation would still have its most important mission before it: preserving wilderness for those human beings who are fortunate enough to know now that it is part of them and that they enjoy it, and also for those in the future who may learn to use technology in a way that does not subvert the human heritage. Carr must have had something like this in mind when he said: "The real reason for saving tuataras is so people can continue to sing them out of their holes."

•  •  •

In the world of scientific specialties, conservation — a Renaissance subject in the diversity of its concerns — has until recently seemed oddly out of place, as if it had come alive in the wrong century. But the century has entered its final, uneasy third, and academic routines have been shaken. Intellectual styles can change quickly under pressure: A synthesis of the related portions of ecology, economics, government, anthropology, sociology, aesthetics, history and law — unthinkable as a standard subject 50 years ago — would now be acceptable in some colleges. Nevertheless, we lack a proper blend of these various disciplines, although each has its own theoretical framework and store of knowledge. During this possibly last, fey surge of population and technology, it may be futile to think of perfecting a still embryonic system of environmental preservation; however, in the absence of reliable prophecy, both optimist and pessimist can agree that there is no other human endeavor more worth the effort.

## FURTHER READING

Carr, Archie, *Ulendo—Travels of a Naturalist In and Out of Africa*. New York: Knopf, 1964.

Crowe, Beryl L., "The Tragedy of the Commons, Revisited." *Science 166*, 1103 (1969).

Dubos, Rene, *So Human an Animal*. New York: Scribner's, 1968.

Ellul, Jacques, *The Technological Society*. New York: Knopf, 1965.

Vonnegut, Kurt, Jr., *Cat's Cradle*. New York: Holt, Rinehart and Winston, 1963.

White, Lynn, Jr., "The Historical Roots of our Ecologic Crisis." *Science 155*, 1203, 1967.

# REFERENCES

1. Cole, LaMont C., *Scientific American*, April, 1958, p. 83.
2. Chesher, Richard H., *Science 165*, 280 (1969).
3. Raup, Hugh M., *British Ecological Society Jubilee Symposium*, a supplement of *J. Ecology 52* and *J. Animal Ecology 33* (Blackwell, Oxford, 1964), 27.
4. Hibbard, Walter R., Jr., *Science 160*, 143 (1968).
5. Ratcliffe, Francis N., *Australian Quarterly 40* (1), 1 (1968).
6. Lévi-Strauss, Claude, *Tristes Tropiques* (Atheneum, New York, 1963), 100.
7. Efron, Robert, *Perspectives in Biology and Medicine*, Autumn, 1967, p. 9.
8. Christy, Francis T., Jr., and Scott, Anthony, *The Common Wealth in Ocean Fisheries* (Johns Hopkins Press, Baltimore, Md., 1965).

# APPENDIX:
## Some Magazines and Journals Containing Conservation Source Material

This is a partial list of conservation-related periodicals; it is presented as a sample rather than a complete survey of the available literature.

### Interdisciplinary Journals

*BioScience.* American Institute of Biological Sciences: Washington, D.C. (monthly). A general biological journal with frequent, broad articles on ecology, environmental quality, and conservation; also political comment and news.

*Daedalus.* American Academy of Arts and Sciences: Boston (quarterly). Leading experts from all fields write scholarly articles on problems of world significance. Often contains important material on population and technology.

*Nature.* Macmillan (Journals) Limited: London (weekly). The principal English general scientific journal. Occasionally contains short technical and survey articles on ecology, environmental quality, and conservation; also political comment and news.

*New Scientist.* New Science Publications: London (weekly). Reports on current scientific topics and discoveries of interest to the educated layman or scientist. Excellent coverage of worldwide environmental and conservation subjects.

*Science.* American Association for the Advancement of Science: Washington, D.C. (weekly). The principal American general scientific journal. Often contains technical and general reports on ecology, environmental quality and conservation; also political comment and news. The most important scientific source for biological conservation.

### Environmental Quality Journals

*Environment* (formerly *Scientist and Citizen*). Committee for Environmental Information: St. Louis, Missouri (10 issues per year). News and scientific articles about the environment for the educated layman. Carefully edited by an advisory board of distinguished scientists.

*Environmental Science and Technology.* American Chemical Society: Washington, D.C. (monthly). An authoritative journal with technical and general articles, news, and political comment on chemical aspects of environmental pollution. Readable and informative.

*Population Bulletin.* Population Reference Bureau, Inc.: Washington, D.C. (bimonthly). A pamphlet containing a wide variety of articles on all phases of the population explosion and its environmental consequences. Useful population statistics.

## Ecological Journals

*East African Wildlife Journal.* East African Wildlife Society: Nairobi, Kenya (annual). Technical articles on general ecology, wildlife and park management, and conservation in East Africa.

*Ecology.* Ecological Society of America: Durham, N.C. (bimonthly). Technical and general articles on all phases of ecology.

*Journal of Animal Ecology.* British Ecological Society: Oxford (3 times per year). General, population, and physiological ecology, with an emphasis on animals.

*Journal of Applied Ecology.* British Ecological Society: Oxford (3 times per year). Oriented toward agricultural ecology and wildlife management. Much material on the relationship between arthropods and food crops.

*Journal of Ecology.* British Ecological Society: Oxford (3 times per year). Treats all phases of plant ecology, including plant-animal interactions.

*Journal of Economic Entomology.* Entomological Society of America: College Park, Md. (bimonthly). Technical articles on all aspects of the relationship between man and arthropods, including many on insecticides and biological control methods.

*Journal of the Fisheries Research Board of Canada.* Ottawa, Ontario (monthly). Management of aquatic wildlife resources, and all phases of the biology of economically valuable animals such as lobsters and salmon.

*Journal of Wildlife Management.* The Wildlife Society: Washington, D.C. (quarterly). Practical wildlife management, especially in the U.S. and Canada. Technical articles on both management and evaluation of management practices.

*Transactions of the North American Wildlife and Natural Resources Conference.* Wildlife Management Institute: Washington, D.C. (annual). Technical survey articles on all aspects of wildlife management; topics range widely from environmental quality, to land use, to human needs, to management of bays and estuaries, and many others.

## Conservation and Wildlife Bulletins

*Animal Kingdom.* New York Zoological Society: New York (bimonthly). Zoo news and informational reports on rare and endangered wildlife.

*Audubon.* The National Audubon Society: New York (bimonthly). Broad coverage of conservation topics; contains the best photography of any comparable magazine.

*Biological Conservation.* Elsevier: Barking, Essex, England (quarterly). A relatively new scientific journal of very high quality. Publishes editorials, world conservation news, and technical and general papers. Truly international scope.

*Conservation Directory.* National Wildlife Federation: Washington, D.C. (annual). A listing of private and governmental organizations, agencies, and officials concerned with natural resource use and management. Complete and very useful.

*Natural History.* American Museum of Natural History: New York (monthly). Often includes semipopular articles on various conservation subjects by noted biologists.

*Oryx.* Fauna Preservation Society: London (quarterly). Comprehensive survey of world conservation news, plus general articles on conservation and related biological topics.

*Red Data Books.* International Union for the Conservation of Nature: Morges, Switzerland. The central listings and descriptions of endangered mammals and birds of the world; they are brought up to date at frequent intervals by supplements. Listings for other endangered vertebrates are planned. The most important source of information on endangered animals.

*Sierra Club Bulletin.*   The Sierra Club: San Francisco (monthly). Current conservation news, plus accounts of little-publicized natural areas throughout the United States.

## Journals in Related Fields

*The Geographical Review.*   American Geographical Society: New York (quarterly). A wide variety of technical papers on the interactions of humans with their different environments. Ranges from urban demography to agricultural systems to resource conservation.

*Law and Contemporary Problems.*   Duke University School of Law: Durham, N.C. (quarterly). An occasional issue is devoted to discussion of an environmental problem such as air pollution control. Contains in-depth analyses of all factors, scientific and otherwise, that might bear on environmental law.

*Natural Resources Journal.*   University of New Mexico School of Law: Albuquerque, N.M. (quarterly). Devoted to technical articles on legal and fiscal aspects of environmental problems.

*Perspectives in Biology and Medicine.*   University of Chicago Press: Chicago (quarterly). Scholarly, comprehensive papers on any subject pertaining to human health or the practice of biology. Includes population control, environmental medicine, human ecology, and other areas.

## Popular Magazines and Newspapers

*Consumer Reports.*   Consumers Union of U.S., Inc.: Mount Vernon, N.Y. (monthly). Contains occasional reports on consumer products that may have an adverse effect on the environment.

*National Geographic.*   National Geographic Society: Washington, D.C. (monthly). Often contains articles on vanishing peoples, wildlife, and communities. Excellent photographs and maps. Well researched.

*The New York Times:* New York (daily).   Most complete and detailed newspaper coverage of environmental and conservation topics. Has a useful index service.

*Popular Science.*   Popular Science Publishing Co., Inc.: New York (monthly). With subjects ranging from lightweight chainsaws to snowmobiles, this long-lived magazine is the major, popular exponent of mass exploitation of the environment through technology. Conservationists should not be ignorant of its contents.

*Ramparts.*   Ramparts Magazine, Inc.: San Francisco (monthly). A politically controversial magazine which has published landmark articles on environmental degradation in the United States.

*Sports Illustrated.*   Time, Inc.: Chicago (weekly). Frequently contains well-written and informative articles which reflect the conservation consciousness of hunters and fishermen.

*Time.*   Time, Inc.: New York (weekly). Now uses its impressive news-gathering services to collect information for a feature section called "Environment."

# Index

Names of persons accompanied by specific literature references in the text are not indexed, nor are species and place names that are cited only briefly. Indexed species are referred to by their common names, unless these are likely to be obscure.